112790

ON EAGLES' WINGS

To Terrance

Who reviewed and
I hope enjoyed,

with thanks

S. Weizman

London   16.3.76

EZER WEIZMAN

ON EAGLES' WINGS

THE PERSONAL STORY OF
THE LEADING COMMANDER
OF THE ISRAELI AIR FORCE

WEIDENFELD AND NICOLSON
LONDON

ISBN 0 297 77034 9

Filmset by Keyspools Limited, Golborne, Lancashire

Printed in Great Britain by Morrison and Gibb
Edinburgh and London

CONTENTS

To the ground and air crews of the Israel Air Force, who made it possible.

FOREWORD

THAT I AM a *raconteur* by nature, and enjoy every minute of it, is not necessarily a reason to write a book about my life. What has prompted me to do just that, however, is that my experiences for the past thirty or so years have been so closely bound up with the story of the Israeli air force, and *that* is one of the most outstanding tales of our times. This account makes no claim to be comprehensive, definitive or objective. It is a history of the air force as I have observed it first-hand over the years. But rather than apologize for the gaps, I hope that the vividness of one man's experience will make up for the lack of an historian's thoroughness.

The purpose of this book is not just to describe, however. A man does not participate in the events I have been party to without learning a lesson or two, and my long association with the air force has taught me at least one fundamental fact about this country and its future: our existence here always has been, and always will be, based on nurturing a standard of quality – and that is not a subject on which we have, or ever will have, a choice. This is a theme that inevitably runs throughout the following pages because it finds its sharpest expression in the story of the Israeli air force. While writing I asked myself whether it was a truism so obvious that it hardly merits mention. But looking around me I think it can't hurt to state it again – especially now – because I think it's a lesson with significance for more than just the three million people who live here.

While on the subject of quality, I want to express a debt of deep gratitude to Dov Goldstein, whose patience, understanding and assistance – in quantity as well as quality – have enabled this book to be written.

EZER WEIZMAN
Ramat Hasharon
August 1975

I

CHILDHOOD

DO I REALLY START this tale by looking back to my childhood? I suppose I do. It seems a long way off for me, and a lot has happened since then. I've been a pilot for two-thirds of my life, fought in five wars, commanded an air force, almost commanded an army and served (albeit briefly) in my country's government, and it seems that I've been a man for almost as long as I can remember. But it all started back in Haifa – at least that's where the memories start – long before there was an air force or an army; when a sovereign Jewish state in the Land of Israel was still only a dream, and my father was one of the dreamers.

I grew up under the influence of a father who was wise and strong, a man with a powerful, dominating personality, who had no need of coercion to impose his will in the home. His will was done because everyone wanted it done. My mother was the direct opposite. She was a beautiful woman, soft and gentle, who imbued our home with tenderness and good taste and effaced herself before my father's strength. In his presence, she walked on tiptoe, eager to fulfil his wishes before they were even uttered. Between my parents (or perhaps above them) hovered the personality of my paternal grandmother, Rachel, who lived in our house until I was fifteen or sixteen years old, when she died at the age of eighty-nine.

Father's Zionism, his burning belief in everything that was being done in the country and his practical involvement in constructive activity still did not totally erase the Diaspora from his character. The names Pinsk, Mottle and Moscow were often on his lips. The Weizman clan has deep roots in this country without losing its grip on the Diaspora. Yiddish – rolling musically off the Weizman tongues with such homespun sweetness – was the bridge between past and present, and this unique melody enchanted me. Whenever Father spoke of the Diaspora, of life in the *shtetl* (the Jewish townships of Eastern Europe), he would call on Grandmother to bear him out: 'Here's Grandmother. If you really want to know, ask her, she'll tell you.' Grandmother's deeds told more than her words: she was the archetype 'Jewish mother' in the flesh, a living testament to a way of life that has since been eradicated. Her hands were never idle – sloth was the only thing she hated – and she would knit socks, bake magnificent cakes and maintain strict supervision over the *kashrut* of her home, yet she was warm and affectionate. At the beginning of each school year, she would send me off with the priestly benediction.

Our house, at 4 Melchett Street in Haifa, had two floors: the lower one belonged to Grandmother, the upper one was ours. My sister Yael and I spent many enchanted hours on the ground floor in Grandmother's company, sensing that she was a representative of the past; when she died, we knew that that world would never again come back to life for us. Grandmother Rachel brought fifteen children into the world, and twelve of them survived the children's diseases of those days. At a time when academic studies were the preserve of the upper classes or of individuals with an unusual thirst for knowledge, ten of them acquired degrees. The most renowned was my uncle Chaim. The other nine include three chemists, like Chaim, my agronomist father (whose profession also led him to dabble in chemistry) and an engineer; the sisters produced two doctors, a dentist and a music teacher. All in all, a most qualified family.

My whole family – both the paternal Weizman branch and the maternal Krishevskis – constitutes an exciting adventure story in its own right, and the time may yet come for it to be told. I don't pretend to know all the minor details, aside from what I heard, which always seemed too little. But my imagination was fired by some of the events that befell both families in the course of their wanderings. For example, my grandfather Ezer, or Ozer (for whom I'm named without having been privileged to know him), was a delegate to a Zionist Congress at the beginning of the century – but he also took along four young compatriots: his sons Feivel, Moshe, Shmuel and Chaim. Much later, that unique picture came to life for me: my grandfather and my three uncles, delegates to the Zionist Congress, with Herzl, the Jewish 'king' with the long beard, and five Weizmans at his feet. After World War Two, when I had the opportunity of going to a Zionist Congress (in a bizarre, adventurous flight by light plane from London), I felt that this was not my first time in the congress hall: I was but returning to a familiar scene.

My father was the *mizinik,* the youngest. He was about twenty-five years younger than the eldest of the tribe of brothers and sisters. His youth made him the darling of the grown-ups, but it also forced him to fight for his position among his elders.

My mother represented a culture of a totally different character. Mother was born in Rishon Lezion, one of the first Zionist settlements established here. She had deep roots in this country and was remote from the East European tradition. My maternal grandfather – I did not know him either – died at the age of forty-eight while serving as a Turkish army doctor.

The Weizman clan roared and trumpeted, constantly erupting into a noisy babble of Hebrew, Yiddish and Russian. They conducted multilingual quarrels and reconciliations; they emitted polyglot bellows of friendship and love, satisfaction and contentment. Mother was reserved, muted and withdrawn, with a silk-like delicacy. She was an introvert, always keeping her feelings to herself. In running the household, she was anxious above all to please Father. She tried to be inconspicuous, not to stand out, not to press her own wishes, giving my father the sense of being in sole control and making him the centre of the family.

For all their Israeli character, the Weizmans always kept something of the flavour of the East European *shtetl.* But my mother's family were local growths, products of the Land of Israel under its Turkish and British overlords, and the colonies patronized by the Baron Edmond de Rothschild. Both families exhibited the same kind of fluctuating ambivalence towards the British. The British were civilized, and, at least in our Haifa home, they never behaved like imperialists denying the Jewish people its independence. They were likeable and pleasant. Everyone was aware that their sole aim was to maintain their hegemony; nevertheless, it was not always easy to dislike them.

This concoction that goes by the name of Ezer is filled with a brew distilled from the powerful, dominating personalities of the Weizmans, from the Krishevskis' deep roots in the Land of Israel, mixed with the scents of Rishon Lezion vineyards and the nostalgic aromas of old Jerusalem.

That was not where we lived, though. My father came to Palestine in 1913 and, as an agronomist trained at a German university, was employed at the Aaronsohn farm in Athlit. He did not belong to Nili (the Jewish anti-Turkish underground headed by Aaronsohn, which worked for the British during World War One), but was a close sympathizer, and for many years he would feed me stories about Nili, which I gobbled down greedily. After the British conquest of Palestine in 1917–18, he was appointed forestry officer in the northern part of the country. He wandered from place to place, until he finally settled in Acre, from where he supervised forestry work in the Galilee. His long journeys brought him very close to the Arabs among whom he stayed, and he had many Arab friends. Whenever I accompanied him on his trek from village to village, I would gaze at the Arab villagers with childish eyes, amazed at the contrasts between them and us.

There were only two or three Jewish families in Acre in 1924, so Mother was sent to bring me forth in Tel Aviv, where Grandmother lived. Strictly speaking, then, I hail from Tel Aviv, but it was Haifa that nourished me, for the family settled there shortly after my birth.

The house on Melchett Street was built according to Father's design, and something of his iron character went into it. It was a fortress, a large stone building with a wide terrace supported on stone pillars; the whole house gave one the feeling of solid strength and impregnability. The Melchett Street 'fortress' was begun after the birth of Yael, and shortly before my cries heralded my *début* on the family stage. The house made such a profound impression on its inmates that when Father died, Mother asked to have his tomb built of the same kind of stone. When her time came, her tomb also was built of stones like those of 4 Melchett Street.

How can I describe my childhood years? Spacious? Bountiful? They were worthy of such terms. But above all, they were eventful, always studded with exciting happenings. We were mobile, far more than most families then, even without elaborate advance planning. Some Saturday mornings Father would decide that he was bored. 'Get up!' he would urge everyone, and before we knew what he was up to, we were in the car, on the road to Beirut. Within an hour and a half, or sometimes two, the aromas of Beirut's inviting dishes were tickling our nostrils. We were seasoned travellers in a world of open borders, not yet sealed by Arab–Jewish hatred. It was not only Lebanon I visited, but Damascus, too; and we were no strangers to Europe either.

I loved to accompany Father on his journeys. He was an innovator who displayed much initiative. He brought the first combine harvester into the country, following it with specialized ploughs. He was like an inexhaustible battery, bursting with energy. He was a wanderer, abhorring prolonged stays in one place. He would visit dozens of new settlements, accompanying them on the day they were founded, guiding their first steps. He was a man of deeds, a creative being.

During my early childhood years, the name of my uncle Chaim (later, the first president of the State of Israel) was always present, deeply imprinted in my whole way of life. He was never Chaim Weizmann, always 'Uncle Chaim'. Although we were thousands of miles apart, his name was always with us: Uncle Chaim is coming, Uncle Chaim intends to visit, Uncle Chaim is ill, Uncle Chaim is better, Uncle Chaim succeeded, Uncle Chaim failed, Uncle Chaim convinced, Uncle Chaim thinks, Uncle Chaim said. There was an invisible thread linking the house on Melchett Street to Uncle Chaim's great battles. Whenever he came to visit us, people would hang on his every pronouncement, while the children sat in the corner silently drinking in every word of the night-long discussions between Uncle Chaim and Father and the various visitors.

To some extent all the Weizmans were overshadowed by the family's most famous scion, and Father did not escape this fate. I often sensed that it was not quite to his liking, although I have no proof. One of Father's anecdotes was that while he was on a visit to

New York, he went into a shop to buy some clothes for himself
and some presents for the family. The bill came to $40.40. When
he went to pay he asked to have his purchases delivered to the
hotel.

The assistant asked, 'What name, please?'

Father replied, 'Weizman.'

The proprietor of the shop overheard and asked, 'Are you any
relation of the great Weizmann, the president?'

'Yes, I am. He happens to be my brother.'

The proprietor was very excited, and in a burst of generosity
told the assistant, 'Never mind the 40 cents!'

Later, whenever some unsuspecting American visitor would ask
Father if he were the President's brother, he would answer, half-
seriously, half in fun: 'Oh, no, I'm the father of the Colonel ...'
referring, of course, to me.

My personal memories of Uncle Chaim date from 1932. We
were touring Europe – an unusual thing in those days – and we
made a stop in England. I was eight, and Uncle Chaim was already
in his late fifties. To me, he appeared old and heavy and wise,
wisdom seemed to flow from him. That was the way I always felt
in his presence. But above all, I remember Uncle Chaim from the
traditional gatherings in our Haifa home, when the whole family
would assemble on the evening of the Passover *seder*, or for the
lighting of the fifth candle of Chanukah, which was also
Grandmother's birthday. These gatherings were a tradition that
withstood passing years and changes, as well as troubles and
sorrows. Whenever Uncle Chaim was awaited, the days were full
of excitement, tension and expectation. Everyone would prepare
for the great event, while the rumour of his coming electrified the
small Jewish community of Haifa, which was no more than a
township in those days.

The *seder* table would be presided over by Grandmother, in all
her majestic splendour, with Feivel, her eldest, on her right, and
Chaim on her left. All eyes rested on Grandmother and Uncle
Chaim, through whose joint presence the room and the family and
the Feast of Freedom all seemed to acquire an added dimension of
omnipotence. Of course, Uncle Chaim did not belong to us alone.
While we were reading the Haggadah and hungering for the

kneidelach (dumplings), the people of Haifa began to gather outside
for their share of Weizmann the Great.

When the bustle outside reached his ears, Uncle Chaim did not
conceal his pleasure. He was a true leader – something of an
exhibitionist – and took a human delight in displays of affection
and admiration. He did not long remain hidden from the
expectant crowd. In a proper leader-like manner, he would amble
out to the terrace and wave to his cheering admirers. Then he
would make his descent, graciously allowing the circle of *hora*-
dancers to surround him, singing along with them in homespun
fashion. He did not know the *hora*. Somehow, inwardly, he did not
belong to the festivity. He had a kind of reserve, the distance of
someone encountering an alien life-style. However hard he tried to
join in, he still remained outside it.

Even within the narrow family circle, I would often feel that, in
a way, Uncle Chaim was an outsider. Not a stranger – he enjoyed
being with the Weizmans – but different. He was Grandmother's
extraordinary son, an extraordinary brother and an extraordinary
uncle. When Father addressed Uncle Moshe, he would say: '*Kum
zingen shach*' (Let's sing chess) or '*Kum reden shach*' (Let's talk chess),
never 'Let's play chess', for it was the custom that a game of chess
be accompanied by humming or talking. Uncle Chaim was never
addressed in this manner. Even within the family, he was treated
with respect, from a distance seldom bridged. This may have been
the influence of Aunt Vera, Uncle Chaim's wife, who, till her last
day, was a 'super-snob', deeply irritated by the various homespun
Weizman customs. Few know how great Aunt Vera's influence
was on Uncle Chaim.

Uncle Chaim's visits left a deep impression on me for a further
reason. Through them I gained access to the mysteries of the
Haganah (the underground Jewish defence organization in mandatory Palestine). At one time I was even personally involved in a
'security problem', allowing me to depict myself as a 'security
man', with many daring deeds to my credit. As tension rose and
the 1936 disorders broke out, Uncle Chaim's visits involved a
security risk: he had to be escorted all the time, to protect him from
the Arab gangs. When Tel Aviv port was opened to shipping,
Uncle Chaim felt obliged to set a personal example and in 1937

decided to disembark at the Jewish port. The British mandatory authority was seized with concern and organized a convoy from Tel Aviv to Haifa, escorted by armoured cars, army and police – none of whom could detract from my private certainty that it was I who was protecting Uncle Chaim. Father had secretly given me his revolver, which I carried amidst all the bustle, fondling it again and again, ready to jerk it out and open fire if anyone threatened Uncle Chaim. I was thirteen years old at the time.

'Don't go down to town today' was one of Mother's sayings in the late thirties, during the 1936 riots. Jews were being killed even then. 'They're coming out of the mosques today. It's better to stay home on Fridays.' Haifa was unusual: unlike Jerusalem and Jaffa, where Arabs and Jews occupied separate quarters, Haifa was a jumble of the two peoples, and life there was much more integrated. The family was on good terms with the Arabs, although this was not always dependable. Father took great pains to treat the Arabs with consideration and understanding, establishing close ties with them. I remember the 1929 disturbances, when I was a small child. Father was away on business in Vienna, and when hostilities broke out, we were alone in Haifa. Father had a friend in Acre by the name of Abbed the Mukhtar (Headman). Abbed was anxious and sent a car to Mother, begging her to bring the children and come to him. 'These days you'll be safer in Acre, under my protection, than in Haifa.' Mother declined the offer politely. She would not leave Haifa during difficult times; she relied on the boys of the Haganah.

When I was about fourteen, I chanced to meet one of the most colourful characters to figure in the long annals of our wars: the Englishman Orde Wingate. He came on the recommendation of my Uncle Chaim and was a regular guest in our Haifa home. Wingate was serving in the Royal Artillery. He was a total contrast to the popular image of the typical British officer. He was of average height, with an aquiline nose and a high forehead; his hair was purposely brushed down, and his strange hat with its RA insignia towered upwards. Anything resembling care with regard to his dress, outward appearance or other external frills was beyond him; he was demonstratively sloppy. He looked much more like a missionary than an officer of the British Empire, and he

would spend hours talking about the Bible. I suppose it was his link
to the Land of Israel and the Jewish people – a mystical,
very personal link.

Wingate was about thirty-five when he came to Palestine,
bringing his beautiful wife, who was half his age. At the time I
knew nothing of the doings of 'The Friend', as I heard him called.
As a child, or at most a young boy, many things were concealed
from me. He would come into the house at all kinds of unusual
hours, bringing the mystery and secrecy of battle – as well as his
muddy clothes and torn socks, which he would hand to Mother for
her to clean and mend, while he himself, his blue eyes smiling
playfully, would hurry to the bathroom for a soak. He provided
me with a good opportunity to improve my English. I cannot
deny that I was deeply stirred by our conversations; I often talked
with him like any young boy who loves to speak with an adult. He
began to let me clean and oil his rifle; my hands would tremble
with agitation when the pull-through refused to slide down the
barrel.

The revolver, Wingate's rifle, the disturbances, the frenzied
arguments about security and defence might give the mistaken
impression that these things were what helped to form my military
frame of mind. I would hesitate to agree. After all, I was only
nibbling at the edges. But I listened, I heard, I took things in. I
remember my fervent support for the 'defence doctrine' my father
expounded in his bitter arguments with Uncle Chaim. Father
versus uncle. Father versus the policy of non-retaliation. Father
calling for action. Uncle opposed; he was in favour of restraint.
And I, shouting at the top of my voice (as loud as it is today, or
even more so): 'Where the hell are we going? Why are we giving
in?'

I wanted to be a pilot. Did I say 'wanted'? I burned with the
desire! But in war, in any war, your wants are one thing, but Fate –
with all the indifference of a self-assured, omnipotent despot –
dictates your actual deeds. In 1941, I was on a Haganah section-
leaders' course at Juarra. The course was an arduous and unusual
experience. At its conclusion I had to pass an examination
conducted by three prominent Haganah leaders. After completing
it successfully, I felt relief, and even satisfaction, though I did not

get much enjoyment out of the course.

The course had included lots of marches; there was a great deal of footwork on those dark nights. Frankly, it was not to my liking – running around, getting thorns in the rear and all sorts of other sensitive places, crawling in the mud and crunching mouthfuls of sand, while gallons of sweat poured off me. I decided that, if I could, I would not hesitate to get out – this kind of thing didn't seem to be what I was destined for. Many years later, under totally different circumstances, young pilots were to hear me reminisce: 'I'd lie there in Juarra or nearby, and four British planes would come streaking across the sky from the Ramat David airfield. I'd say to myself, "Weizman, you idiot, here you are, lying among the bushes and nibbling leaves, when you should be up there, in the clouds, enjoying fresh air and open spaces and the wonderful feeling of being on top of everything." At that time I didn't know that even there, up in the clouds, you sweat – in a different way.'

Nothing, I believe, occurs unexpectedly. No fateful happening ever bursts into your life without announcing itself by a knock on the door, even though it may not always be obvious. The truth is that many events – overt or covert, acknowledged or concealed, conscious or well-buried – leave their imprint. And when I seek an answer to the question – when was it kindled, this desire of mine to fly – I must say: before Juarra, during Juarra and after Juarra. Perhaps it was always there. But there was one small difference. Immediately following my experiences at Juarra, in 1942, I joined the Aviation Club; and paid for flying lessons until I got my first license, after passing British mandatory-government examinations. My first solo flight was in April 1942, in July or August of that year. Bursting with pride, I held my first license.

Aside from it being a kind of internal fever, with everything else having been thrust aside, becoming a pilot was also a matter of a written commitment. Two months before my first solo flight, in February 1942, my cousin Michael – Uncle Chaim's son and an RAF captain – fell in action. He set off in a two-engine plane with a crew of six for a patrol flight between the coasts of England and Spain and all trace of them vanished. The official report quoted their last message, saying that one of the engines was gone and they were trying to ditch in the sea. They were never seen again. I had not seen Uncle Chaim since the outbreak of war in 1939, but from his letters we could learn how grievously he had been afflicted by the terrible blow. He had two sons, Benjamin and Michael, but unfortunate circumstances had forced him to pin all his hopes on Michael.

My relationship with Michael had not been particularly close. We were divided by a double barrier – distance and life-style. He was a few years older than I; he went to school in England and scarcely knew a few phrases of Hebrew. He began to fly before the war; when it broke out, he was already an experienced pilot. But in February 1942, when I heard of Uncle Chaim's grief at the death of Michael, I wrote to him: 'I have decided to join the RAF. I will continue on Michael's path.' Within four or five months, I joined up.

I had become an amateur strategist many years before I began to take it seriously. When I was about fourteen, I joined my father in 'conducting' the 1937/8 Abyssinian War on our carpet. With the pink-hued map of Abyssinia spread out before us, we would move the coloured flags from place to place, following the Italian army in its advance as it destroyed the Abyssinian Empire. Our home was always filled with curiosity and interest in what went on in the world. Every major event found its echo there, drawing members of the family into discussion, argument and commentary. I would buy all the English papers, swallowing every word, working out interpretations, forecasting moves. I had a little notebook with the names and particulars of every British, French and German warship: whenever one was sunk, I would cross it out.

We did not neglect our maps. We pencilled battle-fronts, we sketched thrusts. To this day I can clearly see the map we drew showing the German army reaching the coast and creating the salient called Dunkirk. Breathlessly, I swallowed tales of the British air force and its deeds, I followed the Battle of Britain as though I were personally involved.

After that, to complete my personal involvement, our very hometown was bombed. Everybody – Italians, Germans and Vichy French – dropped their destructive loads on Haifa. One Saturday, at the end of 1941 or early in 1942, I was out walking down the Carmel with a girl-friend when I heard the roar of planes. 'They're hitting Haifa!' I cried. The Italians bombed the Shell fuel tanks, and British planes took off from Haifa to intercept them.

How could I sit still under such circumstances! My mood grew turbulent as I counted the days till the end of my eighteenth year, when I would be able to join the RAF. At that time, gangs of fanatics were attacking anyone who had not joined the British army. One day I was walking down a Haifa street when I fell into the hands of some of these fellows, who promptly showered me with blows, before I could yell: 'Idiots! What d'you want? I'm only sixteen.' I was in anguish, not because of a few punches, but because I was too young to join up. The British were suffering defeat after defeat, the house had a war atmosphere, Haifa was getting bombed – and there I was outside the whole show, unable to contribute my 'share'.

It was then that I heard some story about the Belgian Congo, where they were looking for fellows with a minimum of flying experience to be trained as pilots. The idea caught my imagination. What an adventure! I did not give myself time to think or even inquire whether all this had anything to do with the war. By the time the British Empire graciously permits me to take part in the war effort, I thought, the war would slip between my fingers. Did I, or did I not, have a flying license? And did I, or did I not, have twenty-five hours of flying behind me? And does Belgium want me? Certainly! So what am I waiting for? Start her up and let's go!

It was May, or perhaps June, 1942. The Belgian Consulate was in Jerusalem, so off to Jerusalem I went. I didn't say a word to Father, nor did I share the secret with anyone else. I'm blessed if I know how the whole scheme got to Father's ears. After a productive morning at the Belgian Consulate, I was walking the streets of Jerusalem, joyfully picturing myself as a regular pilot about to receive his plane and take off at any minute, when suddenly there he was, in front of Jerusalem's Eden Hotel, waiting for me.

'What are you doing in Jerusalem?' His gaze transfixed me.

'I've been to the Belgian Consulate,' I replied in the tone of a man emancipated from parental influence.

'What were you doing in the Belgian Consulate?' he continued the interrogation.

I told him.

He listened, and then I saw the harshness give way to concern and tenderness. 'My son,' he said, 'if you're going to fight for anyone, you'll fight for the Jewish people in a Jewish army.'

'But Father, is there a Jewish army? Where is it?'

There was none, but Father was right. He gave me a thorough talking to, showing me that our interests were identical with those of the British army – as indeed they were at that time. After some time, he said, 'If you want to join the British air force, well and good. Let's go.'

With Father there was no great distance between words and deeds. We went to RAF headquarters near the Damascus Gate. My 'old man' had contacts and acquaintances there, but he made no use of them. He brought his beloved son and said: 'He wants to join up. Take him.'

They took me. 'What do you want to be?' I was asked. What do I want to be? What a question – a pilot, of course! With total finality, I was told I could not be a pilot. I wasn't even given a reason. Then the officer in charge said: 'Do you want to be in a ground-crew?' My throat was choked: my beautiful dream, shattered to smithereens. 'Alright.' I barely got out the words.

'Alright,' he said, 'would rigging do you?'

I wanted to tell him to go rig himself, but I only asked: 'Is there any other trade?'

'Driver.'

Might as well be a driver, I thought to myself, if I can't pilot a plane through the sky, at least I can hold a steering wheel on the ground.

On 2 September 1942, in Jerusalem's Notre Dame monastery, I took my oath of allegiance to the King. There were about ten of us – young fellows full of eagerness. In the course of time, this small group produced no less than four pilots: Nahman Meiri, my friend Yitzhak Sela (later a colonel in the Israeli air force), the late Yariv Shenbaum (killed at Dir Amer, during the War of Independence) and myself. But at the time I was far from realizing my dream of flying – possibly further than before I joined up. Up to then I could cultivate my dream, letting my imagination roam: I took off, I landed, I twisted left and right, I climbed ferociously. And then, there was reality, giving my dreams their death-blow, their chances of coming true growing smaller and more remote as the dreary days passed by.

I'm in a regular air force, I kept telling myself, I'm in His Majesty's air force. At night, we were put into some barracks; sleeping on the floor, if you please. We were each given one flea-bitten blanket to lie on, and another one to cover ourselves with, if we wanted it. But there was no need: it was hot in Jerusalem, and our bodies exuded heat and sweat. Scraps of talk echoed all around: a little Hebrew, a little French, a little English. I laid myself down – down on the floor, down in my heart – and mourned my flying career. The air force career I had managed to achieve got off to a memorable start with a spell of 'tater-bashing'. The RAF received a report of some traffic infringement by Private Ezer Weizman of Haifa, a man occupying the lowest rank in the British military hierarchy. Brought to trial, I was sentenced to three days of peeling potatoes. I peeled and peeled and peeled. I think that neither before nor after have I ever seen such an enormous quantity of that disgusting vegetable.

We had uniforms now, and after a few days we got permission to leave our monastery and go into town. We headed for Jerusalem's Café Atara to exhibit our fashionable British uniforms, to glean murmurs of admiration from the girls, to feel like soldiers, to show off. In our khaki shorts, our long socks and black shoes with their clattering heels, with our hats on one side, the world looked less depressing. True, it was not like flying, but it was certainly better than peeling potatoes in Notre Dame's decaying kitchen. And when I strolled down the street and ran into a British officer I snapped out a salute – my first ever – and felt my soul engulfed with a wonderful feeling: contentment and hope at a new beginning.

The air force is full of fine fancies: planes, flying, spreading your wings; the clouds and the roar of engines; and that wonderful feeling of power, of being different. In time I got to know each of these feelings, and I drank my fill of them all. But in 1942, I was as far from all this as the British Empire was from victories on the battlefield. I found myself in the Western Desert, one of many drivers, and it was a lousy life – hard, dreary and depressing. My first encounter with my new existence consisted of bedraggled tents sunk in the deep sand, a dining mess that was a strenuous mile away and mockery of a shower. Hot water? Never! 'And please be good enough to sleep on the sand,' so that you burned by day and froze by night.

We delivered aviation fuel to the British airfields and also ferried up new vehicles for the British army in the desert. We would go to the harbours of Alexandria or Port Said, receive new vehicles and deliver them to the units in the desert. That was our occupation prior to the battle of El Alamein. (On the way from Cairo to Alexandria, I saw the Pyramids for the first time – a thrilling experience.) Subsequently, we became a kind of fuel-transport unit. We would set off loaded down with thousands of gallons of the precious fluid to be supplied to the military airfields.

This was how I made the acquaintance of desert warfare and its problems. Even though I saw everything from the driver's seat, gazing out of the front and side windows, there were things that impressed themselves on my mind and were to be recalled many years later. The desert has its own rules of life and of war; in those wide spaces battle is waged as near as possible to the roads, to the main routes. There is a striking paradox: the desert covers an enormous area, but control of its central routes is enough to dominate it all.

Aside from the desert, I also got to know the British planes. I would see them parked on the runways – the finest planes of their time – and my heart sank. This was what I had joined up for, why I had left my home and family and country. The planes – and the prospect of flying them – were worth the sacrifice. But bumping over the desert roads, delivering fuel! What sort of vocation was that?

There were many men who endured the desert much longer than I did, encountering far more of its cruel and fickle nature. You could distinguish them without any difficulty: sunburnt, brown, brimming over with health. They and their kind were called the Desert Rats. Even the pilots who operated in the desert were a unique breed, parading about in shorts to show off.

I was depressed by one of the first bits of martial wisdom which the experienced Desert Rats tried to teach me. 'Listen feller,' they said, 'you always have to keep three or four jerrycans full of fuel for yourself. Not so as you can go forward, but so as you can go back, if the generals make another mess-up.' They had experienced previous retreats, and they were simply trying to tell me that another withdrawal was feasible; and, in such a case, it is better if a man is not dependent on the favours of others, but can get away under his own steam. However credible (and borne out by experience) it may have been this lesson was bitter as gall for a young man from Palestine who had come to win the war.

An afterthought, dating from many years later, ties in with my memories of the Western Desert: one of Field Marshal Montgomery's most important steps was to unify the commands of the air and ground forces. Previously the two commands were separated by many miles. This was no accident, for ground-air cooperation – which we Israelis, for all our modest means, have always considered vital for success – was as yet undeveloped. Each of the two forces could run its own show, one almost without any connection to the other. El Alamein was one of the first battles with a high degree of co-ordination between air and ground forces, which considerably affected the outcome. In the course of time, such co-ordination became the corner-stone of military doctrine in every army.

I also had an unrequited need. I had to feel far more involved in the war effort of the Jewish community in Palestine. Flying would have given me the feeling of preparing for our war, which would assuredly come when this terrible war ended. Driving a stub-nosed truck was a very minor contribution towards this objective.

At home, the Jewish underground needed arms, and here in the desert there were guns and grenades lying around, with no one bothering to gather them up. I didn't know exactly where this would lead, but I collected three German rifles and a batch of hand grenades and found a hiding-place for them in my truck. Then I waited for an opportunity, and when it came, I didn't miss it. Pick-up trucks carrying various supplies were being driven to Palestine and were left there to be converted into signals vehicles, which were then taken back to Egypt. At Helwan they were looking for drivers to do the job. In a moment, I was on. During the night, I transferred my guns and grenades to the pick-up truck, and the next morning I was ready for my first smuggling operation.

Aside from the troublesome route across the Sinai desert, I was also suffering from fear. Carrying my contraband arms, my heart plunged like a yo-yo at every road-block. There were searches, but nothing was found. At Bir Asluj in the Negev I got hold of my sergeant and told him how homesick I was; I asked permission to push on ahead of the convoy, to go on to Haifa, say a brief hello at home and to return quickly to the convoy's destination. The sergeant was a good fellow, and I got permission. I drove on to Haifa with my precious load. They may not have been like today's Phantoms, but in those days, three serviceable rifles and some hand-grenades were of incalculable value.

I got home to Haifa on Friday, parked the truck in the courtyard and transferred the arms to my father's car. The next day I drove to the late Moshe Zadok, head of Haifa's fire-brigade and my immediate superior in the Haganah. When I gave him the precious load, he did three things practically simultaneously, and I can no longer remember their precise sequence. He reviled me violently, condemning my irresponsibility; gave me an excited hug; and stroked the valuable rifles, as he rushed them to a hiding-place. I was left with the distinct feeling that this single act of mine was equally as important as the long months I had spent in the desert.

Having completed my contraband operation, I returned to the dreariness of the desert. There was only a handful of men from Palestine, a few drops in a sea of Britons and others. But this handful had a certain quality; we lived together and together we dreamed of home and planned our return after the war. I was the youngest, and the others called me 'Baby Weizman'. Although I was having a pleasant enough time, I was full of discontent. Our ancient sages said, 'The greater the expectation, the greater the disappointment.' When I joined the RAF, my expectations were sky-high: I wanted to be up there, in the clouds, and here I was in the desert, with my teeth gritting sand.

We pounded the highways, chugging in the wake of the fighting. Following Montgomery's Eighth Army at the beginning of 1943 gave me the chance of scratching the name Weizman on the great white triumphant gateway (the British dubbed it 'Marble

Arch') that Mussolini had erected at El Agheila, on the border between Cyrenaica and Tripolitania. But it was impossible to overlook the horrors of war – the graves. Every war has its own graves. All along the route, on every side, in every direction, as far as the eye could see, there were masses of scrap metal, tanks, scorched and blackened, and burnt-out vehicles. And the 'bayonet-graves' of the victims of war – a German bayonet stuck in the sand, marking the grave of a German soldier, a British bayonet, an Australian bush-hat, another belonging to a New Zealander or an Italian.

War also has its exciting little reunions, unplanned, but with an enormous capacity for piercing the great wall of grey routine. On the way south to Bengazi there were warning signs: 'Beware of bombing; don't be a bloody fool; keep a hundred yards apart.' And the MPs were on our backs all the time, making us keep the distance so that if one copped a bomb and the fuel he was carrying burst into flame like a giant torch, the other vehicles would remain unharmed.

As we drove along, my senses dulled as I grasped the steering wheel, while the monotonous drone of the engine almost sent me off to sleep. Suddenly I straightened up, wide awake. Outside one of the camps I saw the signboards of 178 Company; I knew that this was a Palestinian transport unit of the RASC, and I recalled that my old friend Danny Agron was serving in it. Danny played a considerable part in arousing my interest in planes and flying. The son of the editor of the *Jerusalem Post* (or *Palestine Post,* as it was called during mandatory times), Danny's English was fluent. When I was only fifteen he was already well versed in magazines on aviation and planes, which he would read avidly; he used to build model planes, and his whole world was 'up in the air'. His fever infected me, and I too found a place in this glorious world. I liked Danny, and I enjoyed his company.

With memories flitting through my mind, I could not restrain myself. I asked my sergeant's permission and sped to the 178's camp. What a joy it was to meet Danny! It was Saturday, and he begged me to stay for lunch, singing the praises of their Hungarian cook – which in no way prepared me for the magnificent banquet we were served. It was great to have a normal meal after all my crazy bumping through the desert. I had a strange feeling, almost as though I were at home in Haifa on a Saturday – a whiff of 4 Melchett Street.

Then back to the truck. What about flying? A remote dream. I did not give up for a moment, but I didn't get much in the way of results. At one stage I thought I'd finished the war as a 'truck-pilot'. I nagged my superiors from the moment we got to Hilwan. I harried every officer of every rank about flying school. Each time we got back to base from a long convoy, I would present myself outside the office of the commanding officer, waiting for hours before I was admitted just to repeat my nagging. In time, the C.O. got to know me. 'Ah, yes,' he would say, half mocking, half pitying, 'the pilot, the pilot'. A nobody from Palestine, number 775869, a 'native' with big fancies. I didn't give up. I wrote countless requests. Once I was summoned to a written examination: English composition, mathematics, geometry, general knowledge. I made every effort to remember everything I had ever learned, regretting the lessons I had missed at Haifa's Reali High School. I completed the examination, with the satisfactory feeling that I had paved my way to the course. But the weeks rushed past, with me in my truck and my spirits at their ebb.

In the middle of the desert, at the spot called 'Marble Arch', my wheel of fate took an encouraging turn. I was ordered back to Egypt for a medical. Around April 1943 I flew to Heliopolis. Excited, impatient and hopeful, I arrived late at night and bedded down on a table in the dining mess. The next day I reported for my medical, obsessed by two worries: my weight and my right eye, which, I felt, was less than 100 per cent perfect. I underwent the test and got posted back to Hilwan, and then on to Cairo – to become the driver of the Chief Signals Officer for the Middle East. So there I was once again, churning the highroads, and I was fed up to the back teeth!

In the summer of 1943, Cairo glowed like a furnace. From seven in the morning till midday, we would work; from midday till five in the afternoon, we would seek relief from the heat, which sucked us dry, leaving us spiritless and apathetic; from five to eight back to work. I would sit around 'Midan Ismailia', getting to know the night life. Together with other adventurous souls, both men and women, I indulged in all kinds of pranks, some of which I regret, others which I remember with a smile, while most have completely slipped my mind.

For two months I was tormented by a British corporal – Jones of accursed memory – who set out to make my life a misery. Every morning I would come to the car park to find Jones in wait for his prey.

'Weizman,' he would say.

'Yes corporal!'

'You want to be a fighter pilot?'

The devil! 'Certainly, corporal.'

'Very well,' he said, relishing his lousy sense of humour, 'go and wash the bloody car!'

So I washed it. And washed it again. And again. And again. Until I was so sick at heart that I wasn't far from some act of folly.

One morning I came to the park, and instead of Jones, I was met by a Jewish corporal, who greeted me with 'Weizman, you've got a posting.' I thought that Jones had tired of his game, and he'd decided to let his Jewish friend in on the fun. But a Jew? Maybe. 'To Tripoli?' I asked hopefully. 'No chum,' he said with a good-natured smile, 'you've been posted to a flying school.'

2

FIRST FLIGHTS

I FOUND MYSELF in the Suez Canal transit camp, on my way to the pilots' course; my heart was singing, and all the layers of frustration and disappointment were peeling off. I smiled and laughed and dreamed at night of the Cadet Pilot badge, and it seemed as though the whole world was smiling with me.

There were five weeks of nerve-racking waiting to endure at the transit camp. My fancies were sky-high, but my living conditions were still miserable, and I was full of nagging doubts. Many of the men in the camp were waiting to go to the pilots' course in Rhodesia. What made life pleasant was a group of Palestinians (in those days, before the establishment of the State of Israel, Jews were Palestinians too). I met Corporal Aharon Midan, later a colonel in the Israeli air force and head of its adjutancy. He fixed me up with three days of home leave, bless him. I picked up the names of Gideon Gordon (now Elrom) and Geda Shocket, who had left for Rhodesia with the previous batch of Palestinians. There was also an English Jew, the Commander, Wing Commander Cohen. From my previous postings, I had got used to the British army's traditional Sunday church parade. Everyone would stand at attention, while the sergeant-major roared: 'Fall out Roman Catholics and Jews.' There were always a lot of Catholics, and a smattering of Jews. It was the same in this camp, except that when the order was given, Wing Commander Cohen would also step forward and join the Jews at prayer.

But the great event at this camp was my meeting with Moddy

Allon, with whom I was unacquainted. He was pure gold, that fellow: strong, thorough, stable. In time, we were to become very close, as we helped the Israeli air force take its first steps. We wanted to be thoroughly prepared for the course. We were eaten up with doubts and fears. Maybe we won't pass the examination in mathematics, or physics? Heaven forbid, we might get thrown out before the course begins!

Moddy was older than I and more experienced. He had been waiting two and a half years for this RAF course. He was also a more established member of the Haganah. I greatly enjoyed my friendship with him, especially our talks about home; he was like a breath of fresh air. We dug up books wherever we could, so that this awesome course would find us ready and worthy.

While we waited for a ship to take us to Rhodesia, every now and then we would go off to Ismailia, to pass the time. But time flowed by with burdensome sluggishness, and my heart was beset by that same old fear of the war ending with us in this transit camp, with no further need for pilots, and I'd be sent home and discharged – ex-driver Weizman.

Finally there was a ship, and we got our orders. But then I almost cut short my flying career in Ismailia, in the company of a charming girl, with whom I am friendly to this day. The evening before we were to embark, I went to Ismailia for a brief good-bye. The good-bye dragged on, and then another good-bye, and another. Finally, I headed back to the camp at a crazy rush, using my last drop of strength to stagger to the ship with my kit-bag and my belongings.

We set sail from Port Tewfik. The ship was French, small and stinking, with 1,500 men crammed into her, some 250 of them pilot cadets on their way to the course. Twelve or thirteen were from Palestine. Three of us were good friends: Moddy, Hans Weissbord (now a senior El Al employee) and myself. We had to get ourselves organized on this little French vessel, which was tossing over the waves, propelled by its steam boilers. Even though it was October, our trip from Egypt to Aden, the first stop for taking on coal, was oppressively hot. The heat, coming together with the heavy stench, was unbearable. Moddy, Hans and I decided to take up quarters on deck. In this way we were rid of the heat and able to inhale fresh air.

We sailed further and further away. It was a slightly strange feeling. In a way, Egypt was still part of home, part of the Middle East; now, we were getting further away, cutting our ties with our homes. From now on, thousands of miles of sea would separate the young cadet Weizman from 4 Melchett Street in Haifa.

War was raging in Europe. There was bloody fighting in India. You go out into the world, placing yourself inside its jaws, and there is no way of knowing when and how they will clamp down on you. You feel as though you're sitting on the tip of a lion's tongue: if he feels like it, he'll leave you outside; if not, he'll pull you in and gobble you up. Sunrise, sunset, another sunrise and another sunset. We spent four weeks at sea on that deck. All that time Moddy, Hans and I were in a kind of sanctuary far from the bustling activity of the ship. It was a floating Babylon – cards, dice and primitive roulette wheels, with money passing from hand to hand twenty-four hours a day. In the end, even though we kept away from the gambling, the crooks took the last penny from our pockets. Apparently a gang of Chinese had combined with a gang of Frenchmen to plunder all the food on the ship. When your belly's full, you can be a man of principle; but hunger doesn't give a damn for all your principles, and you're forced to go to the thieves and buy a little food, to pacify your guts. When we got to Durban in South Africa, all the money was concentrated in ten pockets, while all the rest of us were cleaned out and penniless.

After anchoring briefly at Aden, we set sail at dusk. Off the Somali shore, I feasted my eyes on one of the most beautiful sunsets I have ever seen. An enormous ball of fire daubed the sky a bright red, and millions of rays of afterglow surged over the horizon. After we set sail, we joined a convoy of thirty or thirty-five ships; an escort plane flew overhead and destroyers sailed at our side, to protect us from the naval attack. Every morning and evening we had lifeboat drill, and there was a strict ban on taking off our lifebelts.

Four lousy weeks succeeded in making me long for the Western Desert! Everything was cramped and crowded day and night. Hans and I found a weird kind of two-seated contraption, which we chanced to discover in the ship's stern. We would sit there, enjoying our privacy and blessing our good fortune, as the ship tossed up and down. A great life!

One night we thought our end had come. In the Indian Ocean, not far from Mozambique, Hans, Moddy and I were lying on the deck in our hammocks. It was a wonderful moonlit night, on the far side of the Equator, and there was an air of pastoral tranquillity over everything; we were half asleep, half sinking into the whispering silence. Suddenly we flew out of our hammocks to the sound of a terrifying boom, while the ship tottered from side to side, almost splitting in half. Saturated with stories of enemy submarines lurking in the area, we were convinced that a torpedo had hit the ship, and in a flash, we flung ourselves into a lifeboat and were about to cast off from the torpedoed vessel, when it transpired that our ship's steering had developed a fault, causing her to make a crazy 90-degree turn and collide with one of the other ships in the convoy. Not at all pleasant. I would not like to relive that scene, as hundreds of panic-stricken soldiers stampeded out of the holds to save their lives. Moddy, Hans and I went off, abashed, each to his own hammock, and pretended to sleep, to avoid the need to exchange embarrassed comments.

When our voyage ended at Durban in South Africa, I found that it was very profitable to be a Jewish lad from Palestine. The local Jewish club gave us a taste of national solidarity. In the twenty-four hours we spent there, we were engulfed with the goodies of an affluent society: hot showers and foam baths, regal repasts and piles of pineapples and, above all, love and affection. A day and a half by train from Durban, and we were in Bulawayo, Rhodesia. My heart was in the clouds. I weaved my little dreams: outside the railway station in Rhodesia, cars would be waiting to take us to the comfortable, roomy base. Not quite. At the station 250 of us were lined up in threes to face the onslaught of six British sports instructors in shorts, each one a jolly-green-giant sergeant-major. 'Cadets!' they bellowed, 'By the right, quick march!' And we marched, in step, loaded with our heavy kit-bags, the three miles to the camp.

A pilots' course they called it. It was a hard life, and a young man needed a lot of patience and persistence to endure it. Many of the training methods have not changed to this day. For four or five months we concerned ourselves with various and sundries, without so much as a glimpse of a plane. We were taught basic theory in the preparatory course. We shed a lot of sweat to build up our physical fitness; our nerves were shredded in toughening ourselves psychologically. We were classified and re-classified, to sift out those who were suitable, those who were less suitable, and those who were totally unsuitable. There were lots of courses: flying theory, meteorology, basic navigation, RAF regulations. And there were tests, week in and week out – written, oral, psychotechnical – and obstacle races and route marches and physical exercises. Within me I could sense a tremendous desire to succeed. I had to complete the course, and when I have to do something, nothing diverts me from my goal.

The Jewish cadets were on good terms with the Bulawayo Jewish community. We made ourselves at home in the house of the local rabbi. Once, coming there while he was away, we went into the kitchen and smeared butter and jam on some bread. The rabbi's black cook came in and scolded us in a sorrowful voice, 'Oh, you smeared butter with the meat knife! You mustn't, you mustn't.'

At the end of the preparatory course, the British assigned some cadets to fighter planes and others to two-engine bombers. I yearned for a fighter plane; I didn't want some kind of 'flying bus'. To my joy I was sent to a preliminary fighter-pilots' course at a place called Guinea Fowl, near the town of Gwelo. It was a God-forsaken spot, with two main streets and three bars, whose exterior and interior were equally unattractive. When I entered the camp, I would have remained rooted to the spot, if I hadn't been urged to hurry. I wanted to breathe in the smell, this fragrance I had dreamed of, the odour of planes, that wonderful mixture of aviation fuel, lubrication oil and airplane tyres. Each plane has its own smell. Only someone who has not spent most of his years near planes can think of a plane as no more than a mass of metal and wires. A plane is a living, breathing body, and it should be treated as such.

Many years later, when I took my farewell of the Israeli air force, I was deeply moved as I thought back to the beginning of my flying career. As I recalled those wonderful moments with that magnificent smell of fuel and oil and tyres, I told my air-force colleagues: 'I advise you to treat the machines which have been [e]ntrusted to your care as though they had souls; but you must [ne]ver treat the souls which have been entrusted to your command [as th]ough they were machines.'

[Wi]thin seconds of realizing my dreams, as I was about to take [fir]st flight in a basic plane, my luck took a 180-degree [turn abo]ut, and my career almost came to an end there and then, in [a remo]te little township in Rhodesia. It was five in the morning, [...] after my arrival at the preliminary course. At my [...]side, I was walking – no, not really walking, more like [float]ing – towards my first flight in a training plane. But I [was feelin]g remorseful about not having been completely [... I]t was unfair of me not to have told my instructor [...]k recorded twenty-five hours' flying time in the [cl]ub. On the way to the plane, with the parachute [... discl]osed this fact. He smiled, half-forgiving, half-[...]sed me with a terse: 'Forget it!'

[...] the plane and then *he* made a mistake: [...]on, he asked me to turn the propellor. [... t]urn and heard a kind of cracking, like [... no]t mistaken. The bones of my hand were [... givi]ng down, limp and crooked. A man [... d]esert; he tears his guts out in the [...], close to the climax of his dreams – [... driv]er drove up and rushed me to the [...], 'Do you think it's broken, sir?' [...] 'Looks like it.' British understate-

[...]er and my spirits in my boots. [... w]here I was stuck in the RAF [...]me, so as not to worry my [...]er, telling me that while he [...]got a knock from a bus, [... h]and. That gave me the [... cor]respondence, a kind of [... hosp]ital in Tel Aviv to the.

my stomach. Why

me? Why never me? What is this? I was feeling lonely, and this loneliness was dangerous. I fought it, fearing that my broken hand would break my spirit. Mentally, I looked myself straight in the eye, without any shilly-shallying: 'Weizman my boy, this broken hand of yours, will it cause a total breakdown, or will it be no more than a minor pot-hole on a long route? Will you manage to pick up the pieces?' It wasn't easy. The plaster cast was removed, and the fracture had not healed up properly. It had to be broken again and my torments were resumed. Inside I was shouting: 'Don't give in!'

By the time the damned thing had healed up and could moved and I had gone on leave and returned to base at long la found myself alone, the only Palestinian amidst a sea of stran all Englishmen. Jews, the Land of Israel, our struggle fo independence of our homeland – it was all Greek to them. I g my way carefully. I told them of our dreams of indepen provoking them into heated arguments, which raged on i small hours. The barriers between us fell.

When I first returned to the course, I found things very By supreme effort I managed to convince the doctor who e me that my hand was back in shape. But this was far case: every movement was arduous and painful. Durin month, I could scarcely move my left hand, and whe to lower the plane's flaps – done with a push of the l would kick the lever with my left heel, terrified th would notice and that I'd be sent back to the eventually weeded out of the course – a thought that cold sweat.

One thing that helped smooth over the difficulties friendship I struck with a charming Englishma Brindley, now a captain for British Airways and n day. For both of us it was affection almost Throughout we were room-mates and shared Despite the difference in nationality, we ha common: our love for flying, for planes an connected with them.

I suppose he was drawn to me because of the me, as a Jew. His interest was first aroused by from right to left. That baffled him. He was curious to discover what it was that made up my special world, he was curious about the bizarre people I belonged to – a people who lacked a sovereign country of their own, but lived and prayed for independence. It was this strangeness that gripped his attention. I found him to be a wonderful fellow. His honesty and decency were as near perfect as I've ever encountered. A close friendship developed between us. We laughed together, suffered together and worried together. We were not worried about both of us failing the course. Our principal worry was that only one of us would be dismissed, forcing us to separate.

He was a straightforward Englishman, and that's what he has remained, without intellectual pretensions or neuroses. It was his simplicity that charmed me. Apart from that, he deserves a prize for having lived so close to me for such a long time and having suffered various manifestations of my turbulent nature without responding in kind, without withdrawing – and without even being insulted!

My character has got me into trouble on several occasions and has endangered many of my ambitions. This almost happened while I was training to fly. To explain, I should say a few words about the climate in Rhodesia, which is a plateau, about 5,000 feet above sea level, more or less in the centre of Africa. At certain times of the year the land is shrouded by morning mists. In Rhodesia nature obeys all the rules of conspiracy. It gives no advance warning; suddenly the sky is obscured, with the cloud-base lowering almost down to ground level. This calls for caution, and there were mornings when we did not fly at all before the heat of the sun drove the mists away.

One morning I walked into the mess at 4.30 for my cup of tea and a sweet bun. My instructor said: 'Go up for a solo flight, about 40–45 minutes – a bit of flying, a bit of aerobatics, but watch out for the morning mists! The moment you notice them, you come straight back to the base, instantly, without any playing around!'

'Yes, sir.' How I loved those solo flights! I climbed to 4,000 feet, did a nice loop and one upward roll. Then, out of the corner of my eye, I noticed the *gooto*, as they called that heavy cloud, and it was approaching rapidly. 'What?' I said to myself, 'Just because of a few clouds, give up and go back?' So I did another roll and another nice loop and looked again: darkness, everything obscured. I still paid no attention. I did some aerobatics, and I let myself get carried away by a mixture of levity and foolhardiness. It would not have taken much for me to stay up there in the Cornell two-seater, or crash into the soil of Rhodesia. However, I did decide to try and get back to base and land on the runway, if only for my own gratification as a pilot of practically no experience. (I had then flown for a total of only 40–45 hours.)

I found the edge of the *gooto* and began to descend, abandoning myself to my fate. I watched for a certain solitary tree, near the base, which we all knew quite well, leaving myself time to think that if a wind, or a man, happened to have cut it down, it would be farewell to Weizman. But my luck held, and there was the tree. I went down, below the clouds, hugging the ground, seeing nothing except the tree. I flew straight towards it, lower, a little to the left, a little to the right – and there it was! A line of planes – everyone else had returned – indicated the runway. I glided, touched down and taxied in, as though nothing had happened. But my blood froze as a roar of 'Weizman, where have you been?' pinned me to the ground, and by the time I thawed out, I saw my instructor, ready to take over where the *gooto* had failed – in breaking my bones.

'I was doing aerobatics, sir,' I said truthfully, my voice expressing my astonishment at the strange question.

'Didn't you see?' he demanded.

'I did,' I said.

'Look how everything's obscured! Just look!'

I wanted to tell him that I had noticed before, and there was no need to look again, but why overdo things? Perhaps I could come out of this damned *gooto* without getting screwed. So I said simply, 'But I came back, sir.' I stood at attention, without blinking, praying for him to leave me alone.

'Weizman!' (God, what was he going to say?) 'Take your parachute and get into that plane!'

He got in with me and took the joystick and guided the plane, forcing his way up through the low clouds. He made my stomach quiver, rocking me back and forth, flying to and fro. Down below there was nothing to be seen, because the *gooto* had covered everything. Then he said one short sentence, and his intention became clear: 'Weizman, you've got her.' He handed over the controls, and then he said the last words I was to hear from him that day. 'Take me home.' Once again, a turn here, a turn there. I caught sight of that wonderful tree and flew straight at it, lower and lower, to the runway and landing. Silence. We got out of the plane – still not a word. We walked down the runway and parted without so much as a grunt. That day the following comment was entered in my log book: 'Inclines to over-confidence.' What can I say? He had a sharp eye, that instructor.

There were many pilots who sought that solitary tree, but not all of them were lucky. Those who didn't make it made the cemetery instead. Years after the day that I found the tree, whenever I decided the fate of some brave young boy who inclined to 'over-confidence', I knew that I was dealing with a promising pilot, and it was only necessary to overcome his bravado and to channel his courage and self-confidence into some useful route.

So as not to give my superiors the chance to hold my earlier sins against me, I was doubly careful after that incident. Being a 'goodie-goodie' was not to my liking, but the course was important to me, and no effort was too great.

The course was extremely arduous – far more so than those the RAF ran in 1940, for example. The reason is simple: the way pilots are trained, the requirements and demands made on them, are directly influenced by the degree of urgency with which the air force requires additional pilots at a particular stage of a war. When Britain was fighting for her life, and desperately needed every pilot, she was obliged to be less strict with the cadets, so as to step up the flow of new pilots. Britain's situation was critical in 1940, and the price – lower standards, poorer pilots who gained their wings after no more than 200 hours of flying – had to be paid. On the other hand, in 1944, when I was due to get my wings, Britain was winning, the German knife was far from her throat, and she could afford to put more time into training her pilots, at the same time demanding more of them and sifting the graduates through a finer sieve. The instructors were stricter, more meticulous. I got my wings after more than 300 flying hours, and after

I had been methodically and consistently exhausted – yet another bombing drill, another bout of aerobatics, another night flight, another instrumental flight. In 1940 pilots were turned out in their hundreds, while the attitude we encountered seemed to say: 'Dear cadets, we don't need you very urgently. So if you still want your pilots' wings, you'll have to tear your guts out!'

And we did. We lived under constant pressure, which is exhausting enough in itself. Once, on a relatively advanced course, I had to do a navigation test in a Harvard plane, and I by-passed the objective. I simply missed it. Instead of reaching some bend in the Londy River, I landed up two miles away. I fumed and cursed and raged at myself. That morning I was all thumbs and my head was full of cobwebs. I could not concentrate, and before I got very far I knew that I wasn't going to make it. I got into a complete panic, making me fly even further off course. In my mind's eye, I could already imagine my commanding officer looking at me with pitying eyes and saying: 'Weizman, you're a good chap, but you must understand . . .' Fortunately, that did not happen. They gave me a second chance, and I never missed again.

The basic course finally came to an end, and we set off on a trip across Central Africa, enjoying the wonderful landscapes and views, such as the Victoria Falls. I had good reason to be proud of my Judaism: wherever we went, there were Jews – concerned, dependable, affectionate – true brethren. We walked around in shorts, wearing our RAF forage-caps, in search of minor adventures, feeling on top of the world.

At the time, I did not know what an injustice I had done to Aunt Vera. I had not seen my parents for a long time, and I thought they'd be pleased to get a postcard from the Jewish family of Wasserson, whose acquaintance I made in Livingstone. I asked them to send the card to the home of my uncle Chaim in Rehovot, where my father was living at the time because of his work in the south. It was only many months later, when I saw my parents again, that I found out what had happened. The card, addressed to 'Weizmann, Rehovot', was received by my aunt and uncle, who were thunderstruck. It was two years after their son Michael had been killed, but in their hearts they hoped, like all parents, that some day he would emerge alive and well. And behold, a postcard from Livingstone saying: 'We met your son, he is flying and he sends you his love.' It took courage to shatter that terrible illusion, and Chaim and Vera were bitterly disappointed.

I got my wings at the beginning of 1945, towards the end of the war. Only some 25 per cent of the graduates – mostly Englishmen – were given officer's rank after completing the course. Most of us – Bill and myself included – only made sergeant. But we were pilots, duly installed, and there were no bounds to my joy and satisfaction at achieving that great dream, whose prospects of fulfilment had often seemed negligable. I do not hesitate to say that when a man has his wings pinned on at the passing-out parade, it is one of the most moving experiences of his life. Later there are other events in one's personal and family life, other peaks in one's career but that experience never fades.

The memories of that day and the night that followed have accompanied me for many years – the British general pinning on my wings, the meticulous salute, the splendid ceremonial parade. After the parade was dismissed, I ran arrow-straight to my room, quickly removing the wings the general had just awarded me – they are always of poor quality – and replacing them with the bright new wings that almost everyone had the foresight to purchase. That night's party was quite an event: different groups locked in ferocious battle with fire extinguishers, while their terrifying roars shook the whole camp. But the morning after, a pleasant weariness spread over my limbs, and my soul was bathed in a profound feeling of satisfaction and contentedness.

We were ready to fly back to Egypt, but not before the camp sergeant-major – a dapper Englishman, whose every crease was in its proper place – presented the RAF's brand-new pilots with an itemized bill of damages. Kindly pay up, gentlemen! 'So much for the splintered table, so much for the shattered chairs, and be good enough not to forget the extinguishers; and please dive into the swimming pool and fetch out everything you hurled in during the course of the night's festivity. A party is a party, but RAF property must be treated with due respect.'

There was one prominent difference between me and the Englishmen in the course. Whenever they said 'home' – and they were probably as homesick as any other youngsters – they simply meant father, mother, sister, brother, a room, friends, a girl, a warm fire, family life, Saturday football – that was their home, as it was mine (minus the football). But my thoughts of home contained additional elements, of a kind which the British fellows were unacquainted with: the Land of Israel, the Jewish community there, the future. The Palestinian landscape seemed so alive and near at times that I felt I only had to open my window and I'd be looking out at the blue Sea of Galilee, the rounded form of Mount Tabor and the green Jezreel Valley, with the peaks of Mount Hermon twinkling whenever visibility permitted.

My memories of the landscape at home were accompanied by concern, which I find hard to define exactly or to fit into an explicit frame of reference. What would happen to our land? At that time I did not think in today's terms, my view was not so broad or far-sighted. I could not imagine that when the State of Israel was established it would experience a decades-long war with the whole Middle East. Egypt seemed like a part of home, and the air smelled friendly, not hostile. But I was always sure the Palestinian Arabs would be all over us the moment we proclaimed our political independence. At that time I did not foresee that our efforts to combat the Arabs would produce an Israeli air force. Above all, I did not foresee our fantastic victories, or predict that our airmen could be among the finest and most renowned in the world. All that was so unbelievably remote, not even my dreams went that far.

But I had a feeling that my strenuous training in Rhodesia and the know-how I was acquiring would be of significance in the complex struggle awaiting us, as my people fought for their independence. And with that unclear, undefined sense of belonging to that struggle, there was another feeling: I would bring to it something unique, a previously unknown dimension. Not a Parabellum pistol, or a mortar, or a machine-gun; not dogging through trenches – without, heaven forbid, discounting their importance and the personal heroism involved – but something greater, of more decisive importance. With these feelings fresh within me, I traversed the whole of Africa by transport plane, crossing northern Rhodesia (present-day Zambia) to Lake Victoria, then by way of Uganda to Sudan, with a four-day delay in

Khartoum due to an engine fault. A breakdown like that can involve you in days of dull routine that every subsequent event will erase from your memory without trace. This time it was otherwise. I walked out of the Khartoum airfield, on my way into town to while away a few hours of boredom, with Bill Brindley at my side. On the road I noticed a strange-looking man – blond, European and handcuffed – being escorted by a squad of British soldiers. I stopped and stared curiously, and the handcuffed man grew very agitated when he caught sight of my 'Palestine' shoulder flash. I wanted to talk to him, but his guards hurried him away, and when I walked on and turned around for another look, I saw the man looking back at me, catching my glance. Who was he?

The question plagued me for a few days while other events caught up with me, driving it out of my mind. A few years later, after the establishment of the State of Israel, Ya'akov Meridor (one of the leaders of the then-underground Irgun Zvai Le'umi and later a Knesset member from the Herut Party) said to me: 'Ezer, in Khartoum that time, on the way out of the airfield, do you remember? You were walking along with an Englishman, on your way to town ...' Now I felt my emotions welling up and could hardly believe it. The strange man I had seen was Ya'akov, who had been arrested by the British for his underground activities and was then being brought back from one of his escape bids. Of all the millions of people who rubbed shoulders during World War Two, I had met, without even knowing it – and in Khartoum, of all places – a man who was to become a close friend.

Egypt had not changed much during the long months of my absence: it was still stinking, disgusting, crawling with vice and prostitution. After the pressures and challenges of the courses in Rhodesia, life in Egypt was empty. That is one of the traits of a great war involving millions of people; one has to adapt to sharp transitions, from high hopes to soulless routine, from high tensions to an indifferent dreariness.

I was posted to an air-crew centre near Alexandria. One fine day I was informed that there was a plane from Akkir and that I would be flying home. Undeniably my father's doing. It was winter, and the flight through Sinai was turbulent. The commander of Akkir, a British group captain by the name of Harry Owen (in time, we became close friends), was awaiting me, and he sent me off to Haifa in his car. At home they did not know exactly when I'd be coming. After an absence of eighteen months, I stood, trembling with excitement, gazing up at 4 Melchett Street. Everything was in place: eleven steps up from the courtyard, another small step beside the door mat, then another four, another five, three, and another twenty-three – carefully counted, as before the war. Then Father and Mother, embraces, kisses, excitement. 'Tell us.' 'Where?' 'When?' 'How?' But time was pressing, and my feet were fidgety. A good bath, and the boy from Haifa, 'the imp with the bicycle', in all the glory of his RAF uniform, his chest thrust out to display his wings, strutted into the Atara Café, wafting in on billowing clouds of pride. And if anyone wanted to slap him on the shoulder and say a few friendly words, he did not complain.

That leave was short but good. Then, I returned to Egypt for an operational training course in Faid – an airfield west of the Suez Canal that nearly three decades later was to be successively occupied, operated and evacuated by the Israeli air force. When a young man has learnt to fly and has received his wings, his splendour filleth the whole land. But now the time had come for me to learn to *fight*. You weren't made a pilot so that you could fly around and do aerobatics, or puff out your chest in Haifa's Atara Café. As someone later wrote at the Israeli Air Force's Super-Mystère squadron base: 'An air force without armament is a flying club.'

At Faid, probably for the first time since my decision to join the RAF, I had to make a free choice concerning my future path. I had to weigh all kinds of considerations and reach a decision of the utmost importance. On our first day at Faid, we were called together and told that some of us would do our operational training on Spitfires, Britain's most famous plane in the Second World War, while the others would take on Thunderbolts. The British commander wanted those who chose the Thunderbolt to do so of their own free choice. There were conflicting considerations. The Thunderbolt is an American plane. It is heavier than the Spitfire and aroused greater apprehension among pilots. It was a more difficult plane to fly, and many pilots had paid for that fact with their lives.

There does exist a clear distinction between planes: some are harder than others. In a plane like that, errors are more likely and their price is higher. Such errors stem specifically from the plane's structure. When the designers and engineers are less than successful, it is the pilot who pays the price. The reverse is also largely true: many pilots' achievements are no more than the fruits of the designers' success in overcoming difficulties. At that time the aviation world was still unacquainted with the problems of breaking the sound barrier or the effects of air pressure on the fuselage. The first to exceed the speed of sound was a man by the name of Chuck Yaeger. He was showered with compliments and overwhelmed with praise and universal admiration; a few years passed until it transpired that this achievement, like others that followed it, belonged to the designers far more than to the pilots.

At high velocities, the American Thunderbolt began to touch compressibility problems. At that time, no one talked of Mach 1, Mach 2 and so on. Without being an expert on all these problems and difficulties, I was nonetheless fascinated by a more advanced plane, like the Thunderbolt. But in the last resort, what tipped the scales was an entirely different consideration: I knew that whoever took the Spitfire would be sent to Italy. By that time the war in Europe was over, while fighting continued in the Far East where the war was giving a final wag of its tail. Like a child pursuing a plaything he has been promised, I wanted to give a tug at the tail, to taste something of the cruel flavour of battle.

Bill Brindley raised his hand together with mine. We spent three months at Faid in arduous and intensive training: firing, bombing and navigation – mostly over the Mitla Pass in the Sinai Desert, with which I was making my first aerial acquaintance; my subsequent encounters with it were much stormier.

Besides the knowledge and experience I gained from the course in Faid, I took away with me very pleasant memories of a model commanding officer, Group Captain Frank Cary, as well as acquiring the identification mark that was to be my personal emblem for many years. The C.O. had the use of a black Spitfire with a red nose. At weekends, after days of exhausting training, Cary would settle his nerves by indulging in a most original form of relaxation: he would take off in his black 'Spit' and streak across the sky over Faid and the vicinity. I would stand there enviously. I could not watch him enough. Later, in the Israeli air force, when I was promoted to base commander, I could not resist the temptation, and my envy was translated into action: I gave orders to have one of our Spitfires painted black, and from then on I enjoyed streaking through Israeli air-space in my own black 'Spit'.

A four-engine sea-plane carried us from Egypt to India in a last attempt to catch up with a war whose end was drawing near, thank God. There were thirty or forty of us in the plane. Cairo–Basra–Bahrein–Karachi. It was the beginning of 1945. A shattered world was trying to staunch its bleeding and pull itself together. At home, my folks were longing to see 'their boy', but he was heading East.

In those days, when a Palestinian reached a new base, anywhere in the world-wide British Empire, the first thing he did – before even taking off his uniform, before changing, before unpacking his kit-bag – was to run to the camp notice-board and scan the names on the various rotas, always on the lookout for an Israeli name. And when he found one he knew, he breathed a deep sigh of relief. So it was no wonder that I became excited when I picked out the name of Geda Shochet on the camp notice-board in Karachi. It was a year since I'd seen him in Rhodesia and given him a note to my mother, who used to claim that she had practically raised him.

Karachi was one hell of a camp – miles long. Tired, hungry and thirsty, I trudged from tent to tent, poking my head into the openings as I tried to sniff out Geda Shochet. But when I found him, it wasn't just plain Geda Shochet that I stumbled upon. The commander of a four-engine Liberator bomber was stretched out reading a Hebrew newspaper on a bed in one of the tents, reclining like some sultan, while four or five British sergeants – part of the plane's twelve-man crew of air gunners, navigators and flight engineers who worshipped and obeyed Geda – were playing cards on the floor. I paused for a moment, took a deep breath and roared: 'Flight-Sergeant Shochet!' After that, things happened at flying speed. Geda leaped up off his bed like an acrobat and hurled himself into my arms; meanwhile the British sergeants cleared the tent – why should they trouble themselves with a couple of lunatics from Palestine!

Most of the time, I was in a town called Bangalor doing patrols here and there, ferrying planes about. The war? No sign, no trace. It was over, finished. And just as well.

I lived in India for nine or ten months and got thoroughly sick of the country. Weighed down with human problems, trying to remove the British yoke without bloodshed, it was poverty-stricken and starving. Anyone who wanted to could live like a king in India. Your shoes would be cleaned for a puff on a cigarette; for a slice of bread, you would be served for a whole day. Yet it was degrading. There was no lack of entertainment of various kinds, but when the commanding officer summoned me to ask if I wanted to stay another year and a half, with the prospect of an officer's commission, I didn't hesitate: I preferred to go home. Their war was over, but ours had yet to begin, and I felt that I ought to be at home.

A ship that was making its way to Liverpool dropped me off at Port Tewfik, at the same wharf where I had embarked for my pilots' course in Rhodesia. A telegram to my parents' home in Haifa did all the rest. A heavy plane carried me to Hazor airfield, where Father and Mother were awaiting me. Within a short time, at the base in Ramle – where I had taken my driving test upon joining the RAF four years before – I was discharged from the service.

3

FLYING UNDERGROUND

ONCE AGAIN I was plunged into dull routine. If I had been a grenade expert, for instance, I presume that both the Irgun Zvai Le'umi (IZL) and the Haganah (underground Jewish military organizations) would have sought to make use of my know-how. But I was a pilot, one of the twenty or twenty-five Palestinians who got their wings in the RAF. So what? May his wings bring him joy!

Persuaded by my father, I left for London in June 1946 to study. Post-war London was still black and melancholy. My sister, Yael, who had married an English officer, was living in Pinner. Like London, she had a beautiful past, a grey present and a clouded future. The English were trying to drown their dreariness in barrels of rum and lousy beer, while I was trying to study, but I was homesick for Palestine, then much in the news.

Shortly after I reached London, there was an explosion in the King David Hotel in Jerusalem, which then housed the British command in Palestine. As the radio was blaring the news, Uncle Chaim summoned me to him urgently. I hurried to the Dorchester Hotel. Aunt Vera and Uncle Chaim were sitting in room 212 with Professor David Bergman. There was an air of sombreness and mourning in the room, and you could have cut the tension with a knife. I sat down and studied their sorrowful faces.

Finally, Uncle Chaim broke the heavy silence. '*Nu*, what do you think of it?' he asked in his English, which had never lost its East European intonation. 'It' did not require elaboration. I sensed

Aunt Vera's scorching gaze; she was silent for the moment, but she seemed to be saying: '*Now* we'll see what Yechiel's son thinks of his friends murdering Englishmen.'

My reply may not have been entirely free of flippancy, but I really believed that we had to fight the British with all we had in order to gain our independence. I answered quietly, 'Not at all a bad idea.' Terse. In English. But it was a thunderbolt. Behind me, Aunt Vera, icy as only she could be, fired off, 'If you think it's such a good idea, why don't you go back to Palestine and shoot a few Englishmen?'

I did a kind of half-turn, took in the fury on her face, and said, 'Aunt Vera, that, too, is not at all a bad idea!'

They were polite and family-minded enough not to throw me out. But the atmosphere was ruined irreparably, and the meal was shortened to a tenth of its normal length. When I got up to go, no one bothered to try and ask me to stay. I blasted out of there like a rocket going into orbit.

That was, as I said, in June 1946. It is interesting to mention that the Uncle Chaim I found in Rehovot in December 1948 was quite unlike the man in the Dorchester. I would pass by Rehovot occasionally; Uncle Chaim and I had become very close at that time, and I knew that he gained a lot of satisfaction from my role in the War of Independence. Each meeting with him was a moving experience. He was isolated, almost totally cut off from the events of the war; yet he still exuded traits of leadership and authority, even though there was no concrete outlet for them. After we forced our way into Sinai in 1948 – the first of our three incursions – I told him we had reached Abu Ageila, breaking through the Egyptian defence lines and shooting down some of their planes. There was a great deal of excitement in my voice and possibly in my expression as well. Uncle Chaim listened attentively, his wise eyes sparkling with a kind of moistness, and then he asked, 'Ezer, why don't we go to Cairo?' It was said half in fun, half seriously – I never worked out how he really meant it. In any case, during 1948 I had more than one opportunity to observe that the great Chaim Weizmann had undergone a far-reaching change in his political views. But he was already nearing the end of his days; he'd been pushed to the political side-lines, where he observed the dramatic events like a man whose time was past.

Homesick as I was, my stay in London might have been cut short had fate not led me to an encounter with a unique figure: Boris Senior. We met at the Jewish 'Palestine Club' in London. Boris, an affable young South African Jew, was studying at the London School of Economics. He was a bit of an eccentric, slightly at loggerheads with himself, something of an adventurer and crazy about flying. What more do two young men need to become close, if not a shared craze? It transpired that Boris was a member of the RAF Flying Club, and within three short days, while we were still getting to know each other, we were off to Sweden together in an open plane – in mid-winter! When we reached southern England, Boris broke a finger due to some hitch, and we turned back. The more I heard of Boris, from himself as well as from others, the more I grew attached to him. He was a pilot with a lot of combat experience. He had been shot down near Venice during the war and was brought out in a brilliant rescue operation.

It's strange that it was Boris, a man who did not grow up in Palestine, who should have recruited me into the IZL. Shortly after we made each other's acquaintance, he began to talk me into aiding the IZL in its operations. I did not need much persuading: I'd been looking for some national occupation, some Zionist task to relieve me of the feeling that while great events were taking place at home, I was far away, practising aerobatics. Boris moved in with me, and we travelled to France, where I made the acquaintance of Dr Ya'akov Eli Tabin and Eliyahu Lankin, who recruited us into the ranks of the IZL in Europe. We took underground crash courses in all kinds of sabotage tricks. After that, we were given our first assignment: to assassinate a British general by the name of Barker. Various snags foiled the operation. Scotland Yard had been watching our moves. They may have not known anything precise, but what they knew was enough for them to approach me, with true British courtesy, and proffer me some 'good advice': 'Be so kind as to return to Palestine'.

It would have been unwise to ignore such 'advice'. I returned home to Haifa, by way of France, where I met Eli Tabin again. Papers were concealed in the soles of my shoes, messages from the IZL in Europe to their command in Tel Aviv. I delivered my shoes in Tel Aviv's Allenby Street and was sent to Rothschild Boulevard, where I had my first meeting with Chaim Landau ('Avraham', as he was code-named). I was afire for action, but he cooled my enthusiasm: 'My dear friend, stay quiet until we call you'.

The summer of 1947 passed. 'Stay quiet' was easy to say, much harder to do. There was a political struggle raging throughout the world over the future of Palestine. The country's Arabs were in turmoil, preparing for the war of annihilation, and I was told to stay quiet! I ate my heart out. Father tried to keep me occupied – some tractor-driving here and there – but this was dull and unsatisfying.

This rootless interim period came to an end when I was approached by Haganah leaders in Haifa, who told me that 'there was going to be a serious United Nations decision, and it has been decided to set up an air service'. They invited me to join. I felt a little uncomfortable, because they did not know of my ties with the IZL, and I did not enlighten them. 'Let's go!' I said. Chaim Landau, the only IZL contact I knew in the country, gave me his approval.

On 29 November 1947, the United Nations 'granted' us a state – emasculated and disjointed, without Jaffa, without Lod (Lydda) and without Ramle. But all of us were so eager for some beginning, for some recognition of our right to independence, that we spent the night glued to our radios, counting the 'yeas' and 'nays' of the nations. At one in the morning, the masses poured out into the streets to greet their state, the 'gift' of a generous world.

Boris Senior heard the news in South Africa. He sent me a terse telegram: 'I'm coming'. When the Haganah summoned me to join the air service, I brought Boris along. I told them he was 'A-1' – and I wasn't exaggerating. We found ourselves housed in the Tel Aviv institute for officials of the General Federation of Labour (the Histadrut) and received a living allowance of about £7 a week. Our task? How can I explain it with maximum precision and a minimum of vanity? We were engaged in the first attempt to establish something like an air force (miniature, of course) and to man the first Haganah planes in combat against the Arabs. That was the period when we 'flew underground'.

At the time, the air service consisted of five or six light planes,

officially registered with the Palestine Aviation Club: an Auster, a
Taylorcraft, a Rapid and other such ludicrous objects. The pilots
belonged to two groups: veterans of foreign air forces, who had
acquired years of flying experience, and fellows from the Palmach
(the Haganah shock troops) and the Aviation Club, who had
logged only 140 or 150 hours of flying time. Boris and I belonged
to the first group, as did a fellow named Tolshinski, the late Eddie
Cohen and one or two others. The second group included Misha
Keren, Eli Feingrash, Shmulik Vidlis, Nahum Birn and 'Black'.

The planes were kept at the Tel Aviv airport, Sdeh Dov, where
they were brought from Lod after its capture by the Arabs. There
was a burning urgency to our work: flying over encircled
settlements to bring them ammunition and maintain contact;
flying patrols. And here in Sdeh Dov, we had to pretend that all
these flights were under the auspices of the Aviation Club, with no
reference to our battle for existence. There was a British officer
there, as well as an Arab officer and Arab auxiliary police. Each
flight had to have prior permission from the Arab auxiliary police
and the British officer. Each take-off cost 1 shilling in runway dues,
paid to the Electricity Company (the airfield's sole had been paved
for the company's use).

Take-offs and landings on this runway were difficult. A fellow
named Yehuda Holvitz (later an engineer in the air force) went
with me to buy cloth, a metal pipe and some cement. The cloth
was sewn up into a wind sock. We took a hoe, dug a hole,
cemented the pipe in, attached the home-made sock and behold:
we had operational runway installations!

Of the Jewish settlements cut off by Arab bands, we focused our
attention on eleven Negev settlements and Kfar Etzion and, at one
stage, on Yehiam in the north and Jerusalem. There were nine of
us, founding fathers of the air force, and we were swamped with
work: patrol flights to spot Arab offensive preparation, vital
supplies to encircled Negev settlements and communications.

At that early stage, the planes did not fly any real combat
missions. The first to shoot from the air, firing down out of his
plane at an Arab band, was the late Pinnia Ben Porat, an unusual
man of iron character. Stocky, dark, muscular, a renowned motor-
cyclist, he was married to a wonderful Yemenite girl and they

were both members of Kibbutz Na'an. (Pinnia was killed in July 1955, when an El Al plane was shot down over Bulgaria.) Pinnia was one of the first flying enthusiasts, and he always claimed that the airplane was a tremendous weapon, capable of swaying the tide of battle. He had a pioneering spirit and an active imagination. When the Arabs attacked Nevatim in the Negev, while Pinnia was in the vicinity, he took a Polish plane (one of our stock of wrecks that were not suitable for combat, in any form), mounted a Bren machine-gun on it and took off to strafe the flabbergasted attackers.

One of our first flights was early in January 1948 to Kfar Etzion (mid-way between Jerusalem and Hebron), which was under attack and suffered a severe shortage of guns and ammunition. Aharon Remez, then air force operations' officer, called us one night to plan the operation. Under cover of darkness Sten sub-machine-guns, ammunition, grenades and detonators were smuggled in by sea near the Reading power station and loaded onto three planes. In the morning we took off. Boris and Eli flew the Tiger, Possi (Tolchinski) and 'Black' were in the RWD, and Itche Hanenson and I took the Auster (Itche piloted and I was the 'chucker', charged with throwing the 'toys' out).

Kfar Etzion had no runway and there was no way of landing there. The plan was for members of the settlement to lay tyres on the ground so as to break the fall of the crates. The grenades would be dropped without their detonators, which would be thrown separately, wrapped in cotton-padded sacks to safeguard them. It would clearly be impossible to fly straight back to Tel Aviv after this mission, both because of lack of fuel and out of fear of the British. We decided that after the drop, we would fly to Be'erot Yitzhak, a deserted airfield near Gaza named 'Gaza East', where Eddie Cohen would await us with a Taylorcraft and a few jerrycans of fuel. We would land, refuel and fly back to Tel Aviv, one at a time.

We took off on a stormy winter's morning. Terrible clouds. Unless there are any counter-claims, this was the first time in history that Jews were dropping vital supplies to their soldiers. There was rejoicing in Kfar Etzion, as was customary in those days when every little achievement, every innovation, was a cause for joy. We could make out hands waving in gratitude. I saw the tyres and threw the box out: I'm not ashamed to admit that I prayed for it to fall on the tyre and not smash or suffer damage. From above, some of the boxes appeared to smash: a considerable portion of guns and ammunition were indeed rendered useless, but the rest was unharmed, enabling the besieged defenders to hold out a little longer. What we didn't see – perhaps out of our eagerness for this first operation to succeed – was a British plane, as small as ours, flying quite peacefully, while its pilot kept an eye on us. Pleased at the success of our mission, we landed at Be'erot Yitzhak, refuelled and flew on to Tel Aviv. There was no one waiting at the airfield, but on the table at Haganah headquarters lay a message from the British: one of your planes dropped supplies to Kfar Etzion, and we demand the arrest of the pilot. The British pilot who flew by during the drop had 'succeeded' in spotting no more than one plane.

The total closure of the club would have been a blow to all our operations. To prevent that, it was decided that one of us would 'give himself up' to the British. The options were weighed in a short discussion, which decided which of my dear friends could possibly be considered. It could not be Boris, for he was a South African who held a civil aviation license, which it would be a shame to lose. Eli Feingrash was a member of the Palmach who already had a file, through being imprisoned in Latrun, and would therefore be immediately arrested. Possi? Heaven forbid! He was a deserter from the American army. 'Black' had been interned in Rafiah detention camp, after being picked up on 'Black Saturday', when the British arrested hundreds of Jews. Itche had a civil license. In short, even before anyone named me, I knew that I was 'volunteering'.

At five in the morning, the 'criminal' presented himself at the North Tel Aviv police station feeling very apprehensive. If the British police knew about my links with the General Barker affair in England, then I might have had the best reason of all not to confess to dropping ammunition over Kfar Etzion. With the faint hope that I didn't have a file and carrying two blankets, I knocked on the door: 'I'm the pilot'. Of course, they already knew about the pilot and his transgressions. I was sent to the police station in

Shahar Street, where I spent a not-very-pleasant night. In the morning I was informed that I would be taken immediately to the Jaffa police station. At this point I decided that things had gone far enough. 'No!' I declared is 'Not to Jaffa!' (which was still Arab dominated). So they kept me in Shahar Street another day, until the Jewish authorities organized my release.

There were a few more weeks of operations from Sdeh Dov, and then I was sent down to the Negev. Military command decided that the situation required two planes to be stationed there, and one pilot was to be posted to Nir Am. I applied to go.

One day in January 1948, I found myself in a British Tiger Moth Biplane piloted by Pinnia. I was going to an area, a way of life, customs and people that were a total novelty to me. The headquarters of the Palmach's Negev Brigade was at Nir Am: the commander was Nahum Sarig; Oded Messer was operations officer; and Bibby Niv was one of the intelligence officers. In corduroy trousers, a tiny suitcase in my hand, a British flying jacket over my shoulders and my face sporting a small beard, I went to face the terrors of the Negev, and the Palmach, the *élite* unit of the Haganah.

We landed among the furrows of a ploughed field. Pinnia threw me a hurried farewell, mumbled something like 'good luck', started the engine and took off. Bibby, a tall Palmachnik, was waiting for me. We set off for the Mekorot Water Company's pump-house, where the Negev Brigade had its headquarters.

I had been out of the country for five years. The Palmach, its members and their life-style were totally unknown to me. I was attracted to them, excited by the encounter; I wished to compare my fantasies – based on hearsay and reading – with reality, but we walked along without saying much. Near the headquarters, Bibby stopped. He'd lost his Parker 51. Where? Near where the plane landed, he thought. So what? He was going to search, furrow after furrow, until he found it. 'He's out of his mind,' I thought to myself, and went with him. He searched furrow after furrow, as he promised. There it was! He had followed our footprints. It was lying there in the field, a Parker 51. 'A fine bunch of lunatics you've fallen in with, Mr Weizman,' I said cheerfully. With fellows like these, great things were possible.

The four or five months I spent as the Palmach's pilot, in the company of these splendid men, was one of the finest periods in my life. After my disappointments in the RAF, after the fruitless hunt for General Barker in England, after the frustrations of my father's tractors, after five years' separation from Palestine and its life and people, at Nir Am I returned home. Above and beyond the ideological differences that existed then and widened with the years – in fact, totally ignoring that aspect – I loved them with all my heart – and still do. I loved their comradeship, their frankness, their frugality. I loved their profound Zionist faith – a part of their lives rarely verbalized, but applied day by day, hour by hour, naturally and faithfully.

I enjoyed my life in the Negev. I flew a lot: daily patrols along the water pipeline, which I scrutinized for damage; flying to the cut-off settlements, to bring them medicine, newspapers and mail, as well as vital supplies, such as sacks of flour or packets of yeast. Wherever there was a runway, we would land and deliver our cargo. Where there was none, we would drop it. At Nir Am, I worked hard to make a small runway, improving it whenever I had a free moment. I even built a small control tower. Eli Feingrash – one of the bravest men I've ever met – was my assistant. The two of us threw up a defensive embankment for our two planes.

The planes we flew were unsuitable for air combat and incapable of tipping the balance in land battles; but, with a bit of courage and resourcefulness, we occasionally mounted some unusual operations. I needed little urging. The Palmach lexicon did not contain words such as 'impossible'. We used a bit of everything – a touch of initiative, a bit of 'Jewish brains', a little eagerness and the sharp eyes of those Palmach fellows.

One day I saved the life of some unknown kibbutz girl. Kibbutz Alumim is stuck away in the sand dunes south of Beersheba without a landing strip or anything like one. I swooped down, looking for a level stretch that wouldn't be quite so sandy. There was nothing of the kind; so I landed on the dunes, on a little hill. A girl was brought to the plane, badly burnt and in severe pain from a Primus stove that had overturned and had gone up in flames. I could scarcely make myself believe that I'd be able to take off in all that sand. Then I saw the girl's face twisted in pain; I tried to make the plane feel it too. The machine ploughed deep furrows in the ground, puffed and groaned and creaked and almost fell apart; but we saved her life, the plane and I.

A fellow by the name of Berko had copped a bullet while in a convoy. He was brought to Bet Eshel; his condition worsened, and there was no one in the area who could operate on him. I took off from Nir Am at five in the evening, in pouring rain, with visibility almost nil. Night flights were for the future. They brought the fellow to the plane in a semi-conscious state: one bullet in the lungs, another in the shoulder. He was attached to a blood-transfusion unit. It was dark and raining. I was flying blind, with one hand on the controls and the other on the plasma tube. If I let go of the controls, we were both finished; if I let go of the tube, Berko could say his good-byes. At that moment there was nothing in my life more important than Berko's survival, but it was impossible to see anything in the total darkness. And then, Berko, momentarily emerging from the twilight of his unconsciousness, said, 'Turn right, turn right.' 'Berko,' I said gently, 'Sit still, Berko, you mustn't exert yourself. It'll be OK.' A moment later, in that complete blackness, he begged, 'Turn right.' Once again I tried to reassure him. Suddenly, the truth struck home, sweet and simple: I had flown over Gaza. Damn me if Berko wasn't right! That's the way they were, these Negev Rats. In that heavy darkness, wounded, attached to his blood-infusion unit, alternating between semi-wakefulness and complete unconsciousness – and never before having flown at night! – his instincts nevertheless enabled him to guide me. I corrected the deviation and complimented myself for having told Eli to light a few sardine tins filled with sand and kerosene along the Nir Am runway. That was one of the first night-landings in the Israeli air force.

At that time, Chaim Bar-Lev (later to become chief of staff of the Israel Defence Forces) was in command of the Palmach's 8th 'Battalion' (a bit of an overstatement, as the unit included 120 soldiers at most). But nothing was beyond them. Chaim was based at Tze'elim. A woollen cap on the side of his head, then, as now, he spoke slowly and inspired confidence.

In this outfit there was a Palmach section commander with

bright red hair. His parents must have given him a name, but he was known only as 'Debambam'. If he were better off than others, it was only thanks to his armoured car. At that time an armoured car was a valuable weapon of war, and Debambam took meticulous care of his. One day, he set off with a convoy and ran into band of Arabs. British soldiers came along and helped the Arabs. What a disaster! They took Debambam's armoured car and gave it to the Arabs – an act of piracy that left Debambam eating his heart out. But the crunch came one day as I was flying patrol near Khan Yunis. Suddenly I saw a column moving over the sand dunes. I swooped down low and discovered that they were Arabs. Later, it transpired that they were planning to attack Nevatim. But what did mine eyes spy? This awe-inspiring column was unmistakedly headed by Debambam's armoured car!

In the plane I had a revolver – a weapon eminently suitable for attacks from the air. But a previous attempt at a revolver-strafing did not come off and even earned me an indignant reprimand. It was a known fact that Abdul Kadr Husseini, one of the Palestinian Arabs' leading military leaders (killed later on in the War of Independence), had a white jeep. On one of my previous flights I had been accompanied by Misha, a recently arrived battalion commander from Russia, who could barely speak Hebrew but who owned a big Colt. All of a sudden, he said: 'Abdul Kadr'. I looked down; behold, there was the white jeep. 'So what?' I asked. 'You going down,' he said in an authoritative tone. So I 'goed' down, to the right of the white jeep, and Misha whipped out his Colt, like in the Wild West films, and blazed away, again and again – in vain. Later, I received a harsh reprimand from the 'higher-ups' for my 'cowboy flying'.

So here I was: I could see Debambam's armoured car but hesitated to use my revolver – and I didn't even have a radio. We could, however, drop messages by means of white sand-bags laced up with red string. I scribbled a note to Bar-Lev and dropped it via sand-bag over Tze'elim, and a similar one on Mishmar Hanegev: 'Armed Arabs between Hatzerim, Tze'elim and Nirim, headed by Debambam's armoured car.'

Chaim got the note, read it and got up a raiding party. It was only a raid, because protracted battles were out of question at that time. The British were based in Beersheba and Imra, keeping a watchful eye open. As a result, our forces would stage a raid, do what they had to and clear off to a hiding-place. Chaim got there in time to shoot up the Arab column, making off with considerable booty: the precious armoured car, as well as a white jeep, with a Browning mounted on it, and a shot-gun. Today's equivalent would be, shall we say, a new combat-ready Phantom. Chaim gave the armoured car back to its overjoyed proprietor, De-bambam. The Browning and shot-gun were appreciated by Chaim's own unit. And I, too, received my reward. Chaim came to me at Nir Am and said, 'You spotted them, the jeep's yours.' With the approval of the brigade commander, the white jeep became my trade mark.

To understand the tasks imposed on our few small planes, we have to consider the over-all situation in the Negev at that time: small forces, poorly armed, thinly spread over enormous areas, where the Jewish settlements were many miles apart, and long distances between were partly under enemy control. For the members of the Negev settlements and the handful of soldiers in the area, the missions we flew provided reassurance on two important points: I believe we helped them overcome the feeling of isolation and despair common in those days. We evacuated many of the casualties, giving people the feeling that they were not alone and that, if anything happened, there was no point we couldn't reach, no landing strip, suitable or not, we couldn't land on. Maintaining links had a further value: we dropped food and ammunition everywhere, whatever God-forsaken 'hole' they got to. We revamped our aircraft, turning them into 'transport planes'. We took out the rear seat of the Auster and folded the front seat forwards, making space for a stretcher, which was tied in place to stop it from slipping out, together with the casualty.

Flour and letters were the most sought-after commodities in the distant settlements. We were eagerly awaited wherever we went. In many of the settlements, there was nothing left in the stores except sardines and sweetened condensed milk. The sack of flour we dropped would bring back the taste of bread to the men and women down there, while the letters would cheer them up, bringing a whiff of their far-off homes, family and friends.

There were tragedies too. Conditions were crude and primitive. At times eagerness and haste would claim their victims. A plane once landed at Kfar Etzion, and just before take-off, a girl rushed up to give the pilot a letter for her mother. She ran into the propellor and was killed.

No pilot today would take off in one of the planes we flew at that time, nor would any commanding officer permit such a take-off. That's certain. The engines were rotten; they had long completed their useful lives and positively begged for their *coup de grâce*. They should have been thanked nicely and thrown on the scrap-heap, but we had no others, and we squeezed everything possible out of them – although everything possible had been squeezed out long before. Every pilot was equipped with pliers, a plug wrench and a plug cleaner. Are your spark plugs fouled up with oil? That's all right. Take them out, clean them up nicely, put them back – and away you go! No grouching. That's all we have, and it's just as well that we have that.

For me, it was wonderful to get to know the Palmach and its people. I suppose I must have seemed an outlandish sort of creature to them. First of all, I was a pilot, while they were accustomed to rely on their feet. Not even armoured vehicles were quite to their liking, yet here I was soaring in the sky! And a foreign product, no less. Of course I was a *sabra* (a native-born Israeli), but I'd been branded with His Majesty's mark. I had not sprung from the soil of a kibbutz or a moshav, no roots in the Palmach, never watered by the springs of the Labour youth movements – a total bourgeois. And that illustrious name into the bargain! A queer customer. My life-style only added to my weird image. I would return from Tel Aviv with a bucket of ice-cream and a bottle of cognac. They understood the ice-cream, but the cognac was beyond them, it was a source of bewilderment. Yet, all this did not prevent close friendships from springing up among us. The atmosphere of the Negev was unique, and the Palmach's Negev Brigade was a superior caste. It almost goes without saying that my four months in the Negev were full of fascinating personal experiences – much more so than my four long years in the British air force.

When Israel's independence was declared on 15 May I was no longer there. I was sent to Czechoslovakia to learn to fly a different type of plane, which I was also to bring back with me.

Somehow or other there was a feeling in the air that a new era had arrived, with new problems and new adversaries, and our Austers, with all due gratitude and respect, would have to make room for something a little more formidable. But what, how and when – no one knew.

After I left Nir Am, someone said: 'Ezer has gone to Czechoslovakia to bring us planes'. I was very touched when I heard that, I really felt as though I was their emissary. Later we chose conflicting political routes, but to this day, whenever I encounter the men I knew then, I feel as though, once again, I'm meeting the best of friends and the finest of human beings.

One evening, around March 1948, we were told that an American by the name of Stone was due to arrive at Nir Am. There was a touch of mystery and secrecy about his arrival – as was customary at that time – for no one knew anything about him. It was a winter's night when along came some friendly 'chappie', tubby and bald. We all crowded into a small, smoke-filled room and ate cream cake washed down with cognac (which had become a Palmach recipe, far from laudable, but commonplace by then) and this American – we did not yet know what an excellent officer he was – Colonel 'Micky' Marcus, was drinking and holding forth. As he grew hot and flushed with drink, his tongue loosened. He turned to me and said, 'Listen, we're getting combat planes for you, real planes. Is there any proper combat plane you can fly – a Mustang or something like that?' I looked at him, cold and indifferent, undecided whether he was simply drunk or just shooting off his mouth with this American fairy-tale. There I was, stuck with a rotten plane whose spark-plugs scarcely functioned, whose engine hummed with the refrain: 'It's your last flight, your last flight . . .' and every take-off I'd repeatedly implore it not to pack in on me in flight. A plane's most important components were the bits of wire with which we tied all kinds of parts together, and thin rope, for lashing the machine-gun to the window frame. Tze'elim was out of ammunition, Nir Am was constantly bellyaching for a sack of flour, and when you flew along the water pipeline and saw sections that had been blown up – all you could do was sigh. And then along came this American, from the big world, put away a few glasses of cognac and started blabbering about combat planes. 'I'll show *you* what combat planes are!'

Shortly afterwards, I was summoned to air-service headquarters in Tel Aviv. Remembering the last time I was honoured with such an order, I had no particular reason to rejoice. Clearly I was in for it once more. I racked my brains to remember what I could have done and who was furious at me *this* time. The last time I got a similar summons was after I had flown to Tel Aviv and was told, to my astonishment, that I would not be permitted to take the plane back to Nir Am. Alex Ziloni was head of the air service, and Misha Keren was the commander of the Sdeh Dov airfield. I summoned up all my power of persuasion to make them understand: I had promised Nahum Sarig that there would be two planes in the Negev, and there was no way of making do with less than two. I talked, I explained, I begged. Nothing helped: the answer was 'No!' At the time I closely identified with the settlements and the Negev Brigade. They carried more weight for me than orders from rear command. Enraged, I yelled: 'You headquarters people, what do you understand? Do you know what's happening down there in the Negev?' I grabbed a plane and took off, straight to Nir Am – and almost straight out of the air service. I was in hot water. Nahum covered up for me and defended me, but there was a trial, and the head of the service expressed his astonishment at me, especially with my British air force experience. I claimed that the RAF never had a problem like encircled Negev settlements or the Palmach's Negev Brigade. To cut a long story short, it was insubordination, and I got off with a reprimand. But the Negev kept its two planes.

So when I got the telegram summoning me to Tel Aviv, I told the fellows in Nir Am, 'Somebody's after my scalp.' Ready to do battle, I arrived at air command to encounter the late Moddy Allon, who was stationed then with the Galilee Squadron. Without any preface, the two of us were told to leave our present postings and set off for Czechoslovakia to bring back Messerschmidts.

I stopped breathing. The Messerschmidt 109 was a real plane, a combat plane, like the ones I used to fly in the RAF. For two-and-a-half years, ever since my discharge, I had not savoured the taste of a genuine plane – the kind that hurls you forward with a terrible whack in the rear when you open up the throttle. I caught fire at once. This was the kind of talk that suited a sovereign, independent state: combat planes, Czechoslovakia, Messerschmidt. I went straight back to Nir Am to tell Nahum I was instructed to hand over command of the squadron to Eli Feingrash, whom I had recommended to replace me. But how did one hand over a command? No one knew. I had the only revolver in Nir Am, attached to a very formidable cowboy belt. I took off the belt with the revolver, put it around Eli's waist and muttered something like: 'You're taking command!' Whereupon Eli became the commanding officer.

Moddy and I were the only Israelis in the group. The others were foreign volunteers. We were ordered to leave the country on 9 May 1948, a period abounding with doubts and uncertainty: would the state be proclaimed on 14 May or would our leaders falter at the last minute? What about the Arab regular armies? Would they invade or wouldn't they? Czechoslovakia was under communist domination. The British were still in Palestine. It was a world full of question marks. Travelling on British Palestinian passports, we took off from Sdeh Dov in a Dakota to learn to fly German planes in a communist state.

The plane, piloted by a South African pilot named Claud Duval, a real wizard – pilot, navigator and wireless operator all rolled into one – stopped in Cyprus, Rome and Geneva. From Geneva we went by train to Zurich, where we boarded a Czechoslovakian Airline's plane for Prague. Two men greeted us: Ehud Avriel, the unaccredited and unproclaimed ambassador of a state which had yet to be born, and a Czech air force officer. Ehud dispelled part of the mystery, and the picture began to take on some meaning: the state-to-be had acquired twenty-five Messerschmidts, and we were to learn to fly them. But the problems were still acute and burdensome: no one knew how to bring the planes to Israel.

The political scene also grew a little clearer. The building in Prague manned by a small delegation of Israelis displayed enormous portraits of Stalin and Eduard Benes. This may have been a symbolic expression of our relationships with the communist world. There we were in Palestine, a handful of Jews craving independence, without an army or an air force, about to take on the imperialistic British and drive them out of the Middle East and take the Arab effendis down a peg or two at the same time. We were at the spearhead of the forces of progress, leading the assault on the bastions of reaction. Accordingly, the progressive world would stand by us, as an ally.

Prague was melancholy, poverty-stricken, hungry. We were housed in the Flora, a gigantic hotel that once knew splendour and now had gone to seed. Two days later we took off in a German-built Junkers 52 on our way to the Czech air-base of Budějovice, a grass airfield. We were greeted by two rows of planes – Messerschmidts and Spitfires. The atmosphere was shrouded with mystery. Strict secrecy was the standing order, and we were banned from fraternizing with the Czech officers or men, other than those directly connected to our training. We were issued with German flying kits – the Czechs did not have any of their own, and they largely used German army leftovers, which had been abandoned there or were received from their Russian patrons – flight overalls, flying boots and a parachute. Before the Messerschmidt, we were taught to fly a German training plane called the Ardo. We lived in shacks and the food was lousy, not because we were treated unfairly, but because there was nothing better, and everyone had to make do with what there was. Our instructors were charming. Kind and unassuming, they were genuinely eager to help and give us as much as possible in a short time. They knew English – for they had served in the RAF – and we had no language problems. The commanding officer, Colonel Hlodek, had also served in the Soviet air force.

At the weekends there were no lessons and no flying. Once we were sitting in our shack swapping yarns when, suddenly, a plane streaked past with a roar, almost bringing the roof down on our heads. We went outside to see what was about. Within a short time, the whole camp was in total confusion: one of the chief instructors, together with several officers, who had had their fill of the communist regime and its blessings, had taken a plane and made off for nearby Austria and pitiful attempts were made to keep the matter secret. But the story of their escape was making the rounds within a few minutes, as the mechanics whispered it from ear to ear.

We flew and trained and advanced. Our hearts were in Palestine, so our ears became glued to the radio. On that fateful Friday, 15 May, we heard the news we had been waiting for: the State of Israel had been proclaimed. It was a painful experience, being far from home at a time like that – even knowing that my being there was in order to guarantee some solid backing for that very proclamation. Moddy and I were restless; we scuttled around, frantic as mice, foraging for any crumb of news. We heard that Tel Aviv had been bombed from the air. All of a sudden things acquired a new significance, a new dimension. I began to get ants in my pants. It was terrible not being *there*. We couldn't sit sill, didn't have the patience to study. The affable Czechs invited us for drinks, and we raised our glasses to the State of Israel. But our endurance was running out. Tel Aviv bombed, the state hanging by a hair, and I was in Ceske Budějovice, far away from it all.

I had no more than six or seven hours' flying time on the planes when I received a Czech-built Messerschmidt single-seater with machine-guns, cannon and bomb brackets – a formidable instrument, a genuine combat plane and a real delight. As I flew alone in the Czech skies, a message was transmitted to me, in English: I was requested not to go too far. They've had bitter experience with pilots revving up their planes and zooming out of the communist paradise, straight to the capitalist hell . . .

'That's enough,' we proclaimed, 'we're going home.' The Czechs laughed. 'Not yet, you still have a lot to learn, wait.' They were right, of course. Eight or nine hours' flying – that's nothing, it's ludicrous. In the RAF, training on a new plane calls for at least seventy hours' flying time. There's air-to-ground and air-to-air gunning, bombing and night flying. But Moddy and I had had our fill of training, and we were fed up with being far away. On about 18 or 19 May, we phoned Ehud Avriel in Prague, informing him that our training was completed. He was a little surprised, but did not express any opposition. He only said that there were still some problems involved in getting the planes to Israel. He proposed that we come to Prague to think things over together. With these good tidings, we reported to the camp commander, Hlodek. He was amazed. 'What?' You haven't even fired yet! You have to learn to shoot.' Moddy and I replied: 'We'll shoot straight – straight at the target.' Hlodek sent us off with a firm handshake and his blessing: 'Try and catch the Egyptians on the ground. Screw 'em on the ground!' It took us nineteen years before we could carry out Colonel Hlodek's advice, and if he were still alive on 5 June 1967, I'm sure that his heart rejoiced, even if outwardly he had no choice but to join the communist world's chorus of condemnation.

In Prague, Ehud Avriel told us of the difficulties involved in transporting the planes to Israel. The Messerschmidt had a short range, an hour and a half in the air, at a speed of 200–250 miles an hour. Even in Europe, with its short distances, that was scarcely enough to fly from city to city. There was no other way: we had to strip down the Messerschmidt and load its sections into an American transport plane, the C-54, which opened at the side. We examined all the possibilities to see what to load on first and what to add later. In the end the Messerschmidt was stripped of its wings and propeller. The fuselage was placed in the belly of the big plane, followed by the other sections, still leaving room for bombs, ammunition and spare parts. There were three of us there – Moddy and I, as well as Mokka Limon, in charge of security (he was to become commander of the Israeli navy, and later his name was connected with the 'Cherbourg boats').

We took off from Zatec airfield, not far from Prague. A flight lasting eleven and a half hours, with no stopovers or refuelling, took the first transport plane from Zatec to Tel Nof, bringing the newly born air force its first real combat plane. (Further Messerschmidts arrived in DC-4s and other transport planes, which flew by way of Corsica, since they could not come the whole way without refuelling.) We hoped that the crew of the C-54 would find the way, but they didn't until we identified the lighthouse in Haifa. The whole country was enveloped in pitch darkness. We speeded along the coast and landed at Tel Nof. It was 21 May, a few days after the British had left the country. Excitement exceeded all bounds, as though Israel's hour of salvation had arrived.

4

THE WAR OF
INDEPENDENCE

ALL KINDS of important personalities, as well as the heads of the
world's youngest army and air force, came to feast their eyes on the
flying wonder, lying dismembered in the belly of the C-54: a
fighter with gun-sights, wireless equipment and bomb-racks – just
like the movies! Grown men came up to kiss and fondle the cold
metal. But when the festivities came to an end, we were left with
the stripped-down plane that had to be made ready for combat.
We had brought along a few Czech air-force technicians, and we
were met by Yehoshua Gilutz, one of the air force's most gifted
engineers (he later served as chief engineering officer). The plane's
sections were unloaded and carried into a hangar.

By the time this plane was assembled, as well as the three others
that followed it, there were five Messerschmidt 'aces' in the
country – Moddy, Lou Lenart, Rubenfeld, Eddie Cohen and
myself – all itching to take off with our 'Messers' and pounce on the
Egyptian armoured columns, which were advancing rapidly after
having taken Nitzanim and reaching Ashdod. But the planes were
stripped down, and it transpired that they were easier to take apart
than to assemble. We couldn't sit around doing nothing, so we
went back to our first loves, the light planes at Sdeh Dov, which
had remained faithful to us. Lacking other planes, we bombed
Gaza from a Bonanza and dropped incendiary bombs from 4,000
feet.

Around 27 or 28 May, the four Messerschmidts were finally
assembled, and their five pilots returned to Tel Nof, to be near

them. It was only a week later that we were joined by Sid Cohen and Rudy Aurgarten, as well as Sandy Jacobs, a good friend who was killed in an air accident just before the 1956 Sinai Campaign. It was a real squadron: the planes were painted in air-force colours, with a Shield of David, like today, and marked with Hebrew letters instead of numbers.

On the ground the military situation was critical, and in the air the Egyptian air force was king of the skies. Never before (and never again!) did it feel so free. It could do literally anything it wanted. Its Dakotas and Spitfires bombed Tel Aviv and only encountered sporadic anti-aircraft fire (which nevertheless succeeded in shooting down one of the Spitfires). At El Arish, on the northern coast of Sinai, the Egyptians had some twenty-five 'Spits' and a number of Dakotas, which had been converted for use as bombers. There was, therefore, a great temptation, and an equally great need, to take off with our 'Messers', to shoot up the Egyptian armoured columns and to engage their air force and restrict its freedom of operation. However, our command decided to adopt a different tactic – and they were right. The fact that the Israeli air force now had real combat planes, and not just light Pipers and Austins, was unknown to the enemy. Full exploitation of the element of surprise could give us an overwhelming victory. If we used the new planes for an attack on Egyptian ground forces, or for the defence of Tel Aviv, the secret would be out, and we'd lose the chance of making full use of it. Thus, a plan was hatched for a strike against the Egyptian air force at El Arish, to destroy its planes while they were on the ground.

It was the blossoming of an idea that was to bear fruit nineteen years later, when we destroyed the Arab air forces in the Six Day War. Our ground troops were still fighting with Sten sub-machine-guns and 1910-vintage cannon, while we had genuine, factory-new combat planes, with two 20-mm cannon and 70-kg bombs – and machine-guns! To keep the secret, air-force command decreed no take-offs! It wasn't easy to obey. There we were, with our fingers on the trigger of a startlingly new weapon of war, in which we believed without reservation, but it was locked in a hangar, and all we could do was gaze at it, again and again. It was frustrating.

And then on Saturday, 29 May, everything turned upside down. We were sitting in our shack at Tel Nof, when along came Shimon Avidan, commander of the Givati Brigade. He brought grave tidings. The situation on the southern front was acute. One of the last road-bridges before Tel Aviv had just been blown up by Givati sappers. In short, despite all previous decisions, despite the plans to reserve the squadron for an attack on El Arish, Avidan was bringing us an order, from Chief of Staff Yigael Yadin, to take off and attack the Egyptian armoured column near Ashdod. It was a great moment. This clenched fist, whose existence had been kept secret, was finally going to hammer the enemy. Of course there was no time to consider trifles, such as the fact that these planes had never taken off, or even been tested in flight, their parts had not been checked, no one knew whether their systems functioned or if their machine-guns fired. No one was sure that their bombs *would* drop – or that their wings *wouldn't*. These questions had to be shoved aside.

Lou Lenart was chosen to take off first. Moddy Allon was his number two. I'd take off next, and Eddie Cohen would be my number two. We couldn't conceal our excitement as we bent over the maps. The sense of a unique moment showed on every face. I suppose that my ears were as flushed as theirs. At dusk we started up and taxied along the concrete runway. The first pair took off. Eddie, my number two, was dallying. His engine wouldn't start. It didn't take him more than three or four minutes, but to me it seemed like hours. Finally, both pairs were in the air.

From take-off the distance to our combat area was very short. As soon as we got up into the air, we could see anti-aircraft fire directed at us from the direction of Ashdod. We swung out to sea, climbing to 7,000 feet, and swooped towards the Egyptian column. The sight took my breath away: the Egyptian army, in all its power and glory, was spread along the road, and knew, more or less, what stood between it and Tel Aviv – two and a half companies of the Givati Brigade, anxiety-stricken and exhausted. I must confess, I had a profound sense of fulfilling a great mission.

I let go my two bombs, speeding them on their way with a prayer that they would delay the column that was moving northwards. Anti-aircraft fire harried us from all sides. I dove once

more, blasting away with my 20-mm cannon, which soon
jammed. From afar I saw the first pair doing the same. Down
below the Egyptians were scattering in every direction. And then,
amidst the din of bombs and shooting and diving and climbing and
anti-aircraft fire, I saw Eddie, my number two, dive – down,
down, lower and lower. I was extremely concerned that he was
diving too low. And then the crash, shrouded by fire and smoke.
To this day, there is no way of knowing whether he copped anti-
aircraft fire or whether some technical fault on his first mission
made it his last.

We landed. Moddy's plane had also suffered some damage in
one wing and was temporarily out of action. After one operation
we had two and a half planes and four pilots left, in place of the four
planes and five pilots we had before. For an air force to lose 25 per
cent of its planes and 20 per cent of its pilots in its first action is, of
course, unpleasant, especially if that air force is still in its swaddling
clothes. And there was more than a tinge of sorrow to our pleasure
at quitting those miserable light planes and finally flying a combat
mission worthy of the name. Eddie, a South African volunteer,
was a dear man, and we mourned his fate. It was only some fifteen
months later, when the Egyptians had withdrawn southwards,
that a jeep sought out his remains. He was buried near Tel Aviv,
the first of a long and glorious line of Israeli air-force pilots who
laid down their lives for their country.

All in all, this had been an irregular, unorganized action, and its
defects were obvious. The way it was mounted indicated how
difficult the situation was, and it reflected the terrible fear that the
road to Tel Aviv, and to the centre of Israel, was left wide open.

With Israel's combat planes no longer a secret, we went full
speed ahead. The plan to attack the enemy planes at El Arish was
shelved. On the eastern front, the situation was causing serious
concern. Armoured cars with small 30-mm cannon were shelling
Kfar Yona. The Alexandroni Brigade, which had shed much blood
in bitter battles, was in no better shape than Givati. The next
day, 30 May, at 5.30 am, two Messerschmidts took off against the
Iraqis and Jordanians. Rubenfeld and I were piloting, and we
headed for Tulkarem. We dropped bombs on the Tulkarem
railway station and strafed the armoured column spread along the

road. Suddenly I noticed Rubenfeld's plane smoking; I saw him bailing out. Our second Messerschmidt finished. Another 25 per cent of our stock of planes.

In that first bombing raid on the Iraqis and Jordanians, there were two incidents that deserve to be scribbled in the margin of the battle. That morning, the Egyptians, as well as other foes, may have known about our combat planes, but the news had yet to reach the farmers of our own Kfar Vitkin. Seeing real combat planes, they were certain these were enemy aircraft. And then, out of the sky, dangling from a parachute, comes our friend Rubenfeld. Now it so happens that this American, Rubenfeld, is very dark skinned. The men of Kfar Vitkin knew how to put two and two together and decided that this 'enemy' pilot deserved lynching, especially after daring to land smack in the middle of their village. Rubenfeld had very keen instincts, and when he saw the welcoming committee, their expression seemed to bode badly for his future career as a fighter pilot. He racked his brains to recall all the Yiddish he knew and shouted: 'Shabbes, Shabbes, gefilte fish, gefilte fish . . .' Fortunately for him, they got the message and tried to digest the fact that this swarthy fellow was a Jewish pilot who had bailed out of an Israeli combat plane.

As for me, I also had my share of unpleasantness. As I was diving and strafing, amidst some fairly thick anti-aircraft fire, my front windshield was smashed. I landed and was met by the late Yehuda Pilpel, one of the first and best mechanics in the air force. There may have been something over-dramatic in my tone when I said, 'I seem to have been hit.' There was no need to say more. Pilpel groped and poked. And then, with one of his wry smiles, the fellow reached into the plane and pulled out the little bird that had smashed my window.

A story like that never retains its original form. It obeys the law of expansion. For ten or fifteen years the tale was rehashed and retold; it was flavoured and garnished at every squadron party until its aroma pervaded the whole air force. In its ultimate version, Pilpel would wait for absolute silence, and then he'd say, 'So Ezer comes along and, with a tear in his eye, he says, "Pilpel, it's worthy to die for our homeland!"' All right, let's leave it at that.

Everything was embryonic and primitive; we were living from

hand to mouth. No clear doctrine had been forged and tested in the fires of battle. Even a simple problem like quarters for the pilots and ground-crews found no more than a temporary solution: we were housed in the Yarden Hotel, in Ben Yehuda Street. On the premises now occupied by the restaurant, there was a splendid bar. There has never been a tradition of drinking parties in the Israeli army – and there's no reason to regret the fact. But all the same, we would often honour the bar with our humble presence. Rubenfeld's lucky escape was a good excuse to wet our throats, but our boozing resulted in me spending several days away from the Messerschmidt squadron and deprived me of the privilege of taking part in the defence of Tel Aviv.

The morning after the drinking party in honour of Rubenfeld – and the morning after is never as gay as the night before – Moddy, who was already in command of the squadron (two planes and three pilots, just so we keep the proportions right), set off early, leaving me his motor-bike. I was to come along later. However, I was a long time getting there: Arab mines laid at the Beit Dagon cross-roads had left the roadway pitted. Crash – and I found myself with my wheel in a pot-hole and my left hand fractured. I got back on the motor-bike and rode it to Tel Aviv's Hadassah Hospital. Now 33 per cent of the Messerschmidt pilots were out of action. I missed a week of the war, and I also missed one of its great events.

With Tel Aviv totally at the mercy of the Egyptian air force, things were very glum. One day, along came some Egyptian Dakotas, dropping bombs on the Central Bus Station and on the Sdeh Dov airfield; they caused dozens of casualties and a profound feeling of helplessness. Moddy Allon took off in one of the two 'Messers' to intercept the enemy. It was a great occasion for the citizens of Tel Aviv, a real day of rejoicing. As if at some aerial display, crowds watched as the little plane swooped down on the two bombers. He got on their tails and let fly, giving vent to all the fury of Tel Aviv's bomb-ravaged burghers. Both bombers were shot down, and all over Israel the glad tidings made the rounds: We've got combat planes! Soon there was another rumour: the nameless pilots who flew the combat planes and shot down the Egyptian Dakotas were living at the Yarden Hotel. That was sufficient. When we came back to the hotel that evening, we found

Moddy's room swamped with flowers, and the bed covered with every imaginable delicacy: chocolates, cakes, bottles of champagne and cognac – the generous tribute of grateful citizens to a pilot whose name they did not know, but whose feats they so admired.

The destruction of the Dakotas filled the whole country with joy, which grew as all kinds of lurid details were invented to make the bombers seem even more frightening. As for me, I cheered along with the rest. But in my heart, I was feeling a little rueful, as I cursed the craters on the Beit Dagan road and that damned motorbike, which had put my hand into plaster, grounding me until the end of the first cease-fire, late in June 1948.

By the middle of June 1948 we had become a proper air force, at least in our opinion. We had built up our strength; we now had seven or eight planes and a dozen or so pilots. But the Egyptians detected us taking off from Tel Nof, and they bombed the field, hitting one of the hangars. None of the planes was seriously damaged, but all the same, it was decided to move to another airfield. The choice was very limited: we couldn't go south, because Hazor was under bombardment; Lod was no solution, because it, too, was under fire, as was Ein Shemer; while Ramat David, in the north, was beyond the range of our planes. Moddy and I scurried about, shopping for an operational airfield for Israel's combat air force. We explored the vicinity of Herzlia in the company of Eliezer Budenkin – at that time, one of the air force's engineers, and my friend to this day. What caught our eye were the orange groves: they could provide excellent concealment for the planes. We thought it over and decided the place was suitable. We thought it better to use runways that were not asphalted. Some earth-moving equipment was quickly brought in and smoothed out a dirt runway a mile and a half long, running north to south. Within a brief time, the 'Messers' moved to their new home. Whenever they were not in operation, the planes were hidden in the orange groves, and the fact that Herzlia was never bombed proves how well concealed they were.

The absence of organization was unavoidable at first, and our random improvisations even added a certain playful charm. But the time had come for all this to make way for an organized unit,

living and operating according to rules; a normal outfit, with
mechanics, cooks, drivers and armourers. Moddy, as squadron
commander, exerted considerable effort in order to mould the
squadron into regular forms. He brought me into things, even
though I was one of the less-experienced fliers.

'Getting organized' is a meaningless concept if you don't know
how. By sending requests for equipment on printed forms? 'Please
send cooking pots, a typewriter, a jeep and some kettles.' A waste
of time. There would be no response. The attempt to give the
squadron a normal, regular character involved deeds that were far
from being either normal or regular. I got into trouble when I
walked away from air-force headquarters carrying a typewriter
without asking permission. I provided the squadron with a jeep in
much the same manner. Other items of equipment arrived by
similar routes.

To supply our manpower needs, we took anything available,
and the choice was not always the finest. We received mechanics,
most of whom came from the camps in Europe, having acquired
their technical experience through forced-labour for the Germans.
Very few of the Czech mechanics remained with the squadron. In
addition, there were some local fellows, either Technion students
or men who had picked up some kind of experience with the RAF.
Maintenance was headed by an American by the name of Harry
Axelrod (now employed by the Aircraft Industries).

We had fifteen Messerschmidts at Herzlia. There were sixteen
pilots: Canadians, Englishmen, Americans, South Africans and the
Israeli trio, Moddy Allon, Sandy Jacobs and myself. We lived in
unfinished buildings inside one of the orange groves. If the
designers of the planes we were flying had fallen into our hands, I
don't think they'd have designed any more planes. But we had a
fervent belief in our squadron, and if we'd been ordered to bomb
Cairo, no one would have asked: 'But what about the range and
fuel?'

We had great luck with the squadron's adjutant. Moddy
decided we needed someone to take over administration, so we set
out to search. Kalman Turin had RAF experience (later, he was
promoted to colonel as head of the air-force manpower department and is now El Al representative in Canada and the United

States). We found him at Sdeh Dov, loaded him on a jeep and whisked him off to Herzlia. We simply 'confiscated' him. And so the squadron got itself organized: Moddy Allon in command, Harry Axelrod ran technical matters, while I went from one thing to another, doing something of everything. Kalman was the connecting link: he was Moddy's right-hand man; when Moddy was killed, he became Sid Cohen's right-hand man; and when I took over command of the squadron, he became my right-hand man.

So we had pilots and planes and, most important, a fighting spirit, the sense of belonging to a team. The time had come to give the squadron a name and an emblem. These were adopted by a fully democratic procedure, which left the squadron commander, Moddy Allon, in the minority. At the time, the pilots were living in two small hotels in Kfar Shmaryahu, and conditions gave no cause for complaint. By day we would fly, work, perfect our skills – all very satisfying. At night, we would entertain ourselves. Occasionally, we would drop into the Atom Bar in Tel Aviv for a drink and some fun, releasing our tensions in ways that would not, perhaps, have been to the liking of more conservative beings.

Moddy commanded the squadron for only four months. He took over command in the middle of June 1948 and was killed on 16 October that same year. Four months are a short time in the annals of a squadron. Only a unique personality like Moddy was capable of giving that period a dimension that transcended the normal count of days and weeks. During the first period, Sandy and I were the only Israelis serving under Moddy. All the other pilots were volunteers from abroad, seasoned combat pilots, captains and majors, and they left a deep imprint on the unit's life-style. It wasn't exactly a matter of 'eat, drink and be merry, for tomorrow we die', because there was a lot of 'drink' and little was said of 'we die'. They were far from home, and they all shared adventurous leanings and a liking for the high life. They were rather boisterous; they hated curbs and showed little tolerance for harness and saddle. They were a belligerent crowd, but dutiful and willing when it came to the necessities of war. They were ready to act and run risks, but it was hard to be in command of them.

Moddy, who lacked experience as a commander, made up for

all his deficiencies with his fine personality: he was cool, balanced, brave, strong and wise. In dealing with all these 'aces', there was no point in Moddy trying to impose his official authority as squadron commander, or to hand out punishments or reprimands. The great thing about Moddy was that he didn't need all that. The authority he exercised was moral – the kind of authority that every *élite* unit should aspire to, which doesn't need to be backed up by ranks, or the rigid rules of military hierarchy. All it needs is a certain personality. And Moddy had it. We didn't have uniforms so we'd fly in overalls with no rank insignia. What we did have was a model commanding officer. And these seasoned war-horses – tough, undisciplined, rebellious – did his bidding and were overjoyed when he rewarded them with a kind word or a pleasant smile.

The squadron had other problems, which also needed Moddy's talents and endeavours. Mechanics, for example. Nowadays things are different, with the air force taking in graduates from technical schools, where they've been in a disciplined operational outfit ever since the age of seventeen or eighteen. Today, mechanics reach the squadron already possessing clearly defined trades and accustomed to wearing their school uniforms. In those early days, one was from Auschwitz, a second from Petah Tikvah, and a third from the RAF; each one displayed a different degree of proficiency and technical know-how, picked up on all kinds of planes that had very little in common. The squadron supplied most of its own services with the resources at its disposal. There were 250 or 300 men – cooks, armourers, technicians and all the rest. A *pot-pourri* of different backgrounds and forms of training, these men were hurled into the fiery furnace of war, which forged them into a combat unit with excellent fighting spirit.

I may as well admit that the unit exhibited a degree of arrogance, for its men regarded themselves as *crème de la crème*. It also displayed a degree of playfulness, as one or two of Tel Aviv's bars learnt – to their cost. A night of steady drinking would often conclude with a massive demolition of tables, chairs, bars, shelves and bottles if the proprietor raised his prices or his behaviour was otherwise unsatisfactory. The manager of the Park Bar would always plead: 'You fellows, why don't you come one at a time?'

However undesirable the bar-owner found it, that *togetherness* was the very essence of the squadron. We thought together, lived together, dreamed together, went into combat together. Together we took pride in our unit and its planes, even though we sensed, with a kind of collective awareness, that the Messerschmidt was not the best of planes. Of course, for those of us who remembered the little planes, the Austers and others, acquired by the bribes or by illegal 'purchase', the Messerschmidt was an awesome weapon of war, spitting fire from its terrible machine-gun and its two murderous bombs sowing death in the camp of the enemy. However, if we ignore those early improvisations, which used light reconnaissance planes as *ersatz* combat planes, a cool professional evaluation of 'Israel's finest plane' would show up its deficiencies.

The Messerschmidt was unfriendly, 'poker-faced', ungracious and hateful. It wasn't pleasant to fly. The distinction is clear, and every pilot knows it: there are 'evil' planes, which kick back at you, and there are 'good' ones, which don't. The question is, to what extent can you risk an error without the plane making you pay for it. When you make a slight error with an 'evil' plane, it kicks out at you as though you've made a serious blunder; when you make a major error, the plane does its best to make it positively your last. A good-natured plane is like a good-natured person; if you make a slight error, it 'smiles' and 'forgives'. If your error is more serious, it gives you a gentle kick, warning you against further mistakes, as though it were saying: 'Come on now, be careful, I don't want to be hard on you.'

The Messerschmidt had an evil nature. It was intolerant. Like other piston-driven planes, when the propellor turned to the right, it tended to pull to the left, and it was hard to hold straight during take-off. In this sense, jets are easier, for they have less of a tendency to pull you off the runway. The Messerschmidt did not have a trimmer to its rudder. It would overturn at times, and planes would get smashed up. It was hard to operate the flaps, which were lowered mechanically. Its machine-guns fired through the pro-pellor, and, as the synchronization didn't always function properly, a fellow would come back from a sortie with his propellor damaged or pitted with holes from the bullets he himself had fired. In short, the Messerschmidt may have been the finest plane Israel then possessed, but it gave us a lot of trouble.

The story of how the air force rebuilt its first British Spitfire and put it into service was one of the miracles of those days. Freddy Ish-Shalom was one of the key movers in that little group of resourceful spirits that took on the impossible task. They scoured the scrap-yards, picking up Spitfire parts and sections that the British had thrown out as so much useless junk. Only too aware of how much the air force needed a new plane, they set about assembling all the parts, displaying incredible patience until it was completed. Without being convinced that the job had been done properly – and running a great personal risk – Boris Senior clambered into the flying scrap-heap and took off from an improvised air strip. I don't know who was more tense, Boris or us, nailed to the ground as we watched Israel's first 'Spit' on its maiden flight. That jigsaw-puzzle plane not only completed its first flight successfully but continued to fly for a long time. Later it was converted into a photographic reconnaissance plane, and, in November 1948, flying this same 'Spit', I photographed Damascus and its surroundings in an exciting one-and-a-half-hour flight over enemy territory. It was a first-class plane; unfortunately, some technical hitch caused it to catch fire on the ground, and it was burnt to cinders.

The Spitfire was an excellent plane. Its superb performance, dependability, good nature, air-pressure-operated flaps, stability and fire-power made us eager to see it in the service of our air force, and we welcomed the news that Spitfires had been purchased in Czechsolovakia. The first group of pilots who set off to bring the planes to Israel included Moddy Allon, Sid Cohen, Boris Senior and Jack Cohen. They were joined in Czechoslovakia by Sam Pomeranz, who, in addition to being a combat pilot, was also a gifted engineer, and his resourcefulness enabled him to fit out the Spitfires with a new fuel system. The reserve tanks he added gave the plane eight hours' flying time, far longer than its designers had foreseen.

Delivering the first 'Spits' to Ramat David required strenuous efforts. It was a miracle that there were no misfortunes on the way, for the 'Spit' had no navigational instruments. Five planes took off from Czechoslovakia, flying to a Yugoslav airfield that had been placed at our disposal. They went on, guided by a large C-46, which gave them directions by means of walkie-talkie radios. It was a difficult flight. Boris and Moddy encountered malfunction-ings in their fuel systems and were forced to make emergency landings in Rhodes, where they were stranded, finally returning just before the October 1948 offensive. Amidst great excitement, the other three 'Spits', piloted by Sid Cohen, Jack Cohen and Sam Pomeranz, reached Ramat David. (Sam met his death later in circumstances that have never been clarified; he crashed into a mountain while ferrying another 'Spit' to Israel.)

At the beginning of October 1948, the Egyptians were still encamped at Ashdod. The airfield at nearby Hazor was still being shelled, and it was impossible to land there. The women and children of Gedera were evacuated. Kibbutz Hazor was bom-barded by the Egyptians. On 14 and 15 October, we set out with four Messerschmidts, escorting a C-46, to bomb Gaza, Majdal and other Egyptian concentrations along the coast while three 'Spits' attacked El Arish.

The next day was Yom Kippur. 'The Egyptians are beginning to withdraw from Ashdod,' Moddy said to me. 'There are instructions to hit them as hard as possible, while they pull back. Let's go!' I loved to fly with Moddy, but this time, on the way to the planes, we had a slight disagreement. I wanted to fly Number 114, 'a doll of a plane', which I knew well, but Moddy insisted on having it, and I took a less popular one, Number 121. We took off, flying low and maintaining radio contact. We flew along the coast, and I dropped two bombs on the centre of an Egyptian concentration. I continued on to Majdal (today's Ashkelon), strafing with my machine-guns. We lost contact with one another, and each of us returned separately. It was Saturday night. I flew over the roof of my uncle Chaim's home in Rehovot with a feeling of triumph: the Egyptians were falling back, and we were chasing them. Before landing in Herzlia, I noticed a pillar of black smoke near the airfield. My heart stopped beating. The first man I saw when I landed was Harry Axelrod, his face drawn and sorrow-stricken. 'Moddy's been killed.' To this day, it is not clear what happened. Maybe he was hit by enemy fire, or perhaps there was some breakdown on Number 114. He crashed near Herzlia.

Mina, Moddy's wife, was awaiting him in his office. She knew that the two of us were flying together, and she knew that one of us had been killed. She didn't whow which one – until I walked into the office. She was four months pregnant at the time, and Michal was born, fatherless, on 29 April 1949.

We continued our assaults on the Egyptian forces into the winter of 1948. In terms that became familiar to Israelis during the 1973 war, we had completed the phase of containment, and we were moving on to the next stage, which then meant pushing the Egyptians out of Israel. The tide had turned.

The crowning achievement of the land offensive mounted by the Givati and Negev brigades was their breakthrough into Sinai, where they advanced as far as the outskirts of El Arish. That was the first Israeli thrust into Sinai. It is of course possible to claim that had the Israeli army remained there and penetrated further – which was militarily feasible after the collapse of the Egyptian army – there would have been no need for our later incursions into Sinai. There is no way of establishing that claim, and it can be no more than a hypothesis, for political considerations led the government to order a withdrawal. From the viewpoint of air warfare, the decision to pull back from Sinai was of the greatest consequence for a state fighting for its existence.

The air force had been strengthened by the acquisition of additional Dakotas. The Messerschmidts had been withdrawn from service and were replaced by the admirable 'Spits'. Our spirits soared. During the months of November and December 1948, it was evident that the Egyptian army's backbone was breaking. We flew freely all over Sinai: it was the first time that we were to savour the taste of mastery over such extensive areas. Wherever we flew, we spotted Egyptians fleeing for their lives. A less-welcome sight, which caused us much heartache, were the streams of Arab refugees, with their miserable bundles, trudging in the wake of the retreating Egyptians.

The seventh of January 1949 was a grey, winter day. There was talk of a cease-fire; rumour succeeded rumour, with the more reliable reporting that the cease fire would take effect that afternoon, at two. Everyone wanted to grab one last sortie. We flew to the vicinity of Abu Ageila, with that wonderful feeling of complete mastery, to do a bit of strafing here and there. The squadron commander, Sid Cohen, a South African volunteer (now an aviation doctor who has returned to Israel with his family), was in headquarters busy with administrative matters. Rudy (an American volunteer) and I took charge – Rudy as deputy commander, and I as operations officer. It was cold and the Spitfires were unheated, so we flew swathed in flying boots, heavy winter jackets and warm mufflers.

At that time radar was a concept too sophisticated for us. Control systems? We scarcely received any ground reports, and instructions from air-force command (in English usually, for the benefit of the foreign volunteers) would only come through on special occasions. The most convenient sign to distinguish our planes from those of the enemy was that ours only flew in pairs. In the whole course of the War of Independence, we flew a foursome on only three occasions. Our resources were scanty and had to be husbanded scrupulously. If you encountered a foursome, they evidently weren't ours – so shoot 'em up if you can, and if you're short of fuel, break off contact.

Around 9.30 on the morning of 7 January, two of our boys landed at Hazor, to which the squadron had moved in November. One was a veteran of the American air force, and the other had served in the Canadian air force. With an innocent look on their faces, without a trace of excitement, as though it were the most normal thing in the world, they reported shooting down two Spitfires. Before we could congratulate them, they added casually: 'RAF Spitfires'.

It took two or three minutes before we could get our breath back. Everybody crowded around the two pilots, demanding precise details: where, when, how? Somebody even dared to ask why. The two related that they were on patrol near Abu Ageila when they encountered six British planes, they gave battle, knocking out two of them, while the others fled for their lives. Why? 'Whaddya mean, why? Do we or don't we have full air control? And six planes couldn't possibly be from our squadron: we don't fly in sixes, not even in fours. And anyone who isn't ours, is an enemy.' So tally-ho and two planes belonging to the

illustrious British Empire were planted in the sands of Abu Ageila!
These two clowns may have been unperturbed, but we weren't.
We were breathless with agitation. After all, the British *are* the
British. They're no Egyptians. True, the empire came out of the
war with its wings clipped and its treasury empty, but for anyone
who grew up under the tutelage of the British mandatory
government, the British were masters, projecting an image of
power far superior to ours.

In the meantime, while we were trying to predict the British
response, things were happening fast and furious. The boys were
out on patrol, in search of prey, and an Egyptian Fiat G-46 was shot
down. I also went out, but returned empty-handed. At about
11.30, two hours after the first two, two other pilots came back.
One of them did an aerial roll – the conventional way of signalling
an enemy plane shot down – and when his plane came to a halt he
clambered out smiling. Another British plane. A second group of
six British planes – probably seeking traces of the two planes lost in
the previous engagement – and our two took on all six! They shot
down one and thought they damaged another. We reported to
high command, and over the telephone came the sound of agitated
breathing. At 12.30, or slightly later, we got instructions from the
command: continue patrolling, and beware of British planes.

The cease fire was to go into effect at two that afternoon. The
hands of the clock were moving on, the war was coming to an end,
and I'd had a fruitless day. I hadn't shot down anything – Egyptian,
Syrian or British. A crowded day, and here I was, excluded from
the festivity. True, in the course of the war I had flattened some
tanks, as well as some other vehicles; I'd bombed and strafed. But I
never had any luck in aerial dogfights.

Two o'clock. Cease-fire. No more flying over enemy territory.
I phoned air-force command: 'Listen, there's a cease fire? Okay.
But those Egyptians – I don't know whether they'll start again or
not – but I think it would be good for morale to fly over El Arish
with a foursome, to display our presence, and to remind them that
they'd better keep to the cease-fire.' I breathed deeply as I got the
word, 'Go!'

We took off from Hazor at about 2.45. With me were Sandy
Jacobs and two American boys, Bill Shroeder and Caesar Dangott.

It was cloudy and cold; we were flying at 7,000 feet, in fairly open combat formation. Each plane had two 20-mm cannon and two 0.5 machine-guns; sights functioning, the radio in order. We flew on compass bearing: El Arish. Objective: demonstration of force. Motive: a personal hankering for adventure and a search for just one more victory to finish up the war.

Around the international boundary I saw black dots, the same height as we were, at twelve o'clock. I counted eight planes. Clearly not ours. I waggled my wings, signalling 'close formation'. The other three saw what I had and closed up. In air combat, especially with these planes, if you have height you enjoy an advantage, because you can always convert height into speed. So I climbed. At 8,500 feet, they approached from straight ahead. Two foursomes, one slightly higher and to the left of the other. 'Going in!' I called. The planes facing us continued to fly at the same height. Either they hadn't noticed us, or they thought we wouldn't attack them. They did not get into formation and remained 1,500 feet below us, to our right.

Bill was the first to go in to the attack. Within seconds, black smoke was pouring out of one of the British 'Spits': he went into a spin, nose down, and hit the ground. A lively battle – seven of them and four of us. I caught one, sat on his tail and let him have it. I observed hits, but I didn't see him catch fire or crash. In a fight lasting about two minutes we scattered them in all directions. Then the Egyptian anti-aircraft fire was turned on us. I glanced around, looking for the others, but I was alone, which often happens after combat. I noticed another plane climbing, making off alone. I tried to catch up, but the distance was too great. After another turn – perhaps I'll find the plane I hit – I headed back to Hazor. Sandy had already landed, and he ran up to embrace me. He had seen a plane crashing and wasn't sure whose it was, making him fear for my fate. Upon checking I discovered one or two bullet-holes, nothing serious.

We had had a long day. Five planes, the property of the British Empire, were now buried in the desert sands. One of them was mine. It transpired that the plane I hit did a belly-landing near El Arish. Two of the British pilots were killed, we captured two others, and one of them walked back to his base. (A few years ago, I researched the matter and discovered that one of the British pilots had reached the equivalent rank of colonel in the RAF. No wonder. After all, he did have the benefit of a good lesson.)

The excitement was tremendous, both at the base and at air-force command. There was also great concern. Our ramshackle little air force had shot down five British planes in the course of a few hours, in air battle hampered by numerical inferiority. We were certain that the British would send in for a reprisal raid. The most common guess was that a score of bombers, escorted by dozens of fighters, would swoop down on the Hazor airfield and wipe it off the face of the earth. The fearful imaginings of the pessimists went even further.

Panic-stricken phone calls came in from air-force command: 'No pilot is to leave camp!' Clearly, the fate of the bars in Tel Aviv worried them as much as any possible British reprisals. They knew that if we reached Tel Aviv, there would be a riot, a kind of: 'Eat, drink and be merry, for the RAF is coming to flatten us'.

At about 5.30 permission came through for the eight pilots who took part in the battle with the British to come out of 'quarantine' and go to Tel Aviv. We said that either all the pilots of the squadron go, or no one goes. There was some haggling, and in the end the air-force command capitulated: all the pilots set off for Tel Aviv. We refuelled with a few bottles of cognac on the way, arriving at headquarters fully tanked-up. With us in that kind of mood, anyone who came to interrogate us was taking a big risk. We explained the meaning of mastery of the air: no plane must be allowed to make provocative flights across 'our air space'. Moshe (Moish) Pearlman was one of the intelligence officers interrogating us, and I sensed that he caught on. When the interrogation ended, we were given strict orders: 'Everybody back to base!' Moish supported us in our refusal, and then the others also gave in. We went off to Tel Aviv for dinner, and then on to our favourite spot, the bar in the Park Hotel.

The news of our coming preceded us. The story of how we shafted the RAF had already made the rounds, with the details made up of a mixture of fact and fiction. It was a party to beat all parties, with Israelis, American tourists – in fact, anyone who loved a good story and a drink – coming to join us. Whoever it was that carted us back to base the next morning is hereby offered my hearty thanks and good wishes, and I admit that only ignorance prevented me from doing so earlier. If, heaven forbid, the British had decided on a reprisal raid the next morning, they would probably have been surprised to discover that the superb pilots who had knocked down five of their planes were temporarily unfit for combat.

Thus, just before the cease-fire went into force, in effect ending the War of Independence, we enjoyed the experience of combat with the planes of a world power. We definitely had had the feeling that we were running a big risk, and I would by no means say that the decision to engage the British planes was the outcome of cold, sober reasoning. It was a clear expression of our self-confidence, of our belief in our own skills and of our desire to be masters of our country and its skies. The events of that day were treated as a passing episode. In those days, everyone was sure that the fate of this region would be determined by its own peoples.

Had everything possible been done to exploit our victories? That point has been argued ever since, and the debate will probably never end. The fact is that from the operational angle it was feasible to do more and win further gains, but there was a great weariness. A lot of blood had been spilt, thousands of men had given their lives to pay for our independence and liberty, and there was a widespread desire, fully justified under the circumstances, not to prolong the bloodshed, even if that meant forgoing further gains. There was a deep urge to lay down our arms, to put away our planes and to bring our soldiers back home.

In April 1949, Sid Cohen decided to go back to South Africa, and on 1 April I was appointed commander of the squadron. That night we held one of those stormy farewell parties, which never, under any circumstances, ended before the not-so-small hours of the morning. The next day we saw Sid off at Lod Airport. Everyone loved Sid, who is both a brave and modest man, and I doubt if Israel's president, or prime minister, would have earned the kind of send-off we gave him: four 'Spits' from the world's youngest air force attached themselves to his plane, circling in formation and entertaining him with aerobatics until he was 20 miles out to sea.

5

SQUADRON COMMANDER

SHORTLY AFTER I took command of the squadron, we moved to Ramat David. The unit was undergoing a rapid metamorphosis. As more Israeli pilots joined, Hebrew, which had been thrust aside and almost forgotten at the time of the squadron's creation, was reinstated to its proper role. It wasn't just a question of language. Our switch back to Hebrew symbolized the squadron's gradual adoption of an Israeli style of life and relationships. We would now have to face our problems together and try to forge ahead without the foreign volunteers, whose previous combat experience had always given us the feeling that they looked down on us from a position of superiority, allowing themselves an occasional smile at the 'natives'. At the same time I do not want in any way to play down the volunteers' superb contribution to the squadron, its combat skills and its self-confidence. I'm glad they came when they did, but I'm equally glad they left us to face our problems.

Our planes were now considerably better: twenty-five Spitfires – a formidable force. If we had been ordered to fight on, we would have gained significant victories. However, our first war was behind us. It was now vital to strengthen the squadron, to improve its training, to create the strongest possible bonds between the unit and its men. We needed to dampen the tensions between the pilots, with sky-high self-esteem, and the hundreds of ground-crew, who always consider themselves the drab, glamourless rank and file, even though no squadron can live without them.

During this period there were a couple of 'British episodes', perhaps to remind us of the decades of British rule. A British pilot – exhibiting a naive faith in the everlasting nature of the British Empire – evidently had never heard of the independent State of Israel, and piloting a flying boat home to England from Hong Kong, he coolly traversed Israeli air-space.

At the time, we had a number of observation posts; one of them notified me that a large plane was crossing the Sea of Galilee on its way to Haifa. I got the report while I was at air-force command in Tel Aviv. Two Spitfires were ordered to 'scramble' and identify the intruder. 'A British Sunderland,' they reported. 'Bring him in,' I ordered, convinced that I was acting correctly: no independent state permits a foreign plane to pass through without permission.

I took a car and rushed to Tel Aviv's sea front, where crowds of citizens watched the Spitfires escort the flying boat. Out at the Sunderland I came upon a number of shocked Englishmen, scanning their maps for some mention of an additional sovereign state on the long route from Hong Kong to Great Britain. All in all, they were pleasant chaps, I took them ashore, treated them to a beer, let them chatter a bit and then sent them on their way with my best wishes and a polite request to use up-to-date maps showing the existence of a Jewish state.

A year passed. We stepped up our training, acquired further planes and improved our combat tactics. And then, that well-known bachelor-about-town, Weizman, entered into the bonds of matrimony and went to England for his honeymoon. I was a squadron commander, with the rank of lieutenant-colonel. We didn't yet have anything like special air-force uniforms – we hadn't got round to matters like that. But as I was the first Israeli officer to go to England since the British withdrew from Palestine, air-force command saw fit to dress me up in the uniform of an officer in the Israeli air force. At that time there was nothing like General Staff regulations, so I went to a tailor and, using my own judgement, chose a kind of blue – somewhere between the colours used by our police and the Australian air force. I also acquired a cap, pinned on my wings, and in July 1950, set off for England with my wife Re'uma.

Our military attaché in England, the late Katriel Shalmon, did not then have many opportunities to introduce Israeli officers to the British military authorities. Shalmon took a great deal of trouble to arrange a visit to the RAF's Transport Command headquarters, at a place called Lyneham, where a cheerful major greeted me with a smart salute and a pleasant smile and escorted me to the operations room. As it was a transport unit, they had maps of the whole world, with various colours marking different areas as closed or open, friendly or hostile. Now, what would be the natural inclination of any young air-force officer from a newly founded state – especially one who had recently shot down one British plane and then had another intercepted and brought down off Tel Aviv's sea front? To look for his country. And there it was, hugging the Mediterranean coast, squeezed in between Egypt and Syria – it was tiny, but it was there! And what do mine eyes behold? That little state of mine, coloured a sort of vivid purple, had a note attached to it. I asked my host's permission to take a closer look and stepped up close to read it: 'Any plane flying over this area will be shot at without warning'.

At that particular moment, I didn't take the trouble to inform the British that I had any personal connection with the warning note on their chart, yet I felt they knew all about me. Nevertheless, as befits British courtesy, that did not affect their friendly hospitality, nor did it prevent me, a few months later, from being the first Israeli officer admitted to the RAF's staff and command college.

Between that visit and my return to the RAF's staff college, we continued to build up the squadron. I felt the heavy burden of command on my shoulders. My light-hearted tricks and mischievousness had to make way for a good deal of solemnity and seriousness. I felt obliged to take my farewell of bars and parties – or at least to cut down my visits. Actually I didn't find it too difficult to withdraw (more or less) from my light-hearted, easy-going way of life. The squadron was a living, breathing entity, demanding lots of attention, lots of thought, lots of persistence and lots of perseverance. I gained extraordiniary satisfaction from training combat pilots. From the very first, I felt – and that feeling accompanied me throughout my years of service, especially when I was in command of the air force – that I wanted to train the pilot as a man, and not just as a technician who could operate his elaborate flying machine and take it into combat. I wanted to turn these young men into Zionists, totally identifying with their country, with the objectives of Zionism and the needs of the Jewish people. I wanted the pilot to be a good companion, aware of his social obligations; sure of himself and his abilities, but also an integral part of a team, to which he would contribute his share and would be enriched in return.

I had to dedicate myself to my task. I have never feared the word 'dedicate'. I believe that this generation of young Jews is dedicating itself to our people's greatest task: to maintain the sovereignty of the Jewish people in its own land. I put it as simply as that. I've never flinched from the word 'Zionism', and I've always felt myself to be personally obliged – the kind of obligation that cannot be imposed by others – to put my Zionism into practice.

The volunteer pilots from abroad were taking their leave, and a new generation of Israeli pilots joined the squadron. At first, the exodus of the foreign volunteers aroused some concern, and even indignation. What did they think. Here was a new state, facing enormous challenges, and they thought they'd finished their jobs? These fellows had considerable flying and combat experience, and when they began to leave, I felt that the squadron was poorer, sapped of some of its strength.

It was this feeling that provided me with my prime motivation when I faced the decision of whether or not (and for how long) to sign on for regular service in the air force. Like any other army, the Israeli Defence Forces had to have a solid professional core. If I had had the choice two or three years previously, my decision to sign on would probably have stemmed from the feeling that I hadn't learned to do anything else but fly, while that was something I knew I could do well. This wasn't the way I felt now, and I signed on for five years – the longest period then proposed – not only because I loved flying, but because I felt a heavy responsibility for the fate of the squadron. Here we were, building up the unit, acquiring new planes and preparing for new confrontations, when and if they come, and Rudy and Mike and Flint and Jack Cohen and Sid Cohen get up and go. So who's going to do the job? Who will build up the only fighter squadron in the new air force?

There was something else happening which struck me as premature, illusive and deceptive. All around, one heard people say: The war's over! We've licked the Arabs! It is now possible – and even essential – to go back to our original Zionist occupations: building up the country, developing its agriculture, establishing a sound, peace-time society. I was convinced that this was incorrect. I sensed, rather than knew, that we had won only a single battle, that our enemies would pull themselves together and renew their bid to wipe us out.

I had more than one bitter and highly vocal argument on this subject. Kibbutz Degania, the 'mother of kibbutzim', summoned one of our new Israeli pilots, Motty Hod, to return home. They had done without him long enough, while he served in the British army and then fought in the War of Independence. He had done his share; now he should return home to his kibbutz, to a normal life. Three other pilots – Danny, Tibby and Shaya – had no trouble deciding what to do. They were city men, their fate was in their own hands and they signed on. Motty wanted to follow in their footsteps, but he told me regretfully that he couldn'y because he was under pressure from his comrades in Degania to go home and till the soil. Heaven forbid that I should underrate work on the land or kibbutz life! But I felt that his leaving was premature – for us and for him.

I felt affection and esteem for Motty from the very first. Ours was a friendship that withstood many trials. When he came to tell me that he was being permitted to sign on, I said, 'Five years? What's five years? I'll sign on again and again. I'll serve here until we have a first-class air force!' But Motty was tormented by indecision. One day he came up to me and said: 'Listen, come to Degania, to a general meeting of all the kibbutz members. You can convince them to let me sign on.'

'Fair enough!' I answered, without having the faintest idea what a kibbutz general meeting is like or how it is run.

The following Friday evening Motty and I were on our way to Degania in a jeep. It was years since I had last been there, and I dressed for the occasion in an air-force uniform with an American cap and my squadron-commander's insignia. As I walked into the crowded dining room (which also served as a meeting hall), I sensed even before anyone had said a word that there was little sympathy there for me, or my uniform, or the air force that was trying to preserve its existence even though war had departed from the world. They were good people, but their glances at me were as cold as ice. Tanned kibbutzniks, wrinkled and gnarled, their bald pates sunburnt – these were people who had tremendous achievements to their credit, people who had done the same kind of pioneering work in their sphere as I now wanted to do in mine. I was sorry to see myself separated from them by a kind of wall of alienation.

I could sense them looking at me distastefully, thinking that this wasn't exactly the casually dressed Israeli warrior grasping a hoe in one hand and a rifle in the other. I was a stranger, an alien, who had never ploughed the Land of Israel. I was a hired professional who was not content with having chosen a path for himself but was trying to seduce one of their dear young men, their Motty, off the straight and narrow. And I knew that here stories of the Battle of Britain and a plea for the need to prepare for a further war would fall on deaf ears. Suddenly I was not at all certain that I could convince them.

Sometimes, when there's no choice, you have to adopt an unconventional approach. I stood up and spoke briefly and to the point:

'Listen, my dear friends, we've just finished a hard and bloody war. I hope that none of you has any doubts that our young state needs an air force to prevent another war. If, contrary to all our hopes, there *is* another war, we'll need an air force to defend us. Now look, in this war we were helped by the foreign volunteers. They're leaving us now, one by one. The ones left are boys like your Motty and Peretz. If they leave the air force, who will remain? Who? Only characters like me! An air force left to characters like me – is that what you want?'

There was a stir of agitation in the assembly. That was more than Degania could stand – to have the air force left to the likes of me, people without any roots in the soil! What kind of an air force would that be? And what kind of an army? Could you rely on it?

The members of Degenia gave their approval, and Motty signed on. Eighteen years later, as commander of the Israeli air force, he led it to its glorious victory in the Six Day War.

The young state had a military tradition that had been built up, in the face of severe tests, years before the formal establishment of the State of Israel. Admittedly, the defence organizations had always been underground, and there was always an acute shortage of equipment. But in the course of the years, the Haganah, the IZL and Lehi had built up a martial tradition, producing some excellent commanders, who had gained their training in this country. The air force, on the other hand, did not inherit any tradition from the Haganah, or from the other underground organizations, for the simple reason that aerial activity cannot be conducted underground. There were no home-grown aerial commanders who were products of years of preparation for Israeli independence. There were some Israelis with aviation experience, but it was limited at best: a few fellows who flew in the Aviation Club and knew how to operate light reconnaissance planes, logging a few hours' flying time. In addition, there were graduates of RAF flying courses, who also had little experience. They realized their dream, completed the course and gained their wings, but attained no more than the rank of sergeant. No one was given command duties that could have prepared him in any way for a responsible post in the new Israeli air force.

When I was appointed squadron commander, my lack of command experience was a drawback, but it was an advantage as well. The ground forces had the benefit of their commanders' experience, but this also shackled them to fixed patterns, to well-tried routines. We were far more open and unfettered. Instead of imitation – which isn't always bad, just as it isn't always good – we sensed the need to invent, to innovate, to improvise. In creating something from nothing, we didn't say: 'Let's see how others did it and try to do it better!' For us, it was: 'Let's have a look at our own peculiar conditions and do things as well as possible'.

The Haganah possessed considerable printed material, in the form of training manuals and lesson schedules. Of course, as weapons and tactics improved, these manuals became obsolete, and they had to be brought up to date and extended; but the basics, the rudiments, were there. We had nothing like that in the air force. No manuals, no training schedules. Nothing. When I took command of the squadron and we began to induct the first Israelis who did not have RAF experience, I knew precisely what I wanted of them, what I wanted to give them, what I wanted to make them into. My problem was how.

I used to sit up at night writing training schedules and then try them out on the young pilots the following day. Everything was exciting and novel. I tried to combine three components: the knowledge I had picked up during my RAF service, my personal combat experience and the specific traits of the Israeli youngster, with his high intelligence and pluck and his readiness to take risks.

I cannot hide my pride in the first group of Israeli pilots who reached the squadron. About fifteen of them joined us, after an impromptu course at Tel Nof, where they got their wings after some 250–300 flying hours. We taught them to fly Spitfires. Of course, it wasn't just a matter of teaching them the techniques of take-off and landing and piloting the plane. The main problem was how to fight in a Spitfire, how to use it to gain superiority, how to exploit its very advantage and how to overcome its drawbacks – no plane is without those!

Part of the training had to be done as a 'mock-up'; we didn't have the means to teach gunnery by actual shooting, or test-bombing techniques with live bombs. The young pilots often felt a natural need and desire to prove that their lessons had been well learnt, but we had to postpone live practice for real encounters, or to better days when the air force would be able to afford such 'luxuries'.

You can't train a good combat pilot without him being eager to give battle. Every pilot and commander whom I knew was glad of the armistice with our neighbours, but as long as peace was remote and war was an imminent danger, our boys were afire to prove that they had learnt their lessons properly, and, given the opportunity, wouldn't miss their chance. We probably didn't know much about the inner expressions of their desire to prove worthy of the squadron and its spirit and to identify with its successes. But there were visible signs too: their unlimited loyalty and pride, their identification with the unit and its commander and their boundless desire to learn, to advance, to overcome every difficulty. And we'd hear them sigh: 'Oh, just give me an Egyptian

Spitfire, just give me a Syrian Spitfire – just gimme!' They were 'hot' for combat; at times they were even too hot, and they had to be restored to a proper balance.

For all their eagerness, though, our boys were still innocents. They had yet to prove themselves in combat, and combat, of every kind, is a severe test of a man's ability; every battle is an arduous experience in which one is exposed both physically and psychologically. Whatever the dictionary definition of fear, the soldier knows it without the help of verbal definitions. He senses it whenever he is exposed to danger. No soldier is free of fear, nor is any pilot. The difference between a good pilot and a poor one is that the first can overcome his fear, control it and not give way to it. Fear tries to paralyze, to undermine one's judgement, to take away one's willingness to perform his duty. Courage overcomes these dangers and disarms the fears.

Flying, under any circumstances, creates tension. Most people in the world walk, or ride in vehicles as passengers; some drive, or sail boats. Only a small minority pilot planes. And the 'hotter' a plane, the faster and more advanced it is, the greater the tension from the moment you start up the engines. Tension is somewhat contained by various devices designed to protect the pilot. One of these is the ejector-seat. But it is no more than a palliative, and it doesn't really relieve the tension, because the pilot lives with the continuous awareness that one small error can put an end to his plane and himself, even when he isn't in battle.

There's no need of much imagination for one to sense that the danger increases under combat conditions, when a man has to make rapid decisions and perform numerous actions within a brief time. The pilot knows that a tiny error may be his last. An error – any error – is much more fateful for a pilot than for a tank-driver or sailor or infantryman. It's easier to correct a directional error in a tank than in a plane. When a tank's engine breaks down, it has a reasonable chance of withdrawing from the battle and waiting to be repaired or hauled away. It's a bit more difficult to hook your plane to a cloud and wait to be towed to a repair hangar.

But the tension turns you into an integral part of your plane. I'm afraid that anyone who has never piloted a combat plane will find it hard to grasp a pilot's total identification with his plane. You're stuck in a tiny cockpit, and from the moment you get in, until the moment you get out, you're cramped up, strapped to your seat, free to do no more than move the upper part of your body and your feet. You can't stand up, you can't shake off your weariness by straightening up or stretching. There are certain planes that do not even allow you to relieve yourself.

Another cause of tension is the weather and its fluctuations. I have sensed it ever since that peculiar Rhodesian mist, from which I was saved only by a tree. Every pilot knows what tribulations clouds can cause. A thick layer of clouds, covering the earth and obscuring everything, is a pilot's nightmare. Commercial airlines only permit their pilots to land when the cloud level is less than 300 feet. Under combat conditions, when everything is in the balance, when the air force has to shoulder tasks of national importance, many rules are disregarded. But however necessary it may be to ignore bad weather in war-time, it still creates great psychological tension among pilots.

The pilot is the loneliest man in a war. He is in control of an enormously powerful machine and he's on his own. In a Messerschmidt he sits on a tank full of fuel; in the Spitfire, the fuel tank is in front of him. In a jet, he's on top of 4,000 litres of fuel. He knows that a direct hit on his fuel tank could turn him and his plane into a flaming torch.

Even when he's not in combat, the tension wears a pilot out, and this weariness increases his loneliness. I have never flown a bomber, but many hours spent in the company of bomber pilots and crews have enabled me to pin point the difference: it's the total isolation of the fighter-pilot and his feeling that everything depends on him alone. The only words to penetrate the silence come through his earphones. Cold, distant words, which essentially do nothing to dispel his loneliness, which grows progressively heavier. He longs for the voice of a friend, there, beside him. He wants someone to share his responsibility and give him the feeling that he's not alone.

Most people know about flying second-hand. A superficial view of the pilot and his plane reveals nothing but the glamour and glory. Pilots are often objects of envy, because they are a small *élite* whose lives are full of mystery and whose world is hard to scale. There is some justification for envying these 'adventurers'; flying *is* an exciting adventure. But for the combat pilot, a developed, balanced view of flying is among the most important things in his training. He needs the sense of challenge; he needs to build up his bravado, his pluck, his willingness to risk attempting unusual feats. At the same time it has to be kept in proportion, to prevent him from turning the whole matter into an adventure or from being enslaved by the human inclination to excessive exhibitionism – either of which might make him disregard the depth of his responsibility and neglect to use his power of judgement and thought.

There is another seeming contradiction. By nature the pilot is an individualist. A combat pilot, isolated during combat, does not experience the team spirit of a tank-crew. He performs all his combat tasks by himself: he attacks, aims, fires and climbs all alone. Such individualism can make him withdraw within himself. If his experience colours his whole life, it will become a matter of 'every man for himself'. But despite the isolation of the pilots in their cockpits, the squadron needs team spirit, comradeship and mutual responsibility, for its strength stems from a deep sense of partnership, which provides the powerful bonds that hold it together.

The Israeli pilots were not of one kind. The only thing they had in common was the fact of being Israelis – a common language, behaviour and general concepts. But there were all sorts – farmers, city fellows, kibbutzniks, veterans of the Palmach and graduates of the Aviation Club. They had all kinds of attitudes and all kinds of life-styles. There was no book to teach me how to give them the feeling of partnership, or how to cultivate their individual talents – which no air force can forego. No commander should blur his individual men while at the same time trying to forge them into a united social framework. I started with small things – lots of shared living, lots of flying together, lots of social life and the inculcation of a common life-style. Starting in April 1949, I was engaged in building up the first Israeli combat squadron, and it was one of the finest periods in my life.

I presume that for these young Israeli fellows, there was something in me that gripped their imagination, making me an object of their emulation. I wasn't some foreign volunteer who said: 'I came, I saw, I conquered – now I'm going.' I was an Israeli, like themselves, not very much older than themselves, yet I had flying experience and my feats didn't fall far short of those of the foreign volunteers.

When you train a young pilot, one of the ways to kindle his fighting spirit and cultivate his love of flying is by tales and yarns of pilots' feats. Young pilots love to hear them, and old pilots love to tell them. The foreign volunteers were bubbling over with stories of their deeds in World War Two, while those of us who helped found the Israeli air force added our share with detailed accounts of our battles in the War of Independence. (Despite our numerical inferiority and our ramshackle planes, we shot down twenty-two enemy planes in the course of the war.) The young pilots would listen intently, drinking in every word.

But for all the concern and attention I was devoting to the pilots, I was always aware that pilots are no more than the tip of the iceberg. They are charged with the final task, giving incisive, audacious and often startling expression to the efforts of many individuals: the cook, the technician, the armourer and the sanitary inspector. Yet it is the pilot who naturally scoops up all the glory, the renown and the fame, and he is susceptible to the kind of haughtiness that leaves the ground-crew in the shade, full of frustration, disappointment and envy of the 'high-fliers'. I sensed then that one of the most severe tests of an air-force commander was his ability to give the ground-crews a feeling of equality, a conviction of their own importance and satisfaction with their lot, thus enabling them to do their work faithfully, in partnership with their airborne colleagues. One doesn't create that feeling of equality by mere talk. A man can be told, day in and day out, that he's equal to the pilot, but he needs proof, and he will watch your attitude towards him, scrutinizing it to find out if you're sincere and how you, as the commander, regard the partnership between ground and air crews.

At that stage, these were only preliminary thoughts, insufficiently clarified. I was aware of the problem, but I had no ready-made solutions. Three years later, on being appointed commander of Ramat David Base I was older and more mature and able to give expression to the ideas that had been on my mind for years. But on my way from squadron commander to commander of Ramat David, there was an additional posting I took on, one that doesn't allow for transfers or promotions: the command of Re'uma, my wife.

Re'uma has gone a long way with me in loyal partnership. I have many good reasons for feeling grateful to the gods for permitting me to meet her along life's way. One reason concerns the air force; I was never required to choose between two lovers, two loyalties, or two paths. From the very first moment, Re'uma understood, without any need for it to be said, that there was room in my life for another love – for a woman, for children, for my family – but my emotional world had no place for anything to replace the air force. Re'uma was wise enough not to set herself against the air force or to compete with it. Instead, she became a connecting link, fully integrated into my emotional make-up. It is symbolic that I first made her acquaintance – in 1946, in Basle, during my visit to the Zionist Congress – because she wanted to fly back to London with me. I took her to the Auster, which was not a tempting vehicle to fly to London in. Re'uma was always frank; she needed no more than a glance before she said: 'Thanks very much, but with lunatics like you, in a plane like that, I'm not flying anywhere!' Nonetheless, the set back did not prevent us from renewing our acquaintance a few years later, nor from taking a long and pleasant flight together, my lunacy notwithstanding.

Those with a weakness for symbolism will be pleased to hear that our acquaintance was renewed under circumstances also directly connected with the air force. It was April 1949, and I was driving in a jeep with Motty Hod – one of our new pilots in the squadron – to a service in commemoration of Moddy's death, a year earlier. Re'uma stood at the road side hitch-hiking and waved us down. She got a ride – a lifelong one. We drove on past her a short way; it was Motty who suggested going back for her. When she stepped into the jeep, she said: 'I know you from somewhere ... Basel. The Auster. "With lunatics like you!"'

She belonged to one of Jerusalem's oldest and most colourful clans, the hospitable, ever-youthful Schwartz family. A week after that jeep ride, I took half the squadron off to Jerusalem 'to visit the Holy City'. They were sharp fellows, and I couldn't make them swallow that one: they knew that I had a new girlfriend, and they knew she was from Jerusalem. They also knew that their young commander's frequent visits to Haifa and Tel Aviv had left a long trail of broken hearts. I suppose they never guessed that this time I had been hooked for good.

Re'uma became genuinely enthusiastic about the air force. She enjoyed her visits to the squadron. At the time we used to put away large quantities of 'fiery liquid' and Re'uma would spend hours in the bar, quietly, without advertising her presence. She, too, would take a drink every now and then; in fact, her capacity was nothing to be ashamed of!

Soon we became very close, until finally, as they say, 'he chased her and chased her, until she caught him.' Every woman has her own way of catching her man. Re'uma's way was very much to my liking: she made the air force part of our relationship, stilling my fear of ever having to choose between two loves. Re'uma and I came to the air force hand in hand; it was the first time that a woman not only entered my life, but also joined me in the cockpit of my plane. She loved to fly and was captivated by the squadron and its life-style.

Re'uma had always loved music, and when Motty discovered that she wanted me to take her to a concert, he declared knowledgeably: 'Weizman, that's very serious. A concert? There'll be a wedding for sure.' I reassured him, telling him not to worry. But deep in my heart, I knew that, concert or no concert, there would be a wedding. And ever since Motty married his art-loving wife, Pnina, I've reminded him that 'I never went to any concert, but you turned out to art exhibitions like a loyal trooper!'

I would often visit Re'uma's parents in Jerusalem. They kept open house, and I was received with warm hospitality. Less than a week after we met, they invited me, in the most matter-of-fact manner, for a weekend at their home. At one o'clock in the morning, I was stretched out on the couch they had made up for me, when suddenly I heard the door-hinges creak. I pretended to be asleep. It was the 'old man', Re'uma's eternally youthful father, who came in and covered me up with a blanket. I'm not quite sure what that friendly visit was for: to make sure that I didn't get too cold, or that his young daughter didn't get too hot.

She was the younger daughter; the elder had been married to Moshe Dayan for fifteen years and was raising three children. My visits to Jerusalem and my relationship with Re'uma brought me close to Dayan. Previously, I had only known of him by hearsay, and when I first got to know Re'uma, I wasn't even aware of the connection between them. In the course of many years, my relationship with him has known ups and downs, common views and sharp differences. In that period, however, we were very close.

Dayan was then military commander of Jerusalem, and Moshe and Ruth's home was open to all. On Fridays their door never closed, as visitors bustled in and out: Jerusalemites, soldiers, UN observers and just plain citizens and friends. One always found a marvellously informal atmosphere there. Drinks and cakes on the table, Assi dashing around between everyone's legs, and Uddi under the table. It was a cheerful household, a kind of total disorder together with an air of hospitality that charmed anyone who ever enjoyed the company of its occupants and their adorable children.

As for Rachel, Re'uma's mother, she is a story unto herself. The years pass her by, and she remains untouched. When I was courting Re'uma, Rachel was well beyond her fiftieth birthday. I would look at Rachel and think: 'If that's the way my Re'uma looks in another twenty years' time, I'm onto a sure thing!'

At the beginning of April 1950, with five months of close friendship behind us, I took a step to formalize our relationship: Re'uma came to stay at my parents' home in Haifa. She arrived for a weekend, carrying a modest little suitcase. We had never discussed marriage before. Now, sipping cognac in my room, I said: 'You know what, Re'uma? It's no good, no good. It's hard for me to travel up to Jerusalem every week, and it's hard for you to come to Haifa. As squadron commander, I can't go far away. But we could take a room in Tivon. Is that all right with you?' Re'uma was very pale and white. 'Yes,' she said, 'all right.'

It was one o'clock in the morning, but I burst into the bedroom of my astounded parents to inform them that Re'uma and I had decided to get married. And then I saw that Re'uma was even paler than before. Apparently she hadn't regarded the room in Tivon as a formal proposal of marriage, but as a more efficient way of setting up our meetings. However, as my parents were already rushing out of their room and swooping down to hug and kiss her, in the best Weizman tradition, she had no choice other than to accept her 'fate'. Thus we became engaged, and telephoned the red-hot news to Jerusalem, where Rachel and Zvi almost swallowed the receiver in their excitement and joy.

The next day was Saturday. Rachel and Zvi, Ruth and Moshe and the children all came to Haifa to plan the wedding. Plans were bandied about, questions of beds, sheets and furniture, where will they live, how will they get married: 'You may or may not be a squadron commander, but this wedding is going to be a kosher Jewish affair, with all the trappings'. It's a brave man indeed who would dare set his will against the united desires of the Schwartzes of Jerusalem and the Weizmans of Haifa.

We got married in June 1950, at Ruth and Moshe's home. Chief Rabbi Herzog conducted the ceremony, and all kinds of important people and lots of friends came to celebrate with us. My sister wasn't there; to my regret she was still in England. Uncle Chaim didn't come either. The president was old, and two years before his death, his feeble powers no longer permitted him to participate in events of this kind. But he sent strict instructions: the bride was to present herself for his approval!

Re'uma dressed up in all her finery to look her best; she could scarcely control her excitement as I escorted her to the ageing president. When we walked in, Uncle Chaim inspected her with a knowledgeable look, up and down and from all sides, and then his face lost its grimness, to be replaced by a wide smile, 'Well, it could have been worse!' He had set his stamp of approval, and who is a greater authority than the president of Israel?

I had worked out our 'fertility plan' ahead of time: first a son, then a daughter. The order was carried out in full and in the correct sequence: first Shaul, and then Michal. I wanted a son immediately, but I nonetheless suggested to Re'uma: 'Let's leave three months, for the sake of public opinion.' And that's just the way it was. We got married on 6 June 1950, and Shaul was born on 27 May 1951. Public opinion did its reckoning and found everything as it should be.

That year I also faced the question of my future. It wasn't only the foreign volunteers who were leaving us. There were Israelis, too – some of the first to join the squadron, keen flyers for whom flying was their main aim in life, but who didn't necessarily stick to the air force. El Al had its attractions, too: a professional flying career, a long way from combat and material rewards into the bargain. It was tempting, but I'm glad I was strong enough to withstand it. I wouldn't want this to sound like a criticism of good friends who switched to El Al, but I simply did not consider myself at liberty to do likewise. The foundations of the air force were still shaky, I was in command of the only combat squadron in existence, and it had to carry a heavy burden. When Air Force Commander Aharon Remez asked me to stay on and transfer up to his command, that was an added inducement. Air-force command was constructed around three officers: the commander (at that time), Remez, chief of air staff (Dov Peleg, an American volunteer who stayed on, making his particular contribution to the field of electronics) and senior operations officer (whose duties parallel those of today's head of Operations Branch). It was this last post that I was being offered, and I accepted. I was promoted to colonel, and I handed over command of the squadron to Bill Kaiser, a South African volunteer.

6

JUNIOR STAFF OFFICER

Soon after assuming my new post, I was given the opportunity to participate in consultations conducted at a far higher level than I had been accustomed to. The Israel Defence Forces were then holding their first combined exercise. The moving spirit was Chaim Laskov, then head of Training Branch, and the consultations were held under Major-General Yigael Yadin, then chief of staff. The discussions were general, covering all the armed forces. It was a far cry from our debates about whether an air formation should be open or closed and whether it should consist of four planes or only two. These discussions with senior commanders before, during and after the exercise, opened up new vistas for me. I encountered a wide spectrum of subjects I had never met before: the over-all tasks of the air force in any future war, its integration with ground forces, including armour, artillery, infantry and paratroopers, as well as the navy. There were other questions: the defence budget and the portion allotted to the air force; the link between the air force's independence of planning and operations and its role as part of the over-all alignment of forces.

Over the years, there was much heart-searching on all these issues, and solutions were not unambiguous. There were doubts and hesitations, experiments and compromises, disagreements and renewed experiments. The Israeli army was not the only one attempting to establish the correct relationships between its various arms, and Israeli commanders were not the only ones perplexed as to the golden mean between the independence of their units and the need to treat all sections of the armed forces as one single operational entity. Far more experienced armies were coping with the same uncertainties, including that of the United States.

During my RAF service and, later, in the air service and the embryonic air force, to tell the truth, my mind was not on questions like the independence of the air force, or whether it should be under one kind of command or another. Even such practical issues as whether my jeep should be repaired by an air force technical unit, or in a ground forces garage, did not trouble me. But these matters surfaced in 1950, when organizational and operational problems intertwined and were brought under examination in a large-scale exercise.

When these problems came up, I asked myself: if it's so natural and self-understood for every air force to aspire to equality with the ground forces, why do the ground forces resist? It seems there is a certain amount of envy and something of a desire to clip the wings of the high-flying aviators, to bring them down a peg or two and give them a taste of earth-clods and of tank lubricants and of the saltiness of the sea. After all, the destinies of nations had been decided in land and naval warfare, and it was these that had largely shaped the map of the world. Generals and admirals had gained eternal renown by their valorous deeds. And then, all of a sudden, at the outbreak of the First World War, a weird kind of contraption began to buzz through the skies, faster than any vehicle – a kind of bird with fixed wings, carrying a man who from that time on gazed down haughtily at the rest of the world. Furthermore, this object mocked frontiers, crossing and recrossing them, dropping its death-dealing loads, patrolling, taking photographs, reporting, making contact; its bite was painful, and yet it remained comparatively invulnerable. This new-fangled air power had scarcely shown its potential, and here it was, already threatening to dethrone the other military arms from the primacy they had earned through thousands of years of effort and bloodshed. In adequate quantities, the plane was capable of tipping the balance of a battle.

But before the plane could decide the outcome of wars, the world's air forces had to give battle for their rightful place within the armed forces of their individual countries. The Israel Defence

Forces did not evade a battle of this kind. Throughout the years that the Haganah and the other underground organizations prepared to fight for independence, as well as in the first years after the establishment of the state, ours was essentially a ground war. (When Ben-Gurion first spoke to the Haganah command of the need to acquire airplanes, his listeners were horrified: what a catastrophe, the man's gone mad! And the sad tidings were even whispered about.)

There was, therefore, little consciousness of the air force's role in the over-all alignment of the Israeli armed forces. There was a wide gap between the great feats we foresaw for the air force in any future war and the degree of importance it was accorded by the army chiefs, including Chief of Staff Yigael Yadin. We found it hard to prove our claims by the events of the War of Independence. After all, none of its battles had been decided by the air force. Against the Arab Legion of Transjordan, justly considered the best of the Arab armies, the air force's share was negligible, and the Jordanians didn't even have an air force of their own. In the battles with the Egyptians, our role consisted of dislodging the Egyptian air force from the sphere of operations and assisting the ground forces with air cover. Here, too, air power did not tilt the balance, and the air force did not emerge as a decisive factor.

The air force was cursed by its diminutive size. For the Israeli people it had been a fateful struggle. What was in the balance was no less than 'to be or not to be'. Would our audacity in proclaiming our independence give the Jewish people a sovereign state, or would the Jews of Palestine be drowned in rivers of blood? While the ground forces shed their blood and left 6,000 graves in the military cemeteries, the air force lost ten pilots – some of whom were victims of accidents – and emerged from this fateful battle with two and a half planes.

Such were the facts. We claimed that the value of a military force is not to be weighed by the quantity of its equipment or the number of its casualties; we predicted that future wars would require the air force to shoulder burdens unlike those of the past; we pointed out that a victorious army is always in mortal danger of foreseeing the next war along the lines of its successes in the previous one. All our arguments were well founded, but they fell

on deaf ears. Our demands for a certain degree of independence –
and for priority over other parts of the armed forces – were greeted
with bewildered expressions. Our requests for large sums of
money to buy planes were treated as the fancies of young men with
too high an opinion of themselves. Indeed, we were young;
twenty-eight-year-old Aharon Remez, previously a sergeant in
the RAF, was the commander. True, Chief of Staff Yigael Yadin
was only thirty-two, but in those days, four years was a significant
difference.

Yadin's attitude was not purely arbitrary. He was a sensible
man, reflective, thorough, learned. when Aharon Remez tried to
present his point of view, demanding a certain degree of
independence, financial priorities and large-scale acquisition of
planes, it required no small effort for Yadin to control his
astonishment and anger. 'My friends,' he said, 'get off my back!
And get this nonsense out of your heads. With conditions as they
are, and the kind of battles we've fought and will fight in the
future, if we do fight, what do you want? More than honourable
status, something like a brigade, or better even, fully subordinate
to the General Staff?! That's enough! You'll do precisely *what*
you're told, *when* you're told. You'll fight where you're ordered,
you'll be promoted whenever you're promoted. Why should a
pilot be any different from an artillery man or a tank driver? Why
should he have a different standard of living, enjoy better food,
wear better clothes, live in better quarters?' This was not
arbitrariness; it was an understandable miscomprehension.

Aharon Remez was the first man in Israel to see the air force in all
its future greatness and glory. Twenty-two years ago he spoke like
a true prophet. In his mind's eye, he saw the future air force and the
scope of its operations. Today it's clear that he was accurate in his
predictions, but at that time, he would bring sceptical smiles even
to the lips of those who were closest to the air force, who were
unable to see how, with its handful of Spitfires, three B-17s and
twenty assorted pilots, it would spread its wings and fulfil
Aharon's prophecies of squadrons, wings, bombers, combat planes
and gigantic operations. A man needed unlimited quantities of
faith and confidence to break away from the reality of the moment
and its shortcomings and let the wings of his imagination carry him

to the objectives he had set for the air force. This was one of Israel's greatest visions, and Aharon Remez is worthy of being compared with those men who had the foresight to envisage our future industry or our shipping fleet.

A vision is all very well and good, but the chances of convincing the heads of the state and the army seemed extremely slender. There was a tremendous row, which took on the proportions of a severe conflict, between Aharon, backed by the miniature air force, and General Command, which, regarding him as a day-dreamer, confidently rejected his proposals. The disagreements with Yadin grew so severe that Ben-Gurion, then prime minister and minister of defence, had to intervene. The 'old man' was a visionary himself; he inclined, more than others, to show affection and understanding for Remez and his fervent dreams. But, all in all, Aharon gained nothing from Ben-Gurion's intervention. When a decision at the highest level was called for, it came – and Remez went, paying the price for his vision, his persistence and his uncompromising combativeness. He wasn't yet thirty when he took over command of the air force, with general's rank, and he wasn't yet thirty when he was forced to leave his post and lay aside his uniform.

As head of Air Branch, I had a number of opportunities at the end of 1950 to drink in some of Aharon's words of wisdom – and very exciting they were. Aharon was no great organizer and not very systematic. Under his command, the air force didn't exist in the day-to-day reality, rather it lived in the infinite. Aharon's eyes gazed at distant vistas and that may be why he could overlook the confusion and disorder at his feet. He suffered all the tribulations of early beginnings; he became a target for biting criticism. But this did not make him alter his objective. He fought like a lion – and lost. General Command would go no further than giving the air force the status of an air brigade of the ground forces, exactly like the American air force, years before.

Practicalities weren't Aharon's strong side. Everyday questions like what kind of radar we needed and where it should be placed, what kind of plane we should prefer (taking into consideration the severe political restrictions that limited our purchasing ability) and how to train new pilots did not elicit clear answers from him. Four

years after the horrifying blow that descended on Hiroshima and
Nagasaki, many believed that nuclear weapons would sweep all
conventional armaments off the military stage, and our young air
force wasn't free of such notions. As a result, while some claimed
that Aharon was hallucinating and stuffing his listeners with day-
dreams, there were those who attacked him from the other side,
accusing him of being old-fashioned, of having ideas unsuited to
present times and of taking the air force backwards instead of
forwards.

In short, Aharon didn't have an easy time of it. He asked for the
rank of general for himself and demanded that air-force command
be given authority roughly parallel to that of the General Staff. As
he saw it, the General Staff should command the ground forces,
while air-force command should be in charge of everything
connected with the air. Incidentally, this concept has not been
formally accepted to this day. It is in effect *de facto*, but without *de
jure* recognition. But this practical application is a further proof
that Aharon's predictions were correct.

Another one of Aharon's prophecies was proved correct beyond
all doubt some years later. 'The air force is not an auxiliary of the
ground forces!' he said. 'It is a decisive force. Air superiority will
decide the battle. If the enemy doesn't have an air force, or if he had
one and you've succeeded in destroying it at the first stage of the
war, you've won!' That's exactly what happened in the Six Day
War. (The picture changed in the 1973 war, with the appearance of
surface-to-air missiles, but this will be discussed later.)

Aharon was forced to leave. The army still did not dare to hand
over command of the air force to an officer who had emerged from
the force itself; perhaps we weren't ready yet. Moddy had gone,
Dan Tolkovski and I apparently didn't seem sufficently mature.
The assumption was: 'Those air force fellows are good chaps.
They know how to fly, but they need to be organized and fit into
the over-all structure of the armed forces without all those will-o'-
the-wisps.'

If it's a question of organization, all eyes turned to that virtuoso
organizer, Shlomo Shamir. Shamir was transferred from the navy
and placed in command of the air force, while I retained my job as
head of Air Branch – sure of my own ability to reach the top, but

telling myself, over and over again, that I had plenty of time.

Among other things, I also had time to attend the RAF's staff command college, an important addition to my military education. When I entered the college, I expected British experience to provide me with the answers to some knotty subjects: operational concepts, how to deploy combat planes and bombers, combat tactics, exploitation of air-superiority and similar matters. My experience taught me that the British college, like others of its kind all over the world, does not impart much information about tactics or techniques. When I graduated, I knew precisely what I had been taught – and taught well: how to organize my thoughts. I'd call it 'the science of thinking'. There was a well-known saying at the college: 'Here we teach you how to think and write – clearly, concisely, correctly and with conviction.' I attached a great deal of importance to this. Years after completing my regular schooling in Haifa and my studies at the flying course in Rhodesia, it was good to go back to the classroom and study how to take on a problem, to examine it, to see it in its correct proportion, without either over- or underestimating it, to analyze it and discover all its connotations, to attack it in an organized and systematic manner – and to find the right answer.

I can say without hesitation that nothing I learned at the RAF college was as important as my realization that we *must not* learn from others. It's what I call 'the drawbacks of experience'. There is a certain temptation for a young officer to rely on the experience of others. The more prestigious and impressive the object of your emulation, the greater the temptation to accept things blindly, unthinkingly. It's the easy way out, but it is a worthless way. You tend to tell yourself: 'They' (and in this case, 'they' can be the British, the Americans or the French) have fought dozens of wars and learnt their lesson. Compared to them, you're a pygmy. You've fought one war, where you didn't even come to full expression. Learn from them! Learn their lesson! Imitate them, it'll pay off!

Fortunately – I say it without hesitation – some sound instinct helped me withstand the temptation and kept me away from the easy path. Later, I backed up my instinctive reaction with reasoned arguments: we mustn't ape others, whether in organizational matters, in military theory, or in operational tactics, for all these stem from the character of the men who have to apply them. Anyone familiar with French organization and the French way of thinking, in all branches of their army – I presume it is the same in their civilian life – knows that it's the kind of thing that only Frenchmen can cope with. The same is true of Americans and British, and all other peoples. I still believe fervently in what I said then: what counts is *your originality, your improvization and your inventiveness*. I prefer a stupid organization with clever officers to a clever organization with stupid officers. And of course, a clever organization borne on the shoulders of clever officers – glory hallelujah!

I wanted to make our air force into a clever organization based on clever officers, rather than copying the combat tactics and techniques of others. I wanted us to make new discoveries and innovations and to improvise because I believed in the moral and intellectual powers of the Jewish people and its young men. Does this imply chauvinism? Chauvinism can be a useful thing for a small people fighting for life.

This view of mine did not always gain the approval of others. There were times when I was hovering in indecision, trying to find an original Israeli solution purposely unlike the routine of other air forces, and those who disagreed with me would ask me provocatively: 'Ezer, what were you sent to staff college for? What are you wracking your brains for? What's wrong with doing it like the English?' (or, in other cases, when we established links with the French and American air forces, 'like the Americans and the French'). 'After all, they do so-and-so, they have a million times more experience than us, and they've tried it out in war.'

I never tired of explaining, with complete faith and with much fervour, that what's good is what we make to our own measure – to the quality of our boys, to the needs of the region we are fighting in and to the strength of our enemies – insofar as we had the ability to perfect our planes and weapons.

The 1956 Sinai Campaign and its outcome for the British and French provided me with additional ammunition for my claims. What happened to them? Why did they dally so long in carrying out their part of the operation? Didn't the two European air forces have the ability, the know-how and the equipment to carry out their task properly? Of course they did, and they could have done it without any difficulty. But they mishandled it, and the mess they made of it took on almost grotesque proportions after our clear-cut victory in 1967, without anyone's help. And the reason for their abysmal failure is that they were doctrinaire, excessively enslaved to their military theories and unable to free themselves from the cobwebs on their dusty books.

The British made their evaluations of the Egyptian air force in terms of the German air force in 1943. As Egypt possessed 250 first-line aircraft, including new planes from the awe-inspiring Soviet arsenal, they convinced themselves that the Egyptians had a strong air force, which could only be overcome by a powerful task-force suitably prepared for such a formidable operation. Utter nonsense! But because of that nonsensical interpretation, the French and British threw away the time they had. For all their books and their staff colleges, they got bogged down. While the quality and quantity of arms are important, they failed to grasp that weapons are employed by *human beings*, and there are additional factors – no less, and possibly more important – that should be taken into account in making evaluations: combat fitness, quality of command and the intelligence of the commander. When the British and French planned the battle for the Suez Canal, they didn't take these factors into account.

Humanity is always afraid of the unknown. (As they say at Israel's paratroop school: 'Knowledge prevents fear!) Concerning the Russian weapons, the French and British knew little, but their apprehensions were great. It may be claimed that they were grabbed by the tail as a result of political restrictions, but even so, the tactics they adopted were baffing and worthless, and the blame for their failure cannot be placed on politicians. It was a grave mistake by that same RAF which, only a dozen or so years before, had gained a victory that history will record in letters of fire, saving the British from the German air force.

There was a later application of this approach during the Six Day War. There is no single secret to that outstanding victory. It is customary to speak of 'the straw that broke the camel's back', but I believe that many of those who use this expression pay too much attention to the strength of the straw and tend to overlook the weakness of the back. The straw represents a country's strength, but it is very important to get to know the enemy's back and what will dislocate it, to find out what it is that makes him so weak that the straw you hold turns into a murderous weapon that decides the war. Conclusion: the more you know about the weakness of your enemy's back, the more powerful your straw. This does not appear in the staff college's textbooks, but it is written in concrete letters all over the map of the Middle East. Anyone who can't read those letters cannot be a commander in the Israeli army.

Many years after completing that course in Britain, years in which I traversed all the rungs of command and responsibility in the air force, at a time when we were considering what to do and how to use our limited resources to cope with great problems, I was constantly pursued by that staff college, and it became a kind of jinx which I couldn't shake off. Scores, maybe hundreds, of times, whenever I recommended one of a number of options, I would find myself being asked: 'Is that what they teach there, at Andover?' The question and the way it was put exemplified a genuine desire to find out how the English applied their great experience – a desire that was coupled with a twinge of barbed humour. I would reply: 'No, that's *not* what they teach at Andover. They teach the opposite.' This would provoke the inevitable question: 'So what did you do in Andover for a whole year, what did you learn there?' 'I learned what *not* to do.' To this day I'm not sure that all my listeners were convinced I was serious.

The story of my year at the English staff college would not be complete without some favourable mention of my Egyptian friend, Jimmy Affifi. I have fought the Arabs. I have planned military operations whose objective was to defeat them. Whenever they endangered vital Israeli interests, I have helped foil the threat and made them suffer for it. I know it was painful for them; I know they cannot like me. But I have never hated the Arabs as individuals. There are many Arabs for whom I have had a close sympathy. And for Wing Commander Affifi, who was deputy commander of the Egyptian air force in the Six Day War, I felt affection. I liked him.

The staff college was at Andover, a pleasant place in the English countryside, two and a half hours by train from London on the way to Portsmouth. Re'uma and I took a flat in London, so as to take in something of the atmosphere of the capital. Every week I spent five days at the course, applying myself to my studies; on Friday I would come home for the weekend, returning to Andover on Sunday. The course included officers from Britain and various other countries: two American colonels, two Egyptians, two Indians, two Pakistanis, one Burmese, an Irishman, a Frenchman, a Dutchman and myself.

The British Empire might have been in decline, but all the same, the course could not begin without that archetypal British rite, a cup of tea. The officers' club was draped with the flags of every nation that had ever been represented at the course (our flag flies there to this day), and we all stood around holding the traditional cups of tea, which we stirred with clinking spoons. Facing us was Colonel Anderson, our excellent British instructor, who navigated the first British plane to fly over the North Pole after the war. Andy, as we called him, stirred his tea repeatedly, smiling his affable smile. Then, letting his eyes roam over his students one by one, he said, 'What a bunch of rebels!' I had good cause to remember the five British Spitfires we had shot down during our War of Independence. I could only reassure myself with the thought that I was not the only rebel present. After all, which country of any significance has not at some time either rebelled or fought against the British Empire? I presume that Scotland Yard, with typical thoroughness, had taken the trouble to inform the officers in command of the course that my personal record included the destruction of a British Spitfire. But that did not particularly worry me; I knew that the British would be sufficiently gentlemanly not to hold my past 'sins' against me.

I was preoccupied with the two Egyptian officers. They must have heard of my part in the War of Independence, which had ended only two years before. I wondered what would happen, and how our relationships would develop. The more engaging of the two, Affifi, was commander of the airfield at El Arish, a fact whose particular significance I grasped only later. During the early stages of the course, we were strangers and avoided each other. 'Good morning' from me to him, 'Good morning' from him to me, but there was a chilliness on both sides. The British staff school operates on a team system. I was not put into the same team as the Egyptians, for the British were worried about the relationships among their students, and their principal anxiety was how the Indians would get on with the Pakistanis and the Egyptians with the Israeli.

When Israel's Independence Day came round (going by the Hebrew calendar, it fell in April that year), I said to Affifi at lunch, 'Wing Commander Affifi, I'd like to have a drink with you at the officers' bar this evening.' He smiled, 'Yes, Colonel Weizman.' There were some British officers with whom I had become friendly, and I invited them to come along too. We stood at the bar, pouring out the whisky, lifted our glasses and then he asked, 'What's the occasion?' I answered in Arabic, 'Our Independence Day.' The fellow turned green, tipped his drink down his throat and, wasting no time, uttered a terse thank you as he hurried away.

The following day I was approached by Wing Commander Nur Khan of the Pakistani air force. (He was a formidable fellow, and I was glad that he was Pakistani and not Egyptian. Later, he was promoted to the command of the Pakistani air force.) He told me that Gamal Affifi (Jimmy, as we called him) had complained to him about me: 'Look at that bastard, inviting me for a drink on his Independence Day!'

Apparently, however, Jimmy was not resentful, or at least not for long. The ice between us had not yet been broken, but our exchange of smiles became more frequent. Then, one day, he came up to me and said, 'This evening, Colonel Weizman, *you'll* have a drink with *me*.' Without any whys or wherefores, I went along. This time, it was I who asked what the occasion was. His face lit up. 'We're drinking to celebrate the birth of a son to Farouk, my king. To the new prince!' I responded, '*Ahlan wasahalan!*' (Welcome!) If he expected my face to go as green as his, or thought that I'd toss down my drink and quit the scene, he didn't know Ezer! We empted the bottle with all due solemnity, and then, to the unconcealed delight of our British friends, who stood there feasting their eyes at the sight, we staggered back to our quarters, arm in arm, propping each other up and taking deep breaths of the clear English air. Somewhere or other, we stopped: the time had come to say good night. I said, 'Alright, Jimmy, I only hope we never meet at 20,000 feet.'

Drunk as he was, with his arm around me, he said, 'No, we won't!'

'Marvellous!' I said. 'Then there won't be another war between us?'

'No,' he said, 'there won't. There won't be any need for one. You'll collapse economically.'

After that, the ice was broken and the thaw set in. We met more often and talked more. There were many expressions of friendship and personal affection on both sides. Jimmy had a car, something I could not afford. Well versed in the secrets of London's night-life, he would drive up to the capital every Friday, and I would frequently find myself in a bizarre situation – such as could scarcely arise now, twenty years later. Wing Commander Affifi drove, with Wing Commander Attiyeh (the other Egyptian student at the course) at his side, and in the rear sat Colonel Ezer Weizman of the Israeli air force. During hours of driving on roads that were often empty of vehicles, it would have been easy for them to turn off the highway and make sure that the next time there was a war between us, the Israeli air force would have one flight commander less. But I'm sure they never even considered it. They would talk about various matters in Arabic, speaking openly, even though they knew their language was not unfamiliar to me.

On our arrival in London, Jimmy would come up to our flat. He showed a special liking for our baby son, Shaul, who was born in England and with whom he would play and romp. He was very gracious towards Re'uma, and as a connoisseur of London's Oriental foodships, he would advise Re'uma where to get good *humus* and fine *tehina*, and the sweet cakes that he especially loved. Re'uma liked him very much, and little Shaul's face would light up when he came.

My relationship with the likable Egyptian went so far that, one weekend in London, he invited me to his home to help prepare an exercise for his team at the staff school. I did not hesitate for a moment about accepting the invitation, but I notified our military attaché where I was going. Re'uma was a little apprehensive, and I tried to dispel her fears. When I got there, Jimmy introduced an

Egyptian colonel, whom he described as an engineering officer. He may have been an officer in Egyptian intelligence. Jimmy may have been testing me, to see whether I would be afraid of coming. Perhaps they were interested in seeing what kind of solution I would propose for Jimmy's exercise. I wasn't scared. If he did have any hopes of finding out my way of solving the problem, here, too, I did not fall in with his game. Personally, I don't believe he had any designs in inviting me to his home; he regarded it as a normal matter, stemming from our close relationship. Nevertheless, I had to be cautious. Before we parted, he told me he wasn't returning to the course that Sunday and asked me to take his exercise to the instructor.

Our friendship grew closer. At officers' parties, Jimmy would flirt gallantly with Re'uma, exhibiting gentlemanly care in keeping her supplied with food and drink. Whenever I entered the officers' mess, my glance would seek him out, and I would immediately go over; he behaved in a similar manner towards me.

Another interesting experience was Jimmy's meeting with Moshe Dayan, who was then on a course in England and lodging with us. Besides Jimmy, I also invited the Pakistani, the Indian and the Burmese. Jimmy shook Dayan's hand, smiled and said, 'How do you do, sir? I almost killed you one day.' There was an awkward moment, and then we heard the following tale. One day, a few months before the present meeting, Moshe Dayan (then head of Southern Command), accompanied by generals (then majors) Rehavam ('Ghandi') Ze'evi and Avraham ('Bren') Adan, crossed the border into Sinai, which may or may not have been an accident. Driving their patrol cars, they met an Egyptian patrol, which sent a coded message to El Arish reporting the encounter. Jimmy, the commander of the airfield, sought high and low after the decoding officer, who was floating peacefully in the sea at the time. When he was finally found and brought back to decode the message, Jimmy ordered two Egyptian Spitfires to take off and shoot up the Israeli officers. However, by that time, the distinguished company was back in Israeli territory, and the Egyptian planes returned empty-handed. As a result, it was possible for Jimmy and Moshe Dayan to smile and have a drink together that evening.

At the end of 1951, the Egyptians initiated anti-British oper-ations in the Suez Canal zone. As it happened, I played a slightly Machiavellian role here. In the British air force, the day begins with a very solemn ritual – which other people call breakfast. Everyone who comes into the mess-hall picks up his morning paper, takes his place at a table and props his paper on a stand in front of him. Total silence: everyone is motionless, and not a sound is to be heard, except for murmured good mornings. I often felt like picking up a milk-bottle and smashing it against the wall, just to get these glacier-like beings to wake up.

Once, after one of these British breakfasts, an English officer came up to me. 'Did you read the paper?' he asked.

'Yes,' I replied, playing the innocent, 'What's the matter?'

He grew agitated. 'Did you read what those damned Egyptians are doing to us? They shot up a car and killed two British fellows. What d'you think we should do?'

I said: 'You ask me what to do? Give 'em a good hiding, like we did!'

A short time later, Jimmy got hold of me. 'Did you read the paper?'

'Yes, what's the matter?'

'Those English bastards,' Jimmy stormed, 'they sent their tanks to attack the Ismailia police station. What d'you think we should do?'

'Jimmy,' I said, 'You ask me what to do? Give 'em a good hiding, like we did!'

Re'uma was furious. She frowned on my 'divide-and-conquer' strategy. What could I do? Here I was in the country where 'divide and rule' was invented, only a few years after we had thrown the British out of Palestine and after we had sent the Egyptian army home, thrashed and defeated. Now, as Britain and Egypt began to fight it out, I could not deny myself the pleasure from my advice to both sides.

In time, the situation in Egypt worsened, and the two Egyptians were summoned home. In any case, it was none too comfortable for them to be studying at a British course while their countrymen were shedding British blood and the British were paying back in kind. I understood both sides, better than anyone else at the course.

It was exactly how I had felt during my last year in the RAF (1946), with the 'Palestine' shoulder-flash on my uniform, while British army camps in Palestine were being blown sky-high.

On his last weekend in London, before returning home, Jimmy phoned to say that he wanted to come over for a personal good-bye. I was pleased. He brought flowers for Re'uma and a toy for Shaul. He sat down, we drank coffee and talked with great friendliness. Steering clear of politics, we exchanged anecdotes about the course. It was sad to part. I accompanied him to the door. He gave me his visiting card with the address: 44 Tuffik Street, Heliopolis. Did he want me to come and visit him? He didn't say.

I haven't seen Jimmy Affifi since. I did not want to get him into trouble with any overt expressions of friendship, for fear the Egyptians would not receive such gestures in the same way that we would, placing him in an awkward situation. There was only one occasion when I sent him regards and that was under unusual circumstances: after the Sinai Campaign in 1956, we had 4,000 Egyptian prisoners of war, who included two pilots. The Egyptians held four prisoners of ours – three from the ground forces and a pilot, Yehonatan Ettckes, who had been shot down over Sharm el-Sheikh. In 1957 we exchanged prisoners. As head of Air Branch, I went down to Rafiah to welcome Yehonatan. We knew he had been severely tortured by the Egyptians, and his condition was serious.

A batch of some 500 Egyptian prisoners were standing nearby. Suddenly, an Egyptian pilot stepped out of the ranks. Without any fear, before the very eyes of the Egyptian generals standing opposite, he walked up to me, saluted and said in English: 'I know that my countrymen have treated your pilot terribly. I'm sorry!' I said: 'I hope you were well treated in our country.' 'Certainly!' he said. I asked him to convey my regards to Air Marshal Affifi. He promised to do so, saluted, said *Shalom* in Hebrew and returned to the ranks.

At one time Jimmy was director of the Egyptian national airways. At an international conference, he met Shlomo Lahat and Ephraim Ben Artzi of El Al and sent me regards. After the Six Day War, when he was deputy commander of the Egyptian air force, Affifi was put on trial and blamed for the shameful *débâcle*. In my heart, I rejoiced when he was acquitted.

There is another little tale, not directly connected to Jimmy, but I include it here as relating to the same theme. In 1964 an Egyptian pilot defected to Israel with his plane. I have often wondered why he chose Israel, of all places, and not Jordan, Iraq or Libya, none of which were then on friendly terms with Egypt. I don't have a clear answer, but I can venture a guess: his flying instructor was that same man with whom I sent regards to Affifi. As he proved by approaching me before the very eyes of his superiors, he had guts. He may have told his pupil how he was treated in Israel: no one mishandled him; on the contrary, he was taken on a tour of the country. So when the pilot began to consider deserting, he may have thought that, if this were how we treated a prisoner, he would be well received, coming of his own free will and bringing his plane, too. In any case, when I asked, 'Weren't you afraid to come here, after all the stories you were told about the ferocious Israelis?' he replied, enigmatically: 'I *knew* those stories were untrue'. He was not ill treated in Israel. He left for a South American country, but Egyptian intelligence eventually tracked him down and killed him.

As for Jimmy Affifi, if we were to meet today in London, or Paris, or Rome, twenty-three years after our parting in London, I would say: 'Hello, Jimmy!' We would shake hands and walk into the first pub we could find. Then we'd knock back a whisky or beer and get down to analyzing the past years. Just like that. I'm sure of it.

7

BASE COMMANDER

WHEN MY YEAR at the staff college came to an end in March 1952, I returned home more determined than ever that my life would remain linked to the air force. While I was in England, Chaim Laskov had been appointed commander of the air force, replacing Shlomo Shamir. Like Shamir, Laskov was not an airman. In fact, he was an experienced officer in the ground forces, having served in the British army in World War Two, and his appointment as head of the air force was undoubtedly a further step to put 'those air-force rascals into harness'. He also happened to be a childhood friend from Haifa. Yet, despite our long relationship, I felt insecure about the prospects of our future relationship, and I hurried to see him at air force command, praying that my fears were unfounded.

Perhaps I expected him to greet me with a smile and a 'Welcome! Good to see you,' or something of the kind, in keeping with our past. Not a chance. His face impassive, he uttered his distant, cold greeting: '*Shalom*. Sit down. What have you learnt?' in that precise order.

I answered impishly, 'I've learnt how to kill – fast, well and cheap.'

'Very good,' he said, maintaining his official tone. 'You are to set up advanced course for air force officers. Start immediately.'

This was to be the first step in establishing our air force staff command school. I implored him to let me go back to the planes, to flying, to the things I loved. Nothing doing. Chaim uttered a short, sharp 'No!' and gave me to understand that the interview was over.

Looking back, I think he was right. I had quite a good year in England. I studied, I extended my knowledge. Very good! Now I could go and teach others; the air force was in need of good officers. But my whole being rebelled at the thought of a further period away from actual flying. School, lesson schedules, lots of talk and examinations was such a bleak prospect that I permitted myself to approach the then chief of staff, Major-General Makleff, and presented my humble plea: 'Just let me go back to Ramat David!' Makleff promised that if I set up the school, he would see to it that I would return to Ramat David. With that heartening pledge, I went off and began to work on organizing the course. It didn't cross my mind that by approaching Makleff, I would anger my former friend and present commander, Chaim Laskov.

I set up the school, greatly helped by my deputy, Emanuel Yardeni. I found no difficulty in outlining the object of the course: equipping the officers with systematic patterns of thinking. I spent six months on preparations, and then I taught two four-month courses. My pupils included fellows like Motty Hod, then a captain, and a few other promising officers. In addition, I joined the team that founded the staff command college, which would serve all sections of the Israeli armed forces. All in all, the fourteen months I spent at the course gave me a chance to take another look at theory, allowing me to clarify one or two ideas and to examine their application to young officers, whose response I also gauged. All this was good preparation for returning to Ramat David in October 1953, after Dan Tolkovski replaced Chaim Laskov as air force commander.

Military service is by no means only a commitment to the needs of one's country. It is a career that awards satisfaction of many kinds. Anyone who takes it on naturally aspires to rise to the top. My ambition to command, to apply my theories, to shape men, to impart my credo on Zionism, the Jewish people, the Land of Israel and war were some of the desires that motivated me from the moment I decided to sign on as a professional soldier. Up to the time I took command of Ramat David, in October 1953, my opportunities to exercise that kind of control over men were restricted. My command of a squadron was an embryonic period, overshadowed by the urgency of improving our flying capability.

My first steps towards creating a team spirit and giving some meaning to the term 'Israeli combat pilot' were cut short by staff college in England and my work at the air force officers' course. When I returned to Ramat David, full of enthusiasm and plans, I re-entered this complex world: a large command, with its wide assortment of problems above and beyond the rudiments of correct flying.

On the outside, an air-base is no different from any other military base on land or sea: it serves as the place from which squadrons set out, and it's the place to which they return. Every man in the base is there to do a thorough job of preparing them, making sure they set off equipped and fitted out for any task. He identifies with them and awaits their return tensely, cheering them when they come back, whether from combat or training, and then once again he prepares the equipment, and the men who use it, for the next sortie.

That's the general definition of any military base. But it overlooks the basic differences that distinguish an airfield from other military installations. A ship, for example, goes to sea for a long time, much longer than the duration of a plane's flight. Under certain circumstances – whether by choice or necessity, such as the port being shelled, destroyed or occupied by an enemy – the ship can sail the sea for an extended period without returning to its home port. Its size enables it to stock up with relatively large supplies of food, water and ammunition. Its internal organization and manpower is organized to cope with long periods at sea: it has officers and subordinates, gunners and signals' men, a cook and a barber, a chaplain and a small hospital and dining and recreation rooms. On an aircraft carrier, all these things attain town-like dimensions. Nuclear-powered submarines, less dependent on refuelling, go to sea for months, and only return to their home ports after long intervals. Even Admiral Nelson's ships set off for extended voyages without visiting their home ports more than once a year, or even longer.

A tank is different: it can go 100 miles or so from its base, while its fuel and ammunition only suffice for a short time. But various components of its base move up behind it. Without turning back, the tank can be refuelled, have faulty tracks replaced and be supplied with ammunition. The crew can live in the field for weeks, fighting, resting, eating. The infantryman is even less bound to his base, and his personal needs can be supplied during battle through various means, none of which requires proximity to his base.

When we come to an air-base and its planes and pilots, the situation is radically different. The pilot sets out alone – solitude is his hallmark – for a very limited time, which is hard to extend, even by aerial refuelling. He leaves his base for an hour, or two or three, and he cannot continue in combat until he returns to refuel and re-arm and patch up any damage. There is no component of the air-base that can be brought to the pilot. His dependence on the base is of a kind quite unfamiliar to sailors, tank-crews or infantrymen. But it's a two-way connection: an airfield has less of the character of a rear base than any other military installation. The base and its complement are, in effect, an integral part of the battle at every moment. This link creates a deep bond between the combat pilot and his logistic rear echelons, a bond unequalled in land or sea units.

The plane is a strange creature. In the air, refuelled, armed and piloted by a good flyer, it represents an incarnation of power and fighting ability that strikes fear into tanks and ships at sea. But its power is directly related to the time factor: more than any other weapon, it is subject to a limited time-span. If its fuel has run out, or its ammunition has been used up, it is a flabby creature, easy prey for an enemy plane. If it cannot return to its base, or land at another one, it becomes a mere hunk of metal, pitiful and helpless. A shorn Samson, capable of 'dying with the Philistines', it can merely inflict some damage on the enemy when it crashes. And when he has no other choice, the pilot can bale out – but the plane is lost.

If it sheds its tracks, or its engine breaks down, or its fuel has given out, the tank is still a weapon of war. Its crew can fight on. At worst, it becomes a stationary fortress whose cannon can strike at enemy tanks and positions and whose machine-guns can fight off enemy soldiers. But the plane, so powerful in the air, is a despicable object on the ground. Not only is it harmless, it lacks the most minimal defensive capacity. It squats on the runway, clumsy and prostrate, at the mercy of any enemy. Not only is it vulnerable to air attack (which makes air-bases attractive targets in war), but even some humble mortar, correctly deployed, can tear it to pieces. It costs a fortune, it can decide the fate of a war, and yet, it's as helpless as a baby.

When all these thoughts had been worked out and their conclusions were etched on my mind, I began to see the outlines of my task as commander of Ramat David. I had to forge a fighting unit, whose every component breathed, operated and lived at an identical rhythm, with a deep sense of association, and with a feeling of mutual dependency between the ground crews and the pilots. The ground crews had to have the clear conviction that they, too, were part of a combat unit, that without their participation, the base would be exposed to enemy blows and its planes would risk being turned into shattered wrecks. I put my heart and soul into creating this feeling of participation. The difficulties were enormous; they created such conflicts that it often seemed like some hopelessly Herculean task to settle them, or at least defuse them, and prevent them from becoming obstacles to that cooperation which was so vital.

How does one create this sense of partnership and participation? How does one explain to a thousand men (an arbitrary figure) that the field's pilots are no more than the equals of their colleagues on the ground, when they are, after all, the unit's crowning glory and the focus of all its efforts, when they represent the pinnacle of its power? How does one turn the job of 'pampering' the pilot, of making his life pleasant, of ensuring his comfort, of serving him a first-rate meal and preparing a hot shower for him when he comes back from a flight into a combat role? How does one convince a man from the ground crew to do all this for a spoilt *élite* that basks in luxury and lives the good life? And finally how does one get him to defend the pilots, to understand that they need this kind of life, not for their sense of superiority, but so that they can give of their best in the supreme tests they are called upon to face?

Anyone who wants one clear answer to this tangle won't find it. If anyone claims he has a single reliable answer, his seriousness is to be doubted. More than once I was near despair; more than once I've thought that perhaps, after all, it really is impossible to create this feeling of equality, perhaps it's inevitable that ground crews fulfil their duties by virtue of military discipline, according to the well-tried principles of reward and punishment, leaving them to pour their resentments into the ears of relatives and friends.

But my problem was that I don't believe in the value of an order when there is no emotional bond between the man who gives it and the man who is supposed to carry it out. If a pilot is ordered to fly over Tel Aviv and dip his wings over the street where his girl-friend lives, the chances of him disobeying are negligible. Far more is needed if the order is to penetrate a thick curtain of advanced missiles and anti-aircraft guns, when both the man giving the order and the one receiving it have a sober awareness of the chances of carrying it out and of the dangers involved. The more difficult an order is to carry out, the more difficult it is to give. Only second-rate officers believe that an order can ensure good results and overwhelming victories. An officer has authority that stems from the braid on his shoulders. He can say: 'You'll do it because I'm authorized to give you orders, and I'm using that authority!' If, in the course of his military career, he 'pulls rank' more than two or three times – and even then, only when there is no alternative – he's a bad officer, whose contribution to the army will be as limited as his ability to create a fighting team.

The hallmark of a good officer is his ability to create an emotional bond with his men. Full obedience by the man receiving an order does not depend on the awe he feels in the presence of his superiors, but on his confidence in the judgement of his com-mander and the degree of fellowship between them. Serial numbers are a means of identifying soldiers, of allotting them to their units and of processing them in computers, but they are a poor way of getting to know people. If you want to approach a subordinate, treat him according to his true worth. Obedience, self-sacrifice, full cooperation and willingness can only be achieved by getting to know him and giving him a feeling of intimacy.

I knew the name of every man at Ramat David – first name and surname. I knew who his wife was, and what she did. I was fully versed in every detail of his troubles and tribulations, his hesitations and doubts, his sorrows and his rejoicings. I knew about his children, their schools, their interests and had some idea of their achievements in their studies. There wasn't a soldier who felt alien in my presence.

I have always maintained that the separation between a soldier's duty and his social and family life is an artificial division designed to create a restricted framework and thus simplify matters. But Nature rejects such a separation. The soldier is a single being – at home, with his family, in his social surroundings and in his army service. His service, with its successes or failures, its frustration or its satisfaction, his acceptance or rejection by his fellows has a direct and appreciable effect on his life outside the army, and *vice versa*.

This fabric of proximity, understanding and identification is not woven in a single day. There are no miracles. It's not just a matter of strolling through the hangar one morning and slapping Moshe on the back and asking him if everything's alright at home. The soldier can distinguish clearly when his commander pretends to show interest because someone told him he ought to, or because he read it somewhere, and when that interest is genuine and comes from the heart. The Israeli air force was created by men and weapons – in that order; men are the most important, and their weapons help them to express themselves. I've learnt what I could about weapons; likewise, I have not spared efforts to learn what I could about men. It may be because I am inquisitive by nature, or because men are the most interesting subject in life, or because I don't like reserve and so I opened my heart to the soldiers under my command and was rewarded by them opening their hearts to me. The base became a home, not only because more and more men occupied its married quarters (that was another prolonged battle) but because the men felt they could express themselves there. It was an attractive social centre for entertainment, conversation and discussion. It gave the men what so many seek and so few find – an identity, a profound feeling of belonging, a common interest and the pleasure of being together.

Then there's the problem of personal example. The armour units and the infantry cannot forego the famous 'Follow me!'; they cannot advance without their officers going first. If you tell a pilot: 'Fly into Egypt, at an altitude of 100 feet, even though it would be better not to fly at all in this weather,' he ought to know that his commander has performed the same perilous mission, or a similar one, and is prepared to do it again, if necessary. Our wing commanders flew into combat. In the Sinai Campaign in 1956, I piloted Ouragans in various battles, and wing commanders did the same in the Six Day War. It was a clear and concrete expression of personal example, the air-force version of 'Follow me!'

Personal example works with a pilot, but it's ineffective with a cook. You can't walk into his kitchen and say, 'Move over, David, I'll show you how to make scrambled eggs.' You can't poke a mechanic in the ribs and say, 'Look here, see how you fix that bolt.' How then do you establish a link with men for whom your personal example is irrelevant, because their sphere of activity is unlike yours? It is here that close familiarity between officer and subordinate and the cultivation of personal relationships is of striking importance. The Israeli soldier is open to personal relationships that he can respect and enjoy, perhaps more so than soldiers of other nations; but he also belongs to a proud race who hate shackles, and despise attempts to subjugate them. Getting to know dozens of pilots and officers by name and becoming aware of their problems was relatively easy. Getting to know the hundreds of men at the base with whom I had no daily contact or common points of view was far more difficult.

I find nothing wrong in my use of a certain simple technique. I had a detailed album prepared, featuring every non-commissioned officer, with pictures, biography, details of his family and the names of his wife and children, or his girlfriend. In the course of time, I added my personal impressions, and I could therefore display my interest in each man, in various forms. I used to tour the base a lot, not using my car, but riding a bicycle or motor-bike. I also advised other officers to use a bicycle for their transportation inside the base. The bicycle has several important advantages: it's cheap; pedalling is good exercise; and you can display your presence – it's good to let your men know you're around. Instead of sitting inside a car, which hems you in and restricts your view, riding a bicycle gives a wide field of vision, allowing you to see people, their activities, their achievements and failures.

I'd pedal past the 'Spits' and Meteors and the Mustangs (later, as commander of Hazor, the Ouragans and the Mystères) and halt at the entrance to a hangar, throwing out a general 'hello'. Then I'd return to one of the men: 'Good morning, David, how are things this morning? How's Rivka, is she better? How are the kids? Is Dina still limping from scout camp?' The greenhorns would be surprised at first, but the old-timers regarded this as a natural part of life. And when David could tell his Rivka that the commander asked about her and the children, they all gradually became part of the 'air-force family', enabling him to identify emotionally with the air force and the unit.

In brackets I'll add that there were disappointments, too. Such behaviour creates expectations. If there is some sergeant whose wife and children you've enquired after three consecutive times, you've created a habit. The fourth time he won't be satisfied with less. And then, one day, you storm into the hangar – you're in a hurry, or agitated over something, or just plain annoyed – and in your haste you address him directly, without the personal frills. He answers – after all, you *are* the commander and you're entitled to know – but he's disappointed. He's used to a different level of relationships. To this day, my many acquaintanceships exact their price: my embarrassment. Some fellow walks up to me, bursting with friendship and expecting some response, as revealed in his expression. He stands there, waiting expectantly, and I am very embarrassed, and genuinely distressed, when he says: 'But I'm Moshe, Sergeant Moshe from Hazor. How come you don't remember me?' It's been a long time, chum. The years, and, you see, there were other wars, and I got to know a few thousand others. No. He would't understand. He's used to something different. Both of us must pay the price of the years. And there's nothing to do but for me to keep quiet.

Parties are a well-tried way of bringing people together and creating a common life-style. To make the base a place to live in, as well as a place to serve in, we held a lot of parties and entertainments, which were an excellent opportunity to meet the pilots and officers and their wives. And another party for the sergeants and their wives. The atmosphere was free and easy, with an absence of convention. There were lots of manifestations of genuine affection and an unceasing flow of true friendship. I would be completely free in my behaviour at these parties, even a little wild. I would make fun of others and be made fun of in my turn, crack jokes and get them back, dig at weak points and take the ripostes with a smile, joke and dance, drink and sing. Mind your step! Everyone wants a drink with Ezer. Refuse, and someone is insulted. Drink with everyone, and you're finished. You must find a golden mean, where no one is insulted, but you don't get drunk as a lord at every party. You have to make a tremendous effort to find that middle way, and you forfeit your total freedom and the ability to throw off all restrictions.

A good commander always keeps a 'bootlick-meter'. He should hate those who grovel to him. He demands honesty. He learns to know those who try to get in with him. He knows who really values him, and he also knows who is playing up to him so as to gain favours, or because that's just the sort of fellow he is. The genuine fellows are the ones who do not refrain from criticism. A fellow like that will give a warm handshake, look you straight in the face and say 'Well done, sir!' whenever some deed or word of yours has earned his approval. But you should expect – and welcome – him to say, that same day, or the next, or whenever he feels the need: 'Sir, I have to talk to you!' He'll walk into your office and shut the door, and without dropping his eyes, he'll say: 'I think you were wrong'. This principle was the firm foundation of my relationship with Peleg Tamir, who was my right-hand man as administration officer at Ramat David. In our service together in the air force, as well as in civilian life, I knew that, along with compliments and praise, he wouldn't spare the rod of criticism – and at times it would be a painful rod.

For all the effort and energies, it would be no more than fanciful to claim that things invariably ran smoothly, without any friction. Among hundreds of men, you find different characters and mentalities, and it's natural that, here and there, someone will try and shirk, to prove that even a tight military framework has its cracks and openings. But all in all, there were three excellent squadrons, under Motty Hod as operations officer, Peleg Tamir as administration officer and Yisrael Rott as technical officer. These were all first-class men, real 'heavy-weights', enthusiasts for the kind of spirit I wanted to see in the base.

In the course of many years and various posts in the air force, I had many arguments – some of them unpleasant and bitter – on the political aspects of training pilots and ground-crew. Consider the following problems: in strengthening a soldier's motivation, is an officer entitled to claim – and prove – that an additional war with the Arabs is inevitable, by force of circumstances, or is this exceeding his authority? May he tell his subordinates that a cramped little country, even if there is nothing shameful in living in it and defending it, is not the supreme goal of Zionism? Is a commander indulging in excessive freedom of expression when he puts forward the opinion that Israel without *all* of Jerusalem is a crippled country, that this 'infirmity' must be corrected, and that we have the 'surgical' means of doing so?

Whenever I got into such an argument, and whenever I was reprimanded – at times, implicitly, at others, openly – I had only one answer, and I have nothing to add to it today: the Israeli pilot must be overflowing with national identity; he must comprehend why he is required to be the best in the world; he must feel it with all his senses. And that can't be done if we don't constantly and repeatedly recharge his batteries with Zionism and nationalism – seriously, and in depth.

During the early fifties, I was continually aware of the incomplete nature of the state. I sensed how vital it was to make up the deficiency at the first opportunity. I tried to discover why we didn't do more during the War of Independence. At that time there was an evil spirit afoot in the land – something I called 'pygmyism'. The average Israeli would fall into the trap and boast of the smallness of his country. From a national viewpoint, this was a perverse view – and may I be forgiven by the many good people who were bewitched by that evil spirit. Excellent pilots would come to me and say: 'Oh, it's great – as soon as you take off from Ramat David, you have to turn, otherwise you cross the border.' While some regarded this as 'pygmy power', I considered it a total perversion.

In none of the positions of command that I filled in the air force did I conceal from my subordinates the sense of constriction I felt inside the over-tight strait jacket of Israel's 1948 boundaries. I didn't keep my views to myself. I did not regard this in any way as being political indoctrination, and the whole matter was far from the alleged 'politicizing' of the armed forces; I regarded it as an integral part of a pilot's training to be 'the best in the world'. I was convinced he would not be worthy of that title if he didn't know why and what he was fighting for.

I attached a great deal of importance to the 'commander's evenings'. I wanted them to be conducted amidst an atmosphere of real freedom, so that every officer, sergeant or private would know two things with certainty: that his opinion on any subject would be heard and considered and that he was assured freedom of expression, without suffering for any criticism he might utter, however unpleasant it may be. Participation depended on the subject under discussion: pilots alone, or officers alone, or officers and sergeants, or meetings of the whole base. The evenings consisted of two parts. The first part dealt with immediate problems: was there or wasn't there hot water? Was the food varied, or was it dull and monotonous? Was leave satisfactory or not? Were the quartermasters polite or rude? Everything, the whole spectrum of minor matters, which combine together to make up what we call the quality of life, would be investigated. I specifically wanted the officers to hear the private from the motor transport workshop complaining about the cold omelette and the cold water and the overflowing sewage tank and the carelessness of the cooks and the stupidity of the guard at the gate and the harshness of an officer who takes it out on his men whenever his wife treats him as he deserves.

But, consciously and deliberately, I also turned these evenings into a fruitful opportunity for the national education of my men. Early on in our independence, I had observed a phenomenon, characteristic of the average Israeli. Deep down in his heart there was some hidden fear, filling his world with gnawing doubts: were Israel's victories in the War of Independence a true expression of her collective ability? Did they represent the essence of every value belonging to our persecuted people? Did they indicate the superiority of the Israeli Jew in his homeland, or were they some fleeting 'miracle', like luck, which is governed by chance? Did we just exploit the enemy's temporary weakness, which occurred in one war but will not recur? Will the Arab multitudes finally overcome their frailties and wipe us off the face of this earth? Of all the unpleasant things that happened to us during and after the 1973 war, I would not hesitate to single out the worst: the war encouraged those who have always predicted that the Arabs would overcome their weakness and, at a later stage in the unfinished struggle against Israel, convert quantity to quality. Not only were these people strengthened in their view, but many of those who had once believed otherwise, and inspired others by their confidence, thereby becoming well-known leaders admired by the masses, have now crossed the lines and fallen into this dangerous trap.

At the beginning of the sixties, that feeling of fear was nourished by the Nasserist revolution in Egypt. Those whose emotional make-up made them predisposed to nervousness now had something to justify their anxieties. Our fears are coming true! The Arabs are ridding themselves of everything in their society that's bad and rotten: they're on the way to recovery! What we had defeated in 1948 was a feudal society, now they have a progressive leader, who'll cure Egypt's ills! We defeated them because of the divisions, now there's a leader who will unite them under his flag. He'll lead all those millions, he'll make them overcome their defeats and disappointments, and then, like a great tidal wave, they'll overrun this little country of ours. When Nasser added the contention that the 1948 defeat was due to rotten ammunition and poor arms, there were many people in Israel who actually supported his claim. When he flung off Egypt's traditional dependency on Britain and the West and crammed his arsenals with modern Soviet arms, Israel was filled with despondency. People would give each other gloomy looks and say, with a tone of final farewells, 'I knew it! That's it!'

Facing the greatness of this new Saladin, whom the whole world applauded, facing the saviour and modernizer of Arab society, facing the beloved leader, the man who was to cure Egypt of its ailments and liberate it even from hashish, stood an Israel that was confused, eaten-up from within, losing its self-confidence and full of self-recrimination. This was an especially difficult period for Israel. There was large-scale immigration from backward countries – hundreds of thousands of destitute people, transit camps and tin shacks and economic difficulties – and a feeling that the burden was too heavy for us, that we'd taken on too much. Inside the armed forces, the Palmach generation was proportionately in decline; the Palmach veterans called the younger men 'the *espresso* generation', spreading the word that the youngsters cared only for their own welfare and worked only for themselves, that they were light-weights, lacking values. 'Look at them and look at us! There's no comparison!'

So everything was clear. The Egyptian soldier was improving, his arms were better, while the Israeli soldier was progressively deteriorating and Israel had no modern arms, and nowhere to get them from. That's it. The dream was over; reality was gloomy and disheartening.

This despondency was increased by the successful *fedayeen* raids deep into Israel, sowing death and destruction, killing women and children and innocent workers in orange groves. The *fedayeen* were hard to catch, and reprisal raids didn't always work. And there was a feeling that the armed forces were losing something of their skill and audacity.

This whole outlook was swept away like a house of cards by the Sinai Campaign. But before that, it was no easy task to convince people that their fears were in vain and their anxieties groundless, that the Israeli soldier and pilot of the fifties was in no way inferior to his forerunner of the forties, and that if our enemies sought further confrontations, we would smite them again and again, because *we are better*. It was terribly hard, uphill all the way. Only a further military contest could prove it beyond all doubt. I often suspected that deep down in their hearts the boys were thinking: 'What's he going on about with all this ranting and raving? Maybe he doesn't believe it himself, and he's only trying to encourage us with his stories, to put some wind into our sails? Why is he so arrogant?' It was a depressing feeling, and I would often fall silent, because I sensed that I just wasn't getting through to my subordinates.

We tried to present before the men well-verified facts about the aptitudes of the Egyptian and Syrian pilots and their failures in operating their new equipment. Even more important were the operational sorties. Whenever there was an opportunity, I'd grab it: photographic reconnaissance, escort, anything that could give the boys that 'operational feeling'. When we made our incursion into Syria and took pictures of Damascus, I asked the boys: 'Well?

Where's the Syrian air force?' When we took pictures of El Arish and Sinai, I could ask: 'Where is it, this Egyptian air force which is growing stronger and more fearsome every day?' When the photographs were taken from Mosquitoes, we escorted them with our fighters. Later, a Meteor was adapted for photography, and we took accurate pictures of the whole length of the Suez Canal. The fact that Egyptian planes almost never pursued ours and that we never lost a plane contributed something to our morale and our sense of superiority.

Was I always eager for combat, from the first, as some have claimed? This is a question which demands a great deal of study and consideration. I could never tell my subordinates that I was satisfied with the outcome of the War of Independence. It was definitely an incomplete job, with Old Jerusalem snatched from the State of Israel, the Gaza Strip like a thorn in our side and Judaea and Samaria filched from us. It was the Land of Israel without the Land of the Bible. I could never accept all this, and my intimacy with the men serving under me, and their need for a Zionist education, made it impossible for me to conceal my opinions and feelings. I also felt the need to analyze why it was that the War of Independence ended the way it did. The conclusion – painful, smarting, but realistic and honest – was that we weren't on the West Bank not because we didn't want to be there, but because we were kicked out. The Carmeli Brigade had been there, and it got booted out. The Palmach and IZL were in the Old City, but they were forced to leave it. The same goes for Kfar Etzion and other places. There was, therefore, no point in concealing the truth, and I felt that I must foster the longing to return, rather than stifle it with the false contention that even a small Israel was an inhabitable place.

The fact that the political echelons have the responsibility for preventing wars is well known and accepted. Yet in his subordinates' eyes, a commander must show his eagerness for combat. That is *his* responsibility, and it is no lighter than that of the political echelons, nor does it contradict their duties. If our enemies had been honestly and truly willing to accept Israel within those narrow borders, to make peace with her and give up their hatred and their desire to exterminate us, I would have remained dissatisfied with the borders and the exclusion of the historical portions of the Land of Israel from our boundaries, but I would not have demanded that we initiate further wars. But that's not the way things were. While we were dreaming of the Land of Israel, the Arabs held on to their demented vision of destroying our state. Under such circumstances, an officer whose task it was to lead his men to war – and win – had to be eager for battle, if he were a sound commander. So I admit it – I hungered for prey. I sought out enemy planes. When I stood up before my subordinates, I would say: 'Just let us have some Migs. We'll tear them apart. Let the boys have the chance and we'll hit the Egyptians and Syrians a bull's-eye.' And whenever we encountered opportunities, we did not let them pass.

The section at Ramat David was solidifying, but during the years 1954–5 my attention was drawn to a very negative fact: the boys did no more than their regular two-and-a-half years mandatory service. Along comes some fellow, gifted and worthy of all the outlay and effort required for his training; he goes to flying school for a year and a quarter, or a year and a half; serves another year in the unit; and that's the end of his flying service in the air force. The boy gets his release and off he goes to pursue a civilian career. I was convinced that the investment in him was out of all proportion to the return we were getting, and the matter required adjustment. I had no way of forcing those boys to sign on for additional service, other than by persuasion. With the approval of air force command, I let it be known that I would not receive pilots at Ramat David unless they signed on for three years of service from the day they got their wings. I was especially unwilling to invest further effort and money in training them as combat pilots on the Mustangs, 'Spits' and Meteors. Whoever did not want to sign on was welcome to fly B-17s, Dakotas or Mosquitoes, which were, of course, much less attractive.

In its life-style and its high degree of motivation, Ramat David was unlike the other air force bases at Hazor and Tel Nof. Slowly but surely, the word got around: 'The best to Ramat David!'

I also put a great deal of effort into persuading ground crews to sign on. Like the pilot, a first-class technician needs time to attain a high level of proficiency. Like the pilot, a first-class technician is snapped up on the civilian market and can easily double or treble

his pay. I have never lost my faith in 'a bit of Zionism', and in this
sphere, I can boast of no few successes. I would persuade the boys,
and in many cases, we reached an understanding. When I left
Ramat David in 1956, I left behind some sixty technicians who had
signed on for five years. (They included sergeants taking their first
steps in their profession; in the course of time, they spread their
wings and took their places in the senior command of the air force.)

There was a saying at Ramat David: 'That idea was born on the
terrace'. Never in the underground operations rooms, surrounded
by large-scale maps and aerial photographs. Lounging out there on
that terrace, our minds would join together at the highest level of
cross-pollination and feedback, with everyone learning from
everyone else. Whenever a flight was completed, whenever some
combat technique had been tested, we would sit around the
terrace, without superiors and subordinates and military trappings,
and exchange impressions. We would relate everything, down to
the minutest details, seeking answers to problems, drawing
conclusions: what was the best offensive formation, what was the
best way of attacking enemy air-fields, how headquarters should
operate, how to bomb, night-flying tactics, when were cannon
better than missiles or *vice versa*, how to operate against anti-
aircraft systems, feints and decoys, how to use surprise, how to
overcome weather dangers, how to get 100 per cent service from
our planes and every one of our pilots.

When I left Ramat David, the section had become a combat
unit. It was a major social and organizational force, with hundreds
of men and many planes ready for any mission, however difficult
and dangerous, and possessing a clear awareness that the base was
more than a conglomeration of offices, runways, hangars, work-
shops and dining-mess, but a home, in the deepest sense. Home is a
place you don't leave; there is nothing temporary about it. It
envolves a permanent and continuous bond. That was why I put
forward the idea of men living on the base. This required houses
being built, and there was a great deal of opposition to the idea. I
had to do a lot of persuading before I won over the opponents,
even half-heartedly. Re'uma and I took up our quarters in a small
three-room wooden hut with Shaul, who was four, and six-week-
old Michal. I knew that when Re'uma, and other wives, began to

breathe in the petrol fumes and accustom their ears to the roar of airplane engines, so that they knew whose plane was landing or taking off, the gap between the family and the airfield would close, engendering a unity that would produce total identification with the air force and its tasks. From then on a wife was a sort of woman-soldier, involved in flying, its smells and dangers, and identifying with this wonderful madness called the Israeli air force.

That's the way I'll always remember Ramat David of the fifties, whatever far-reaching changes were made later. It was like a big kibbutz, with red-roofed houses – a home. Attractive girl clerks netted their bridegrooms there. (Motty Hod got to know a pretty operations sergeant by the name of Pnina, his wife to this day.) And the terrace. You came back from a flight, soaked in sweat, with everything sucked out of you, and sauntered over to the terrace, opened up your overalls, legs upon the parapet, a glass of cold milk or fruit juice – and free rein to your tongue. And I'll always hear the roar of engines being warmed up in the morning. It was an ear-splitting sound, which ripped into our sleep and echoed through the eucalyptus grove where Re'uma and I lived with the children in our little hut.

But my days were not filled by planes and flying alone. There was always a mass of administrative problems: food and sanitation and promotions and the wing's entertainment troupe, with an occasional contribution to its repertoire; and a tour of the stores and the garages and the vehicle unit and the dispensary and the meteorological unit, with a jibe here and an affectionate word there. And visits from air-force command and long discussions with other senior officers and conferences at headquarters to plan for the future and discuss combat tactics. It was a schedule without a dull moment. And when, at twelve or one in the morning, I could finally go home to Re'uma in the house among the eucalyptus trees – which I would only visit briefly in the course of the day for a cup of coffee or a word with my wife and children – and throw my weary body on the bed, I always felt that I still hadn't done all the things I had planned.

It was also at Ramat David that I acquired my 'black Spit'. A commander should have some kind of personal hallmark, which sets him apart from everyone else. There is a certain degree of theatricals in a commander's personality – the way he speaks, his tone, the way he bounds up the platform to address his men, and other such expressions of his natural desire to win their hearts and be the object of their emulation. My 'black Spit' was a personal emblem of this kind, and it became known throughout the air force.

At the end of 1955, the time came for the Spitfires to be withdrawn from service (we had about forty of them). It was a plane with a whiff of history about it: both in the World War and in our War of Independence, it was largely the 'Spit' that had tilted the balance of the air war. It took no more than to hint that I was thinking of retaining one Spitfire for my personal use, for a crew of mechanics, electricians and technicians to swarm all over one of them and give it a thorough overall: fuselage, engine, circuits, radio. We decided to disarm it, as it would not go into combat again. I asked to have it painted black, with a red nose, a lightning streak down the side, and the insignia of the squadron – red–white, red–white – and of the wing. That was how I got my 'Spit'. I felt I was part of the plane. The 'Spit' permitted me to attain three objectives: private pleasure, the personal emblem I had been seeking and a memento of an excellent plane, as an historical relic of the Israeli air force. I can only regret that we didn't do the same with the Mustangs and Mosquitoes and B-17s, which we allowed to disappear like so much junk when they went out of service.

I was gaining much satisfaction from Ramat David and enjoying the fruits of my efforts. Meanwhile, however, the political wheel had made one of its turns, bringing Israel and France into close cooperation and friendship against our common enemy. The French wanted to hold on to Algeria, while we were trying to keep our foothold in the Middle East and beat off the waves of Arab agression. The new friendship brought us Ouragans and Mystères, our fastest and most advanced planes to date. Dan Tolkovski, commander of the air force, offered me command of the wing at Hazor, which was to receive the new Mystères. Well-wishers said: 'Are you out of your mind? To leave this wonderful base, where you've put in such great efforts, and to take over a base like Hazor, with all its problems?' But I had three reasons for agreeing: the challenge of taking a new base and reshaping it; the attraction of the new planes, which every commander would be glad to contend with; and the feeling that, with an additional war round the corner, whose sphere of operations would be the Egyptian border, Hazor, with its new planes, would play a more important role than Ramat David.

I departed from Ramat David in February 1956, with mixed feelings of regret and satisfaction. I flew to France, for my first contact with the French and their aviation industry, and to feast my eyes on the Mystères. I was responsible for ferrying the first planes to Israel, under the command of Benny Peled, who headed our first Mystère squadron. I had received air force command's permission to take several excellent fellows with me from Ramat David to Hazor, including Motty and Benny, and together we began to build the Mystères and Ouragans into a formidable force, which shortly afterwards, in October 1956, bore the brunt of the Sinai Campaign.

8

THE SINAI CAMPAIGN

HAZOR – a new base, new people, new problems. The first problem was whether a new war would feature World War Two-type air battles, or would the introduction of air-to-air missiles and the speed and power of the advanced jets fundamentally alter the character of air warfare, eliminating the conventional forms of short-range combat. (The question of missiles appeared when we got the Mirage jets, but it was only with our most advanced plane, the Phantom, that we entered the missile age, equipped with the right system, the right missile and the right computer.) In my view – supported by some, rejected by others – we would be able to gain air superiority in a future war only if we succeeded in 'conventional' combat. We had to learn to pilot fast planes at low speeds, for when you turn sharply in air combat, your speed increases. If you fly a Mirage at 500 knots and you make a sharp turn, your speed drops to 300 or 200 knots. As your speed drops, you are in danger of going into a spin. The technical skill and the psychological willingness to fly Mach-1 planes (and, later on, even faster ones) at low speeds in air battles was one example of the Israeli pilot's tip-top brinkmanship, as he combined perfect mastery of his plane with the daring required to make it behave at its best.

Later, in 1955 and at the beginning of 1956, another argument raged in both military and political circles: should we buy the Mystère 2, or should we have the patience to wait for the Mystère 4, which was more advanced. I sided with the French view that we

would do better to take the Mystère 2 immediately and wait for
the Mystère 4. To understand the argument, we must consider
conditions in the Middle East at that time. Egypt had completed
her deals with Czechoslovakia, backed, of course, by the Soviet
Union. She now possessed 150 Mig 15s – an excellent plane at that
time, superior to our Meteors and Ouragans. Facing them, we had
only twenty-five Meteors – they were jets, but they flew at
subsonic speeds – and some twenty Ouragans. We were doubtful
whether the Israeli jets would be able to contend with the superior
Egyptian planes, so there was an understandable desire to equip the
air force with the Mystère 2. The French also urged us to purchase
the Mystère 2, for their own economic reasons and also because
they were interested in strengthening the Israeli air force, to
prevent it from falling behind growing Egyptian air power. The
Mystère 2 was ready and could be supplied immediately, while the
Mystère 4 would require another few months – a further argument
in favour of the less sophisticated model. All these arguments were
hurled at the air force commander, Dan Tolkovski. Chief of Staff
Dayan, Deputy Defence Minister Shimon Peres and I, as well
as many others, were in favour of purchasing the Mystère 2, and it
was only Dan's stubborness (in retrospect, completely justified and
praiseworthy!) which kept the Israeli air force from acquiring the
plane. Dan presented his case with his usual ability and logic: the
Mystère 2 was an excellent fighter plane: it was fast, reached high
altitudes and had excellent combat qualities. But it was no more
than a fighter – and that didn't dovetail with our view that an
impoverished country, whose air force would always suffer
numerical inferiority, must have versatile, multi-purpose planes
and bomber-interceptors. There was therefore no point in buying
a single-purpose plane, when the advanced Mystère 4 was multi-
purpose. Eleven years later, Dan was proved correct. In the Six
Day War, the Mystère 4, still a first-line plane thanks to Israeli
modifications, made a valuable contribution in destroying the
Arab air forces.

The top military and political circles in Israel may have been
holding their preliminary discussion of the Sinai Campaign, but I
knew nothing of that. I simply regarded the task of ferrying the
Mystères to Israel as an operation of the greatest importance. The

excitement over receiving the first Mystères in Israel was so great that the French ambassador (a true friend of Israel) was nicknamed 'Mystère Gilbert'. A group of our pilots was already at an air-force base in southern France, where they were being trained to fly Mystères. I flew to Cambrai in France, to see the first Mystère 4 squadrons, which inspired me with great excitement and admiration. Then I went to visit our pilots.

When I arrived in France, we were still undecided about how to ferry the Mystères to Israel with a minimum of stops on the way. It was, of course, a problem of distance. The Ouragans had followed an awkward route: France–Rome–Athens–Israel, an unpleasant experience that induced us to seek a route without a stopover in Athens. For this purpose we had to find an airfield in Italy as near as possible to Israel, so that the Mystère's range would suffice to bring it to Israel with minimum exposure to Arab eyes.

Benny Peled, the present commander of the air force, was in command of the pilots in France. Then, as now, he was a smart fellow, and he had mastered the Mystère perfectly. Dan Tolkovski gave me the authority to decide, on the spot, how to bring the planes to Israel. I had a long and detailed talk with Benny, who explained that if we could stop over at an airfield in southern Italy, near Brindisi, the Mystère, with detachable 620-litre tanks attached to its wings and with a good following wind, would be able to reach Israel without refuelling. Winds usually blow from west to east (that's why commercial jets can fly direct from New York to Lod in ten and a half hours, but take longer in the opposite direction). We calculated that, without any wind, the Mystère would reach Israel with a tiny quantity of fuel – no more than five or ten minutes' flying time, a perilously small margin (and despite all our calculations, two of the Mystères had to make emergency landings in Cyprus). Even at best, with the most suitable winds, the margin would be no more than fifteen minutes. At the altitudes we flew the Mystères – 30–35,000 feet – the winds were very strong, 50–100 knots. In choosing the day, we had to make sure the weather was good, so that the planes would not have to waste fuel because of difficulties on the way.

I informed the French that we would fly the planes to Brindisi – although we did not yet have Italian permission. The French,

unsure of the Israeli pilots' skills, proposed that one of their pilots
lead the first six Mystères. (The Meteors had been brought to Israel
by British and Israeli pilots, and the Ouragans by French and
Israelis.) I had full confidence in our pilots, and Benny reassured me
that he would lead and would carry it off, providing that
everything was alright on the route to Brindisi and, from there, to
Israel. And so it was decided, with the approval of Dan Tolkovski.
Shimon Peres, then in France, also took part in the discussion. Our
air military attaché in France was Paul Kedar, and in Rome,
Shlomo Harel (commander of the navy in the Six Day War). It
was agreed that I would fly to Rome and keep in telephone contact
with Paul to report the arrangements at Brindisi and announce the
day chosen for the flight. Everyone involved in the matter was
very excited. The tension was inevitable: it was no small thing to
ferry Israel's newest planes, which cost 360,000 dollars each, a
fortune in those days.

Shlomo had done an excellent job of preparation. He had
organized things at Brindisi, settled everything with the Italians,
and the only thing left for me was to go there and co-ordinate final
arrangements. In a Nord piloted by Uri Yaffe, I flew to Brindisi,
which I had heard mentioned in my childhood when immigrants
to Palestine had come through there. My visions of it were
shattered when I found a dull and dreary semi-Sicilian township,
whose harbour had long given up the ghost. I met an Italian
colonel, who headed the security services in southern Italy, and, as
sometimes happens, we quickly became fast friends. We took over
the airfield and established direct contact with the pilots in France.
One day, when we discovered that the next day would bring fine
weather with suitable winds, we sent off a preliminary alert,
notifying both France and Israel. We informed the Greeks that the
planes would cross their territory, near Athens, and estimated that
if all went well, the flight to Israel from Brindisi would take two
hours. The next day I phoned Paul: 'Take off!'

The pilots set off early in the morning for the one-and-a-half
hour flight to Brindisi. The affable Italians did not protest when we
gently shooed them out of their control tower and took over
communications – in Hebrew. Benny, leading a formation over
Europe for the first time in his life, performed in a masterful

manner, as though he had been doing nothing for the past ten years but ferrying combat planes from France to Israel by way of Italy. When I heard his 'Hello, Brindisi. Hello, Brindisi' in the control tower, my suspense evaporated, to be replaced by joy. 'Hello Benny,' I replied in Hebrew, 'this is the Brindisi control tower.'

There were no snags. They landed, swallowed a cup of coffee, refuelled and took off, with the Nord flying along with them and reporting their progress. The small group of Israelis who remained at Brindisi counted the minutes. We knew no rest until we got the news that the Mystères had landed safety. Then we celebrated their arrival with cognac.

In Israel, all the high-ups were waiting at Hazor. Ben-Gurion fondled each plane with his eyes, Dan was overwrought with joy, Moshe Dayan was excited but wordless, and Eshkol 'protested' at the glaring waste of money – 360,000 dollars and only one seat!'

Two or three weeks later, in May 1956, a further six Mystères were ready to be ferried to Israel. Having already been through the experience once, I was requested to repeat 'Operation Brindisi'. Again I flew off to France in our Nord, and when I'd made the necessary arrangements, I went on to Brindisi. When the plane came to a halt, the door opened, and I was about to get out when I suddenly saw a little Fiat tearing down the runway only to halt with a screech of brakes and disgorge my colonel. He didn't know that I was again in charge of the operation, and he was so overjoyed at seeing me that he grabbed me in his arms and hugged me tight, Italian style, shouting at the top of his lungs: '*Buon giorno, Colonnello bambino!*' ('Welcome, colonel baby!'). Because of his fifty-six years and because he was so kind-hearted and helpful, I forgave this slight to a thirty-two-year-old colonel of the Israel Air Force.

With the combined assistance of the over-courteous Italians, extra fuel tanks and suitable westerly winds, we brought twenty-four Mystères to Israel. When these were added to our twenty-four Ouragans, we began to regard ourselves as an air power. In the meantime, far-reaching plans were being hatched, and in July I was summoned to Dan Tolkovski, who let me in on a closely guarded secret. It had been decided to acquire another thirty-six Mystères, for a total of sixty – an extraordinarily large number for those times. Why all the hush-hush treatment? First of all, because any arms purchases by Israel always aroused delicate political problems at various levels; secondly, because this time the French government had given its agreement on condition that the whole affair, including the planes' delivery to Israel, be conducted under a thick veil of total secrecy.

We needed to train Mystère pilots as quickly as possible in order to fly the additional thirty-six planes. We couldn't tell the boys at this early stage what the objective was, as we had been ordered into total secrecy. So we told them that we had been offered training facilities at French bases in North Africa, and then sent off the pilots in two groups, the first commanded by Benny, the second by Motty. None of them had the faintest suspicion that Israel was buying Mystères on a grand scale. Secrecy was so tight that it was only when the El Al Constellation was approaching France that Motty and Benny were told: 'Dear friends, forget about North Africa and training and all those fairy-tales. You are going to France to fly thirty-six Mystères to Israel by the route that Benny has used and knows well.' Benny heard the tidings with his characteristic calm; Motty, the commander of the Ouragan squadron, was a little more shaken. I wasn't there, but I'm told that it took the pilots several minutes before they could digest the wonderful tidings.

Everything was prepared: the planes were waiting, the pilots were ready and eager to bring them home. There was only the problem of the Italians. The high degree of secrecy meant that this time they could not be allowed in on the plot. This gave rise to a ruse, which was a mixture of ingenuity and tongue-in-cheek humour. Shlomo Lahat, who was in charge of bringing the planes to Israel, sold the Italians a 'tale of woe': 'The Mystères we bought from France, the ones which refuelled at Brindisi, have developed defects. We have to fly them back to France for repair, otherwise we can't use them.' The Italians fell for it. The higher levels of their government may not have been convinced that the story was the unadulterated truth, but the lower rungs at Brindisi did not show the faintest suspicion.

From then on, everything was simple. The first eighteen planes took off from France and landed to refuel at Brindisi, where they were described as being on their way from Israel to France for repairs. The Italians even expressed their sympathy over the additional trouble we were being put to. The planes then took off 'for France' and flew straight to Israel. With the next eighteen, there were no problems at all. They were marked with the same identification numbers as the first eighteen and followed the usual route from France. As far as the Italians were concerned, these were the same planes, on their way back to Israel after repairs.

After all the excitement and subterfuge, the best story came from Shlomo Lahat, the man in charge of the whole operation. When the 'repaired' aircraft took off from Brindisi to Israel, that charming Italian colonel stood next to Shlomo, as a heartwarming demonstration of goodwill, and watched the 'newly repaired' planes fly away. Then he whispered to Shlomo: 'Listen, *colonnello*, when your first six Mystères passed through here, and your *colonnello bambino* was here, I told my friends that the French are shafting the Israelis. There's something wrong with the planes' tails. I even wanted to tell the *colonnello bambino*, but I didn't. Really, you should be more careful with them, otherwise they will screw you . . .'

He was wrong, that dear Italian colonel of mine. The Mystère 4 was an excellent plane. Then, in the summer of 1956, with sixty Mystères in our hands, our sense of strength was not just an expression of our well-known propensity to a fervent belief in our strength, even in a position of numerical inferiority; this time it was genuine, high-quality power, with which we could embark on the Sinai Campaign at the end of 1956.

My desire to set a personal example required me to learn to fly every new plane acquired by the air force, and, moreover, to perform well on it. When a wing commander leaves his routine tasks and returns to 'the classroom' to learn to fly the latest plane to reach the squadron, he enjoys a large measure of sympathy at first. Everyone tries to help him overcome his difficulties and teach him as quickly as possible, lest he give up in despair. The Mystère was like the Phantom, a plane heralding a new era. I was taught by Benny himself. I took a lot of trouble over my training and passed the tests successfully; then the time came for me to spread my wings in a Mystère 4.

Aside from learning the Mystère's advanced systems, I also made the acquaintance of the new French pressure suit, which is deserving of a few words. Under certain flying conditions, such as executing a sharp turn, you have to endure strong centrifugal pressures – two or three or five times the weight of your own body (2G, 3G, or 5G, as it is called). What happens is that the blood from the upper parts of the body is forced towards the lower limbs, and while you don't lose consciousness, your eyes 'blacken out' and you can no longer see. There's no need to say that a blind pilot is a dead pilot. The pressure suit was designed to prevent this temporary blindness, by pressing on the arteries in the legs and stomach. As the pressure of the plane increases, it opens the valve, releasing air into the parts of the suit covering the legs and belly, thus preventing the blood from the top part of the body from flowing to the feet. The pilot's vision, which depends on a continuous supply of blood, is thereby protected, although the suit cannot stand unlimited pressure, just like the plane (a Nord can only take 2 or 3G, a Mystère can go up to 9G before it gets into trouble).

The half hour in the air on my maiden flight in a Mystère 4 was a pleasure hard to describe. Strapped into this superb pressure suit, with my face in a modern French oxygen mask, I climbed to new heights, banked like crazy, feeling my whole body being torn by the new pressure. My heart jumped as I flew at full velocity. The plane was 'mine' – tamed, broken in and obedient.

I began to land, at 150–155 knots, with everything rushing past much faster than I was used to. The wheels touched down, half fondling the runway, half protesting at the friction, as though they wanted to lift off again. Stop. This is the great moment of the mechanics. Look at those grinning, 'bloodthirsty' faces. They are flushed and breathless, impatient to get hold of their commander and perform the traditional ceremony: upon landing after a maiden flight in a new plane, every pilot, whatever his rank or status, is doused in buckets of water. In preparation for my ducking, I delayed my exit from the cockpit, making good use of the time: off went my shoes, off with superfluous clothing, I rolled up my socks and laid aside a fresh pair of dry underpants. That's it. To my baptism! Sloosh! A bucket over my head. Sloosh! Another bucket. May it bring them joy.

The months of August through October witnessed exceptionally feverish activity. My first aim was to put the Mystères into full operation, with the pilots being given the best possible opportunities to polish up their performance, as they took the 'mystery out of the Mystère'. At the same time, we were craving for actual combat operations and hoped they would bear fruit. For eight years, ever since the War of Independence, the air force had been enjoying peace and quiet. It had been building up its strength, but its eagerness for real trials of strength in air combat was only satisfied piecemeal and at lengthy intervals. Still the question of how Mystères and Migs would face up to each other remained unanswered.

As the hands of the clock turned and the Sinai Campaign drew near, I felt that I was facing a personal test. It may have been because I'm pretentious, or so highly identified with the air force, or so deeply involved in filling the bases I commanded – above all Ramat David – with new and original content. But the Sinai Campaign of 1956 was to give the air force its diploma, and I felt that I, and my methods, were facing their test.

A man needed more than a little faith to fortify his heart during those days. There were even those who alleged that it was only my excessive self-confidence that rescued me from depression. While Nasser was cheering his army on and equipping it with the finest Soviet arms, the *fedayeen* were sowing death and destruction in Israeli population centres, destroying the average Israeli's sense of security. Soviet support for the Arabs was only at its early stages, but it added an additional dimension to the fears and anxieties of the Israeli. Russia – gigantic, mysterious, with its traditional hatred of the Jews – filled hearts with fear. A new term appeared in our lexicon: Frunze – the place in the Soviet Union where the Egyptian officers were sent to study the art of war and improve their capacity to destroy the State of Israel. For us, Frunze symbolized the process by which the Middle East conflict was expanding into an international conflict, with Great Power involvement.

This was the situation when Moshe Dayan became chief of staff in 1953. The intervening years have taken their cruel toll of him, undermining his self-confidence and tarnishing his image, but at that time, in the early fifties, he was a brilliant commander, an unconventional, first-rate military leader. He filled our defence forces with a renewed sense of strength and purpose, of tenacity and faith. Officers and men were infected by the great spirit that Dayan brought with him and which was expressed in his confident behaviour. He exhibited a personal example: he was never absent from any operation, and could rarely be dissuaded from taking an active combat role.

Again there were wide-ranging debates within the Israeli armed forces. How should we face up to the new realities and their rapid fluctuations? How should we apportion the minute budget? Which arm was to have priority on the allocation of resources: more armour, more planes? How was the armour to be organized and deployed? Dayan was at the storm centre of the debate. His attitude to the air force was ambivalent. On the one hand, he couldn't – or perhaps, he didn't want to – understand why a pilot should get higher pay and enjoy better conditions. One day he came to the pilot's school to talk to the cadets. Squatting on the lawn they laid aside all barriers of rank and spoke openly. The cadets tried to explain that the form of training, the conditions, the high standards required of a pilot, the dangers and the costly equipment called for the pilot, and the air force, to enjoy a special status and a different life-style. Moshe's eyes flashed angrily. 'What the hell are you talking about? Our commandos go out on raids across the border with a cheap knife and perform extraordinary deeds – without hot showers or steaks or higher pay!' But his own argument did not prevent Dayan from looking into the future and viewing it correctly. An air force was needed, so he fought, successfully, for sixty Mystères, giving the air force enormous power, in terms of the fifties.

At the same time, our *affaire* with the French and British, who were later to prove false when they were seduced by the aroma of Arab oil, reached dizzy heights, as the Sinai Campaign drew near.

The tricks of fate, I thought to myself. Only a few years earlier we were making ourselves at home in Czechoslovakia. We learned to fly planes produced in that same 'Avia' factory that was now turning out Mig 15s to help Egypt overcome the Czech-trained

Israelis. In my mind's eye, I saw the Czech colonel, Hlodek, putting his beefy arm around Jimmy Affifi's shoulders and asking him: 'Tell me, colonel, do you know Weizman?'

'Sure,' says Jimmy, 'we studied together in England. I would bring presents to Re'uma and play with Shaul in his crib.'

'In that case,' says Hlodek, his eyebrows raised, 'listen carefully. When Weizman took his leave of me a few years ago, I told him: "Catch 'em on the ground and shoot 'em up!" You understand, at that time we were still . . . And now, I'm telling you: you must catch the Israelis on the ground and shoot 'em up, before they can take off.'

Even the air force wasn't free of its sceptics: 'Look, Weizman, a Mig 15 is no joke, and you know the Czech air force. So what do you mean by telling us that we'll beat them with Ouragans and Mystères?' I considered this a sign of declining self-confidence, and these fellows annoyed me considerably. They claimed that the only plane that could stand up to the Mig 15 was the American F-86. But the Americans were deaf to our pleas; at that time, they didn't dream of supplying us with planes.

This kind of feeling had always accompanied Israel, or parts of it. These people try to justify their lack of faith by claiming that this time the enemy has weapons we can't contend with. Either it's some plane with awe-inspiring numerals, like Mig 21, 23 or 25, or some missile, anti-tank, anti-aircraft, air-to-surface or surface-to-air, or surface-to-surface. Of course it's idiotic to overlook the dangers stemming from the modern weapons acquired by our enemies, but there is no greater danger than helplessness, fear, self-abasement and a paralyzing national confusion. We must always tell ourselves, over and over again, untiringly, that the Arabs have always had a greater number of superior modern arms, and we've always defeated them – and we always will. The moment we give in to the idea that the enemy's acquisition of some new weapon prevents us from acting, we've lost the war. That was what happened in the War of Attrition of 1969–70, a subject that I will return to.

The strength of the Israeli air force on the eve of the Sinai Campaign consisted of the following: one squadron of Mystères, one of Ouragans, one of Meteors and one of Mosquitoes, two squadrons of Mustangs, one of B-17s (consisting of two airplanes), and one squadron of Harvard training planes fitted with rockets. In short, we had some 100 jets and fifty piston planes – 150 planes altogether, quite a formidable force. We knew that the Egyptian air force was of a similar size, numerically, but we assumed that its planes were better.

In comparing the Mystère with the Mig 15, the great fear was that the Mig would out-climb the Mystère. I was sure we could overcome this, and I was furious with those pilots who fell into the trap of scepticism; in fact, I almost had them released from the unit. I say 'almost' for, after all, it's only human to fear the unknown, and the Mig 15 was definitely unknown. Not surprisingly, therefore, the subsequent disagreement over the air force's role in the forthcoming conflict stemmed from conflicting estimates of its capability.

Even if it wasn't specifically stated – and in matters like this, it is customary not to go beyond generalities, leaving plain speaking for well-guarded conference rooms – the objectives of the campaign were to free Israel of the Egyptian menace for an extended period of time. Contrary to the picture usually drawn about all of Israel's wars, I still maintain that the 1956 campaign was not a war to prevent our annihilation. It was an operation with well-defined objectives: to open the Suez Canal to Israeli shipping, to lift the Egyptian blockade of Eilat and to destroy the *fedayeen*.

The Sinai Campaign was not preceded by weeks of suspense, like the 1967 war. Sinai was not filled with 1,000 Egyptian tanks, even though the 250 that did appear there, which was a large number for 1956, sufficed to give us sleepless nights. The secrecy surrounding the operation and the wide-spread feeling that the objective of the attack would be Jordan, not Egypt, reduced the suspense and the rumours. Given the circumstances and the objectives of the war, it was totally justified. It should be stressed that the campaign was not mounted under the pressure of a hawkish right-wing opposition. Our government was headed by Ben-Gurion, with Golda Meir as foreign minister, and the left-wing Mapam party as a member of the coalition.

According to our preliminary instructions, the operation was to begin on 24 or 25 October (for various reasons, it was delayed until the 29th). A week before the scheduled attack, our preparations were at their peak, and we were very worried by irksome problems such as a shortage of ammunition and spare parts and the need to bring all the air force's planes and installations into full operation at the decisive moment. The Mystère was the first plane fitted with the excellent French-made 30-mm cannon, but even the French were short of ammunition for it. When we received the planes in March and April, we were supplied with small amounts of ammunition, far less than what was needed for the most modest war. Only a day or two before the operation, a French transport plane landed at our base and unloaded eight small crates containing 20,000 30-mm. shells. We didn't have any bombs for the Mystère, and we scarcely had any 68-mm. rockets. The plane was not fitted for carrying bombs – a most serious defect in what was then our most advanced plane, which was only corrected later.

Naturally, my total involvement in the air force and its plans prevented me from taking much interest in the operational plans of the land forces, which I knew only in outline: a thrust into Sinai, occupation of Sharm el-Sheikh and of the Gaza Strip and defeat of the Egyptian army in Sinai. It was clear that the depth of our penetration into Sinai was strictly limited: we could only go as far as 10 miles from the Suez Canal, where we were to halt and await developments.

The operational plan we were shown was audacious, no less than that of the Six Day War. Sixteen Dakotas, escorted by Ouragans, Mystères and Meteors, were to drop some 300 paratroopers over the Mitla Pass in the late afternoon, around five o'clock. The pass was some 20 miles from the Canal and 100 miles from our border, and it would be at least twenty-four hours before additional forces joined the paratroopers. The parachute drop was to take place while the Egyptian air force was at full strength and eminently capable of attacking the small force so far from the rest of the army. When the plan was shown to the wing commanders, we asked directly: 'What about the Egyptian air force? What about destroying it?' It was shortly after the Korean War so a parallel was drawn: 'For us, the Suez Canal is the Yalu River in Korea. We mustn't cross it. We can do anything we like in Sinai, but we must not, under any circumstances, go beyond Sinai!'

There was only one Egyptian airfield in Sinai, at El Arish. The order not to cross the Canal tied our hands. With the Egyptian air force fit for combat, we feared for the fate of the paratroopers. We tried to persuade Dan Tolkovski to give us permission to hit the Egyptian planes on the ground, at Faid, Kabrit, Abu Sawar and Cairo West. 'We can get there, give them a good booting, finish them off and come back. We can do it!'

But we were facing a brick wall, made even higher by political restrictions. I have no doubt that if the choice were between the offensive as it was carried out – with all the political restrictions – and not launching the campaign at all, the first was undoubtedly the better choice (even though everything we captured had to be vacated, and we were obliged to wait eleven years before we could repeat the operation free of political restrictions).

Still, there was one exception to the order on restricting our activities to Sinai, and it proved that had our request been approved, the results would have been as good as in 1967, and perhaps even faster and better. Orders were to shoot down only those Egyptian planes trying to operate in Sinai. But concern over the paratroopers led to Benny Peled being ordered to take a formation of Mystères to patrol over Kabrit, the Egyptian airfield nearest the Mitla. The patrol was under strict orders not to attack, not to hit, not to bomb! 'Just patrol and report!' Benny returned frustrated: the Egyptians were taken totally by surprise by the whole operation, and he could have ripped their Meteors and Vampires to pieces on the ground.

 With all plans set – although up to the last hours before the attack even I wasn't completely sure the operation would get off the ground at the appointed hour on 29 October – Motty escorted the sixteen Dakotas with his Ouragan squadron. The Meteors were led by Yoelli, and the co-pilot in the plane leading the Dakotas was Yael Finkelstein (now Rom), the only woman with pilot's wings in the Israeli air force. When Motty returned from his escort mission, he had his own special way of expressing the doubts we had all shared in fearing that the operation would be called off at the last moment: 'The view from above was wonderful. Seeing the boys jump – it was just out of this world! But until I saw the parachutes open, I was still waiting for an order to collect the paratroopers in the air and bring them straight home because the whole show's been called off. It was only when I saw the parachutes open that I knew it was on its way.'

I had a minor ambition I wanted to satisfy in this war. I had never hit a train or a ship from the air. My 'naval ambitions' stemmed from some of the debates of those times. I claimed that it was a pity to waste money and manpower on the navy; if an enemy ship entered our territorial waters, our planes would tear it apart before the navy got their engines started. Operations room had standing instructions that I was to be called at any hour of the day or night if an enemy ship appeared. My wish was granted. Early in the morning of 31 October, the telephone heralded that an Egyptian destroyer was shelling Haifa. Quick as a flash, I ran out to the squadron and 'incited' Motty to 'take this run with me'. Motty knew that when 'my beloved Haifa' was being shelled, I couldn't remain indifferent and let someone else do the job for me. 'Let's go!' he said. 'You lead!'

Two Ouragans were armed for us. The Ouragan is a pilot's dream, like some ageing prima ballerina who has not lost her grace. Each of these excellent planes carried sixteen rockets and we were eager to give the ship a taste of them. Then we were stopped short: ground control informed us that the ship had capitulated. For years a debate raged over what hit her: a shell from one of our warships, or a rocket fired by one of our pilots in the area. Supporters of the opposing views went so far as to measure the hole in the ship and to compare calibres, but, even so, they haven't reached agreement to this day.

What was beyond doubt, however, was that Motty and I were 20,000 feet up, on our way to Haifa with our rockets. We were aloft, armed and charged with fighting spirit. We requested permission to return to Sinai. When we reported that we had enough fuel, permission was granted. The ban on attacking Egyptian ground forces had been removed the previous day, and our men had already engaged the Egyptians in air battles. In effect, we already had mastery of the air.

Motty and I headed south. At El Arish we saw Egyptian Vampires parked on the runway. We reported this, and two of our planes went up to attack, scoring good hits – unfortunately, it transpired that the planes had been dummies. We continued southwards and discovered an Egyptian column on its way up from the Canal hauling cannon. We swooped down, rocketing, strafing and scoring good hits.

At seven in the morning, we landed back at base, where I discovered my brother-in-law the chief of staff, Dayan, who was hungry. We brought him his favourite – tomatoes and cucumbers. Moshe insisted on telling me that, as commander of the base and the wing, I shouldn't fly operational sorties. But he soon cooled down and, munching his cucumber, told the assembled pilots how the war was going. He spoke well, and the fellows listened in great excitement. He munched and talked, talked and munched. Then he got up and started towards his Piper. 'Where are you off to?' I asked him. 'To the Mitla,' he replied.

It was 31 October, and the British and French hadn't even touched the Egyptian air force. Egyptian air attacks were common in Sinai. Our pilots were busy shooting down planes. Some of the paratroopers had just got themselves bombed. A tank brigade was bogged down in the sand. Chaim Bar-Lev was having trouble in Rafiah with the First Armoured Brigade. Everything was hanging by a hair, and the chief of staff wants to fly to the Mitla?

'My good man!' I said, 'You're not flying to any Mitla! I've just come back from there, and there are Migs hovering around. If you want to, give us the order to attack the Egyptians from the air. I can understand that. But you have no business flying there.'

We argued: it wasn't easy to dispute him. In the end, he gave in a bit and agreed to fly to Abu Ageila. We didn't have helicopters for flights like that, so he flew there in his Piper, landing not far from a mine field and falling straight into the raging battle. Things weren't going well, and after examining what was going on, Dayan decided to replace a brigade commander – not the most usual thing to do during a battle.

Meanwhile, itching to keep on the move, I drove around the base, from hangar to hangar, in a mobilized civilian vehicle. To maintain the atmosphere of one united family, I took the mechanics into my confidence, letting them know how the war was going, to make them feel they were in on the whole affair.

Our base was in a state of frenzied activity. We knew that the

British and French were due to go into action, but they were apparently still engaged in working out their doctrines and decoding intelligence reports, missing all their chances and displaying astounding operational ineptness. Finally they moved, and it was a 'semi-misfire'. The English launched a night raid, full of apprehensions about the Egyptians and their 150 fearsome Migs. What we could do by day with bombs and well-aimed rockets, they tried to do at night, in the dark, with long-range bombers from Cyprus and Malta.

After the bombing raid, whose results were disappointing, they began the landing at Port Said. The French had a little more guts: they permitted their pilots to mount a bombing raid on Luxor. One of them (today one of the French air force's best-known generals) took four F-84s and with his four machine-guns, destroyed twelve Ilyushin 28s on the ground, a foretaste of what we were to do in 1967.

Even though the French and British air forces did not gain any far-reaching results in their raids, the Egyptian air force was sufficiently mauled for us to extend our operations on 1 and 2 November, with the air force aiding the ground forces. The Ninth Brigade, on its way to Sharm el-Sheikh, was given air assistance, as were other forces. We also had an unpleasant mishap in that area. Early in November, with the fighting at its height, we were notified that a ship was in the waters off Sharm. A group of Mustangs and Mystères set out to attack it, doing a good job. When we found out that it was a British destroyer, four of whose men were killed in the attack, we could only – and inadequately – express our regrets.

We went into the war with sceptics doubting whether the 'home-grown' Israeli pilots would compare in skill and performance with the audacious founders of the air force. We came out of it confident, for the young pilots showed wonderful ability, courage, skill and willingness. The participation of the French and British air forces prevented the Israeli air-force pilots from showing their full ability and strength, but the boys carried out all their missions with great success and proved their resourcefulness and daring.

They were especially concerned about the planes. They had

always been aware of the political and financial difficulties involved in acquiring the aircraft Israel needed; they knew what the state had to forego in order to channel large sums of money into purchasing modern planes. There is no need to stress that human life was holy, and we told the commanders and pilots that no plane, however costly, was as precious as the life of its pilot. However, as in many other cases, these reiterated orders left some room for individual discretion, and it was this, rather than blind obedience, which indicated the pilot's attitude to his plane.

One of the first six Mystère pilots – a fact that he must have regarded as placing him under an obligation – either miscalculated his fuel or for some other reason found himself over enemy territory with an engine that ceased to function. Any 'normal' pilot would have obeyed instructions and bid a sad farewell to his plane, as he bailed out by means of his ejector seat. But when the engine stops, a plane still has some momentum, the equivalent of a limited amount of energy. He made good use of this momentum (he had been flying at 560 knots when the engine stopped) by climbing to 15,000 feet and gliding back to base, planning it so well that he completed an accurate landing on the runway. It was a brilliant feat, and he was justly pleased at saving his expensive plane.

Benny Peled had the privilege of being the first pilot in the Israeli air force to save his life by bailing out of a damaged plane by means of an ejector seat. Benny, then a young major and commander of a squadron, was out with a foursome, giving air cover to a brigade that ran into Egyptian armour and fortifications on its way to Sharm el-Sheikh. The foursome attacked the area, especially the Egyptian shore batteries, and Benny's plane was badly hit by Egyptian anti-aircraft fire. When he found that he had lost control of the damaged plane, he operated his ejector seat (which did not yet work automatically) and jumped. On landing, he suffered a slight fracture of the ankle, but hobbled off to the hills above the coast. The Egyptians had seen him jump and sent vehicles to winkle him out of his hiding place. Israeli Mustangs worked hard, strafing the Egyptians and preventing them from reaching Benny. While they were doing so, another one of our planes was hit, and the pilot parachuted into captivity.

The nerve-racking 'game' went on for several hours: Benny on one side, the Egyptians on the other, and our planes protecting him from above. We didn't have much experience in rescuing pilots. In the end, Benny was rescued in one of the most exciting feats of those days. A young Piper pilot (now a successful lawyer) set off from Eilat and scoured the area where Benny was supposed to be hiding. His plane lacked any equipment for finding Benny, who was sitting in a narrow cavity, suffering sharp pain from his ankle and still convinced that his salvation would come. When he saw the Piper, he spread out his parachute and waved. Now that Greenbaum knew where he was, there was just one small problem: where to land the Piper?

He found one dune, slightly larger and flatter than the others, and executed a daring landing. With his ankle giving him intense pain, Benny limped to the Piper and squeezed in. Greenbaum was not at all sure that his wheels would get through the deep sand. Benny crossed his fingers, the plane began to move and just managed to take off. After an hour and a quarter, they were in Eilat, and a Dakota flew Benny to a base near ours. When we heard of his return, Re'uma, her sister (Ruth Dayan) and I rushed to welcome him. He was carried off the Dakota on a stretcher, his ankle already placed in plaster at Eilat. How do you welcome a friend who has been rescued and brought back on a stretcher? Standing orders do not specify. I kissed him.

A day earlier, I myself had encountered a problem in the air, which I only solved with the help of Sheika Barkat, a youngster who had grown in the air force and whom I liked very much. In the Sinai Campaign he was operations officer of our base and was burdened with problems, but he was a model of efficiency and diligence. Fellows were taking off and landing and the base was full of stories and everyone was oozing with combat, experiences. Sheika got fed up and came to me tearfully.

'What's up, Sheika?'

'Sir, the war's about to end. What will I tell my grandchildren?'

The man's right, I thought to myself. 'Chum,' I said, 'saddle up!'

At that time, our aerial operations were very varied and instructions flexible: 'If you have a plane available, take off and let 'em have it, just as long as as you keep 15 miles from the Suez

Canal. Anything Egyptian down there that's moving, make it stop moving.'

We saddled up two old war-horse Ouragans. At that time I hadn't had more than ten hours on an Ouragan, and it would be quite an exaggeration to say that I knew it inside out. Loaded with rockets, we set off for the northern highway, El Arish–Port Said. We had just taken off when Sheika informed me, 'You have a leak in your right tank. Do *vide-vite* immediately!' Now I know what *vide-vite* is. It means a rapid emptying of the fuel tank. That's fine. But what I didn't know was how to do *vide-vite* in an Ouragan, or even where the button is. In cases like that, I follow the rule: what you don't know, ask. The fact that half the Israeli air force – in the air or on ground bases – was listening in to our radio conversation was not pleasant, but then, the number of options was not very large. So I was obliged to ask: 'Excuse me, Sheika, how do you do *vide-vite* here?' Sheika was very patient with his ignorant commander and he carefully explained how, on the right side, upwards, so-and-so many finger-breadths from this board, there's a little button that you press. . . . I released a certain amount of fuel, still leaving me enough to shoot an Egyptian train, strafe and rocket and get back to base safely.

Five years passed and I got a further opportunity to discover that the minor events, the things that occur on the sidelines of the war, are nevertheless etched deeply, never to be erased. As commander of the air force, I took part in a passing-out parade and afterwards I stood with the young pilots, enjoying their company. The stories began to flow, and memories gushed out. Among others, I told them my *vide-vite* story, in all its tiniest details.

Some of them had already heard the tale, and they were comparing versions. For others, the story was new. But the commander of the base, Shmuel Sheffer, stood on one side, ecstatic, grinning from ear to ear, but not saying a word, as though he were keeping a little secret to himself. 'What are you so pleased about?' I asked him. 'Is this the first time you've heard the story?'

'First time?' he replied, 'I've heard it again and again. But there's something I've never told anyone yet. When you took off with Sheika during the Sinai Campaign, I was also up in the air, and I also had a fuel leak, and I also had to do a *vide-vite*, and I also didn't know how. The only difference was that I was shy about asking. As the fuel poured out, my shyness was getting more and more dangerous. And then my salvation came. I heard you over the radio, asking Sheika how to do it. At long last, somebody was in the same spot and, fortunately, he wasn't shy.'

Compared to 1967, the Sinai Campaign was a mini-war for our air force. We didn't throw in our full power, and it wasn't the air force that decided the outcome. A large part of the work was done by the French and the British air forces. We gained air superiority over the battlefield, but it can't be overlooked that we didn't do it alone. Thus aside from its undesirable political results, the Anglo-French-Israeli partnership, to some extent, prevented us from proving to the last of the sceptics what enormous power a modern air force with first-class combat-pilots can wield.

Nevertheless, this war encouraged lines of thought that we had followed before, but had never gained much of a response in the Israeli high command. When you gain total air supremacy over the battlefield, an air force becomes a tremendous factor, operating in two different directions: your ground forces can carry out their task of dealing with the enemy ground forces without fearing enemy attacks; and if you strike serious blows at them, putting a large part of them out of action and disrupting their communications, their strength is sapped to such an extent that they are unable to halt the advance of your ground forces. When this concept was adopted, it was a significant addition to the Israeli armed forces' combat doctrine.

There were a number of operational conclusions from this overall view. Maximum co-ordination of ground and air forces and full use of their joint strength made it necessary to put the two high commanders under one roof and to unite the headquarters of the combat units. Up to and during the Sinai Campaign, air-force command was in Ramle. The lessons of the Sinai Campaign induced us to move our headquarters to Tel Aviv, and this was one of my duties as head of Air Branch (and, in effect, Dan Tolkovski's deputy) after the 1956 war.

As for my personal advancement, the Sinai Campaign may have speeded things up. But back in September 1956, Moshe Dayan told me that Dan Tolkovski wanted to appoint me head of Air Branch, the second most important post in the air-force hierarchy. I was a little surprised – my relations with Dan were not always very smooth. But Moshe asked me if I agreed, and I did, there and then.

During the last stage of preparations for the war, Dan Tolkovski called and said, in English: 'You don't change horses in mid-stream.' In other words, my new post would have to wait till after the war. That was just the way it turned out. During a commanders' meeting, Dan sent me a note: 'When can you take on the job? The earlier the better.'

There was no need for details. I wrote back: 'Tonight!'

9

STAFF OFFICER

AFTER A SHORT PERIOD as commander of Hazor – and although it may have been short, it was full of storms and battles – I left the base and its wing in the good hands of Motty Hod and on 1 December 1956 found myself in a little shack in Ramle, as Dan's deputy and head of Air Branch.

A natural gap exists between any high command and the ranks of field commanders who actually get in there and do battle. The former tend to claim that the pilots, so caught up in their planes, don't see anything beyond them. The pilots and their commanders come back with the cry: 'What do they understand, up there in the rarefied atmosphere!' As a wing commander, I hadn't spared air force command a fair share of gripes, when I first sat down behind the desk of head of Air Branch, I felt a sharp sense of obligation. 'Weizman,' I told myself, 'for the lieutenants and captains and majors and colonels and all your good friends from the airfield, from now on *you* are air force command. And you have to prove that your partnership with them hasn't ended, that it has grown even stronger. You have to prove that command staff isn't alienated from the units and their needs.' I also knew that there were staff men lying in wait, eager to pounce on me: 'Now that you're here, don't you see that your complaints were groundless? Don't you see? Now you tell Motty and the others that's what we've got, make the most of it and get off my back!'

There's a great measure of dreariness in staff work: torrents of tedious papers and a diary overloaded with appointments, often

The Weizman family on a picnic in the early 1930s.

Yael Weizman, Ezer's sister, before her marriage and departure from Palestine.

Ezer *centre* with his close friend Bill Brindley *left* and another pilot cadet during their RAF training in Rhodesia.

Ezer leads a lorry in an
attempt to release a plane
bogged down in mud at
Nir Am in the winter of
1948.

Moddy Allon, the
commander of the first
Israeli fighter squadron.

Ezer with Sid Cohen who
took command of the
fighter squadron after
Moddy Allon's death.
(courtesy of Auraham Gihon)

ABOVE Base Commander Weizman gets a shower from the mechanics after a solo flight in a new plane.

TOP Ezer during the War of Independence.

Air Force Commander Weizman cheers as the air force soccer team takes the cup for the third time. Sharing the excitement are his children, Shaul and Michal.

BELOW Ezer shows a model of the Mirage to Ben Gurion and deputy defence minister, Shimon Peres, after the signing of the agreement to purchase Mirage planes.

Going out to meet the first Skyhawk to arrive in Israel: *from left to right* Motty Hod, Levi Eshkol, Chaim Bar-Lev, Moshe Kashti and Ezer Weizman.

Ezer with Moshe Dayan on Mount Scopus during the Six Day War.

The photograph found in Syrian intelligence files after the capture of the Golan heights during the Six Day War: *from left to right* Ezer Weizman (head of General Staff Division), David Elazar (head of Northern Command), Shlomo Erel (Commander of the Navy), and Yitzhak Rabin (Chief of Staff).

Ezer under Egyptian bombardment on a visit to the Suez Canal during the War of Attrition.

Citizen Weizman receives a copy of the air force album from Air Force Commander Motty Hod.

Ezer and Re'uma.
(photo by Ilani)

kept unwillingly and endured impatiently. There is a tremendous difference between the responsibility resting on a commander and that of his deputy. As commander of a wing, one listens to opinions and suggestions and takes decisions affecting human lives. As head of Air Branch and deputy of the air force, one offers advice, trying to make it as sensible and well-balanced as possible; but the decisions are taken by the commander, and it's he who issues the orders. In other words, the duty of a staff officer is to advise; the fate of the commander is to decide.

I wanted to throw myself into my new post totally, heart and soul – and I ran into difficulties from the start. One of the tasks of the head of Air Branch is to handle the air force's operational policy and to submit his recommendations on the subject. This must be done on two levels, which do not necessarily go hand in hand: the here and now, and long-term planning over a period of five or seven years. A man needs a daring imagination and the ability to perceive the mass of fluctuating factors in our region and in the world at large in order to get near whatever it is that the future conceals. In Israel there is an additional difficulty. Because of its political isolation, Israel cannot buy arms at will – neither the types nor quantities she needs.

My encounter with the complex problems of the Air Branch was full of challenges and required me to learn a lot: combat doctrine, day-to-day supervision of flights and training, air-force intelligence (now a separate branch), training, supervision of the equipment branch (in effect, the engineering branch), short- and long-term planning and co-ordination of all the other branches of air force command (which resembles the Staff Branch in the High Command, a post I was to fill in later years). Lots of meetings, lots of discussions, lots of paperwork, lots of thought – and my brain working overtime. All these did nothing to diminish my desire to remain in close contact with the units in their bases. I would visit the squadrons and take up a plane to prove that I hadn't forgotten how. I wanted to spend time in the company of the the pilots during their recreation evenings, to listen to their views and their problems. I wanted them to have the feeling that someone out there was listening to them and passing on what he heard to the air command staff. Throughout my years as head of Air Branch, and later as commander of the air force, I regarded the role of connecting link between the senior command and the operational commanders as a matter of the greatest importance.

While serving at air force command, my access to accurate intelligence reports of Arab re-armament, and especially of Egypt's growing strength, as well as analyses of Arab opinion, strengthened my assumption that the 1956 war was not the last, and that further rounds were to be expected. I assumed the Arabs would not let us live in this region, but would make repeated attempts to wipe out the shame of their losses and defeats.

Even though the plight of the Palestinian Arabs did not cause the Arab rulers to lose any sleep, and it was no more than so much political propaganda for them, they still had good reason to dream of another war against Israel. Israel's victories in 1948 and 1956 (and later the greatest victory, in 1967) humiliated them, delivering a mighty blow to their national image. The entire international press praised the Israelis, so few in number but so clever, thereby rubbing salt into the wounds of the Arabs, who were represented as numerous but backward. Hence their dilemma: there are tens of millions of Egyptians and Syrians, Iraqis and Jordanians, Saudis and Kuwaitis, Libyans and Tunisians, Moroccans, Abu-Dhabis and Algerians. They have inexhaustable stocks of oil, vitally needed by the Western world. They control international waterways, indispensable for international commerce and shipping. And two and a half million Jews, in an impoverished state, without any oil and scarcely enough water to irrigate their fields, have been shafting them and beating them repeatedly, putting them to shame in the eyes of the whole world.

To the Arab, this state of affairs must seem like a passing episode, a temporary aberration of history. We have adopted the view that the Arabs are mystics, while our strength stems from our rationalism. But an objective consideration of the circumstances and the numerical proportions reverses the picture: it's we who are the mystics, and the Arabs are rational realists. We claim that, despite everything, three million Jews will withstand 100 million Arabs. They believe that, in the long run, their enormous numbers and their fabulous wealth will give them the advantage. 'To win,' they reason 'we don't have to be as good as the Jews on the battlefield. It's quite sufficient to be a lot worse than they are for our quantities will overcome their qualitative superiority. The Jews have tensed their muscles as far as they will go. Now we'll press forward – not to draw level with them, but just to reduce the gap between us. That will suffice to beat them and wipe out disgrace.'

This powerful motivation, combined with the excellent weapons and political backing of the Soviet Union, their flirtations with Europe and, to some extent, with the United States, have produced the Arab belief that the wheel will ultimately spin in their direction, even if they have to wait for a fourth, fifth or sixth round.

It was under this cloud that I lived and worked. It was not a pleasant outlook. It demanded a sober view and an avoidance of illusions. It required the construction of an enormous force, which would ensure our security despite everything. And it cried out, again and again, to retrieve Zionism from the corner where it had been flung and restore it to its previous status as the driving force of everything we do in this country. This is what had guided me as a pilot, as a squadron commander, as a wing commander, as head of Air Branch, as commander of the air force, as head of the General Staff Division, and as a minister in the Israeli cabinet.

When I commanded the air force, I would address my subordinates in metaphoric terms: 'Imagine that you're Arabs, living on the hills, facing the Mediterranean. What do you see? The State of Israel doing a strip-tease, that's what you see. A strip-tease! Green, flourishing, prosperous, twinkling at night with a mass of lights. And whatever the Arab eye doesn't see, his imagination invents. Now, you know what happens to a healthy man when he watches a rousing strip-tease act. Right, that's exactly what happens to him! Therefore, there won't be any choice. The Arab will have to be moved away from Israel's naked borders. It's the only way of knocking these exciting ideas of a masculine conquest of Israel out of his head!'

In more prosaic terms, the Arab burns with hatred, he is consumed by envy. He cultivates his illusions of possession: this was Kakon, this was Aksil, here was Jaba, there Ain Razal and there Sumal! It's all mine! But what do I have in their place? Refugee camps and poverty; a dog's life and national disgrace! It's wrong. Not just morally wrong. It's wrong because there's no reason why it has to go on! Because we Arabs are a great people, and they, the Jews, are a small people; we're rich and they're poor; we have oil and they have sand; because time is on our side, because they are a passing episode, like the Crusaders, and we are masters of this region, which will spew out any alien!

All this isn't attractive. I love people, and I've never hated the Arabs. But instead of building and developing and living in peace, the Jew is forced to learn to kill more Arabs in less time. This prospect depressed me and saddened me, no less than the 'professional peace-mongers'. But I knew there was no way out. I knew there would be another confrontation, and it still wouldn't be the last.

In the wake of the Sinai Campaign, during the early days of my service as head of the Air Branch, we were still living under the delusions of a 'Great Israeli Kingdom', as Ben Gurion used to call it. A week after my appointment, I took Re'uma for a flight in a Piper over the Sinai Desert. Suddenly, our vistas broadened: we flew on and on and on, and there was no end to it. Below, we saw the sights that later became the hallmarks of the Six Day War: columns of burnt-out wrecks, which only a short time earlier were the pride of the Egyptian army. Aside from the exhilarating spirit it typified, the 'Great Kingdom' also had a practical significance for the air force, which was supposed to operate the airfield at El Arish (a town that had a special place in the hearts of those who had fought in the War of Independence, when our air force bombed it and the ground forces reached its gates before being ordered to pull back). This time, too, those who were making plans for El Arish had no luck. After a stiff political struggle, talk of an 'Israeli Kingdom' ceased; instead, we packed up and pulled back from everything we had captured.

I suppose I was as indignant as anyone else at the time, and I, too, protested against our withdrawal from the Sinai. But now, from a more distant perspective, it is impossible to overlook Israel's not-so-splendid isolation. Withdrawal was forced upon her by irresistable political pressures – above all, by the Soviet-American alliance against Israel. England forfeited all influence, and Anthony Eden had to pay with his political career for what appeared to his countrymen as a pointless adventure. France was shaking with fear of Soviet threats, later to be revealed as empty but which seemed real enough at the time. Abandoned and threatened – even by America – Israel was not left with many options. The shock of being isolated in a hostile world recurred on the eve of the Six Day War. Some of the doubts and hesitations of the stand-by period of May 1967 stemmed from the fear that, once again, we'd shed our blood, and once again, we'd be forced to withdraw.

Our withdrawal in 1957 was accompanied by a mood of depression. Characteristically, the chief of staff, Moshe Dayan, left El Arish in the last half-track. It was the last point we held in Sinai, although we occupied Gaza for a little while longer. I offered to fly Moshe to El Arish, where he would join the retreating Israeli forces. On the way, he asked me to circle over one or two sites that he had marked out for archaeological digs. When we landed at El Arish, the town itself had already been vacated. The sight was grim. A heavy silence. The Israeli troops had assembled into a column of fifteen half-tracks. You could have cut the silence with a knife. I have seen soldiers with grins of victory on their faces; I have seen them in the pain of defeat; but this was neither. Their faces showed the gloom of uncertainty, of questions: Why? Is this going to do any good? Is it bad? Was there any alternative?

The soldiers stood there by the half-tracks, sour-faced, in full battle-kit, ready to move off. Anyone who knows Moshe's face when he's angry could see that he was burning with fury. I asked him to return with me in the Piper. He refused, but he permitted me a farewell flight over El Arish, although UN troops had already entered the town. Some evil instinct made me fly very low, between the palm trees, zooming over houses and courtyards, with a terrible anger in my heart. I almost shouted, 'We'll be back! Remember, we'll be back!' It was what I felt, without knowing exactly why.

I turned the Piper round and headed back to 'the cage': to a small Israel without any open spaces, where one has to land soon after taking off, where one is strictly bound to constant caution: Stop, Border Ahead. No Transit. Border!

And inside that beloved 'cage', there were heavy apprehensions. With France torn and divided, paying the heavy price of democracy as her governments rose and fell with breathtaking speed, could she maintain her special relationship with Israel and continue to supply the Israeli air force with planes? After getting her fingers burnt in the Sinai Campaign, would she change her policy? It soon became clear that there was nothing to worry about. Up to 1967 at least, France remained a loyal friend of Israel. The especially close links between the two armies led me to believe that the French army felt it had been covered with shame and its plans put to nought only because of the French politicians and their hesitations. I, for one, didn't agree with this concept – at least not then. I regarded the military command, the political leadership and the economic system as inter-connected, each affecting the others and being affected by them. Today, too, I reject the theory of 'a victorious army and a defeated government'. The inter-relationships of military and civilian leaderships make them partners in victories and defeats.

The Sinai Campaign taught us another lesson, which I have done my best to pass on both inside and outside the air force. In Israel's wars, the factors of time and speed are of critical importance. Probably more than any other people or any other army, we have to fight with a stop-watch in our hands, for our chances of a decisive victory diminish as the hours tick by. There are two inter-connected aspects to this time factor. A small people has only limited breathing space. Our standing army is small, and war requires mass mobilization of our reserves, which paralyzes the whole economy. A long war means a lot of casualties and heavy bloodshed; it also means that a lot of *matériel* is used up, emptying our stocks. (One of the serious causes of our present political weakness, which has exposed us to possible US pressures, was our urgent SOS to America during the Yom Kippur War. The American airlift to Israel was essential for the conduct of the war, and as such, spelt salvation for Israel. But the political bill was not long in following their supplies.)

Time is critical for another reason. The world can't quite stomach a triumphant Israel. This was evident not only in 1956, but has been proven repeatedly thereafter. In the Six Day War, when the Soviet Union grasped the dimensions of the Arab defeat, she moved heaven and earth to obtain a cease-fire. But then it was a bit too late; with the Arab armies out of action and Israel occupying territory, the defeat was great, though not total. The Yom Kippur War, was prolonged beyond Israeli expectations because of governmental errors, lack of military preparation and surprise, allowing the Russians plenty of time to watch the progress of the battle. When the balance tilted in Israel's favour – with our foothold on the western bank of the Suez Canal, the encirclement of the Third Army and of the city of Suez, the threat to the Ismailia–Cairo road and the possibility of the Second Army also facing encirclement – the Soviet Union issued its threats of massive military intervention and summoned Henry Kissinger to the Kremlin. With America approving the cessation of hostility before a decisive victory could be reached and exercising pressure by conveying the Russian threats, Israel's political hour-glass ran out.

That is the tragic meaning of a 'stop-watch war'. As long as Israel is under pressure and the Arabs appear to be in a promising position, the hands move slowly, as though the Arabs have all the time in the world to strike their blows at Israel and shed its blood. But the moment the experts in the Kremlin see the scales tilting in Israel's favour, the hour-hand begins to twirl rapidly, as if to make up for the delay of the early days of the war. The outcome: Israel can only lose. The world doesn't allow her to win.

It is exactly because of the inter-play of these really unique factors – time pressures and the political limitations of Israeli diplomacy – that our army has never been ignorant of our country's political problems. On the contrary, we were well up on them and much involved in discussing them.

The ten years between the Sinai Campaign and the Six Day War were of the greatest importance for our air force's development. The Super-Mystères, the Voutoures and the Mirages purchased during those years became our first-line planes. The great victory of the Israeli air force in the Six Day War was achieved with combat planes of exclusively French manufacture. Shimon Peres, then director-general of the Defence Ministry, deserves every praise for his success in strengthening our military ties with France.

He displayed a definite French orientation. When some people said that we should put our faith in the Americans and gain a foothold in their arms market, Peres would answer: 'By all means! Does anyone have any bright idea how to do it? Does it depend on us?' When Shimon left the Defence Ministry, I was commander of the air force. As a farewell gift, I gave him small silver models of our planes and wrote: 'To Shimon, who turned our air force from a bird into an eagle.' (Peres, in Hebrew, means 'eagle'.) His contribution to the growth and strengthening of the air force was truly enormous.

The best and most advanced plane we purchased from the French was, of course, the Mirage. It is an excellent plane to this day, even though we have since acquired American Phantoms. Shortly after the Sinai Campaign, in the summer of 1957, we had our first opportunity to feast our eyes on a model of the Mirage, which was brought to Israel by Serge, the son of Marcel Dassault, the owner of the airplane factory. They reported that the plane was still in its preliminary planning stages, but set our imaginations afire: the Mirage would fly at Mach-2. No wonder we didn't rest until we saw this wonderful plane in the service of the Israeli air force, streaking across the sky at its demented speed.

The open French market and the opportunities of buying new planes made us step up the replacement of planes by withdrawing the old ones from service and buying new ones, as far as our perennial shortage of money permitted. We planned to remove the last of the piston planes. The Spits had gone earlier; now it was the turn of the Mosquitoes, the B-17s and the Mustangs. And so, as far as combat planes went, the air force decided to 'go jet', in the full sense of the term: Meteors, Ouragans, Mystères, Super-Mystères, Votoures and Mirages. Eventually, with the arrival of the Phantoms and Skyhawks, American aircraft began to replace the French planes.

The Votoures were delivered under conditions of complete secrecy: because of international political complications, the French did not want it known that we had been supplied with the bombers. The planes were stored in secret hangars for six months, before they were brought out for display on air-force day in July 1958, two weeks after I took over command of the air force.

The knowledge that we would always be in a position of numerical inferiority vis-à-vis our enemies' air forces forced us to develop ways of exploiting our planes to the utmost. This, too, is a sphere in which the Israeli air force has achieved astounding successes. The operational capacity of our planes has been extended by shortening the time between sorties. Speeding up turn-round demands a number of fundamental conditions: skilled and devoted ground-crews, who refuel and re-arm the plane at record speeds, as well as repair any faults that can be put right quickly without need of repair hangars or factories; additional pilots, over and above the number of planes, so that a crew can be replaced when it is tired or when there are casualties.

The great time and expense needed to train a jet pilot altered the length of service in the air force. Previously, we used to think that signing on for five years would solve the problem. Even that made it difficult to find volunteers. Now, five years were no longer enough. I expounded the notion that the air force was a way of life, which a man should choose for far longer periods, so that we could make full use of him. The number of volunteers was not always sufficient, and we were sometimes tempted to reduce our demands and make do with a little less, so as to acquire more pilots. But we fought that temptation and overcame it. Matters reached their low point when I once pinned pilot's wings on a single cadet, the only one who successfully completed the course. It was sad and kind of ridiculous to hold a passing-out parade for one solitary pilot, so I invited him to my office, where I pinned the insignia on him. Even he did not show any joy, though he was the first cadet in the history of the Israeli air force to receive his wings in the office of the air force commander, who joined him in celebrating the event with a glass of cognac.

While I was totally immersed in planning and thinking and co-ordinating the branches of air-force command, trying to foresee the innovations of the new era and how to prepare for them, there was another worry at the back of my mind: Dan Tolkovski's retirement was approaching. Evil tongues reported that Ben-Gurion did not want him any more and that Peres would not be unduly sorry if he went. I remained strictly loyal to him, but the possibility that he would shortly be leaving brought me to a high pitch of tension. Would I be his replacement or would it be someone else?

I have always found it difficult, if not impossible, to be loyal to a man I don't respect – whether as a man, a commander, or a leader. I respected Dan Tolkovski and considered him suitable for his position, which made it easier for me to accept his authority and act loyally towards him. I was loyal, but not subservient. A man of independent thought, who has confidence in his personal contribution, cannot content himself with 'Yes, sir!' and receiving instructions from whoever is above him in the chain of command. In developing my ability to think in an organized manner, I learned more from Dan in the eighteen months I served under him than I did even at the British staff college. It was a pleasure to hear Dan conduct a discussion. He is tops as far as clear methodical thinking is concerned; he knew how to present a subject and analyze it, to take all the facts, evaluations and considerations and lay them on the scales in a manner that always aroused my admiration.

Dan was supposed to recommend his successor, and much depended on his recommendation. He had good reason to propose me, but he also had good reason not to. Our characters were so unlike that arguments and misunderstandings were unavoidable. Meanwhile, people were spreading various rumours: Weizman in, Weizman out. Full of doubts, I wasn't far from accepting the appointment of someone else, if that should be the case, as long as the suspense could be over! Then Dan called me to his office, and, in his own special way, though possibly unintentionally, he proceeded to crucify me slowly, with utter Tolkovski thoroughness. As he is shy by nature, he was slightly embarrassed. He honoured me with a long address about the air force and the need for continuity, and he didn't fix his eyes on me, but glanced about, up and down. I grew more and more convinced that the lecture would end with something like: 'Ezer, you're not ripe for it yet'. As he went on and on, I began to fear that I wouldn't have the strength to hold out to the end.

Although it seemed like hours, an objective check later convinced me that no more than three and a half minutes had passed from the moment Dan began his speech up to the moment when he concluded it with the words: 'I have therefore decided to recommend you to replace me.' What should I say? That I was in a state of rapture? Heaven doesn't know such rapture.

But one has to know Chaim Laskov to understand that Dan's speech was nothing compared with what awaited me from Laskov, when I was summoned to him. I entered and saluted, my body tense and my soul even more so. Now it was Chaim's turn to orate. 'I have considered and re-considered, I've had lots of hesitations. I did a written evaluation. I wrote pages upon pages about your traits and those of another candidate.' (He'll talk the life out of me I know. I'll leave this room on a stretcher, straight to hospital. The pistons in my heart were working overtime, at a crazy pace.) 'After all my hesitation' (get it out, for God's sake!) 'I've decided to appoint you commander of the air force.'

Joy. Pride. Satisfaction. There's nothing wrong in feeling all that. In the army, promotion and receiving a command are, quite naturally, regarded as signs of success. But I had to remain within bounds; to take my success and get over it; not permit it to pull things out of proportion; not to float in the clouds; not to stick my nose up in the air; not to push my chest out; to remain faithful to my duties and friends. At that time, promotion was far more significant than it is nowadays. There was a curtain of secrecy over the army, and very little got through to the public. Attaining command of the air force stripped you of your anonymity; you became well known and found yourself at the focus of public interest.

A phone call home, and the sweet words: 'Re'uma, I'm in!' Ever since we had made each other's acquaintance, she had been totally involved in the air force; she knew all about the doubts and uncertainties and mental torments. She, too, had been preparing herself to swallow the disappointment, if I were to be passed over for the command.

At air force command, some of the officers were pleased, others less so, and there were those who must have been worried. Then, as now, I had a loose tongue, and it was an open secret who enjoyed my esteem and who did not, who could regard my appointment as a good opportunity for advancement and who could do well to think of a new career.

Doubts. Fears. Apprehensions. Suddenly I found myself in an enormous pair of shoes. I had always been sure that they would be a perfect fit, that they were just made for me; and if, heaven forbid, someone else were to try them on, they'd be far too big. But now that they were on me, suddenly I began to measure them; here and there, they squeezed my feet, and I wondered what to do – loosen the laces? I had just been handed control of the most important section of the Israeli armed forces; the responsibility was a tremendous burden, and I stooped under the load. It was surprising, because I had never felt like this, the weight had never been so heavy, never had so much depended on me. I added up my pride and joy, my satisfaction and exhilaration, my confidence and the consciousness of my new burden, together with the plans, long in my mind, whose time had come; and when I totalled it all up, I got a kind of overwhelming passion to build an air force that would be something quite out of the ordinary, the crowning glory of Jewish aptitude, talent, persistence and the determination to hold on to this country, with our very fingernails, if need be, never letting go.

10

AIR FORCE COMMANDER

THE CEREMONY for the transfer of command, on 25 July 1958, was stamped with Dan's seal: calm, quiet, solid, free of any exhibitionism, rounded off that evening by a party. Early next morning, it was the great day of my loyal driver, Avraham, who came to collect me from home and bring me to the air force command, making no effort to conceal his glee. He attached the little blue-and-white ensign to the front of the car: he was driving the commander of the air force, and no one was going to deprive him of the accompanying pleasure. Ever since, I have comprehended what the ensigns are for: they were designed for the gratification of drivers, much more than the ostentation of senior officers.

During my early days as air force commander, I was still a little excited. I derived pleasure from the compliments and expressions of confidence in me. The first appointments were my aide-de-camp and my secretary. These would be my closest assistants, and I would be exposed to their inspection; they would witness all my doubts and weaknesses. I intended to be very particular in choosing them. They would soon discover what a powerful position they had, close to my ear. When that time came, I would be wise to replace them.

All kinds of ideas, thoughts, plans and solutions spun during various periods of my service now began to weave themselves into a single fabric. The foremost of all these thoughts was filling hearts and minds with the need to build a victorious air force. I never once used the term deterrent force. If you build a victorious air force, you have given the senior political echelons, who are empowered to make the final decisions, a tremendous weapon. They can apply it to whatever national objective they find fit: deterring the enemy from instigating war; overcoming the enemy and destroying him, if the deterrent fails; or instigating an attack on the enemy, to forestall the danger of war, to disrupt his movements and to help the ground forces in their tasks. But effectively attaining any one of these objectives, or a simultaneous combination of two or more, is feasible only if it is a victorious air force, one of great power, whose men possess a burning faith and are confident of their strength and their superiority and *know* what they're fighting for.

In all my posts in the air force, I cultivated freedom of expression. I disliked officers who tried to find a short cut to promotion through blind agreement with my opinions. I've never liked yes-men. What the air force needs is an officer who thinks, who has his own way of analyzing issues and uses it openly. I was certain that we could be the dominant air force in the region, despite growing Arab strength, but I never thought my certainty obliged everyone to accept my view without argument. I welcomed confrontation with those who disagreed with me – a genuine confrontation, honest and open, allowing both my opponents and myself an equal opportunity of proving our views.

During 'commander's evenings' I would encourage pilots and officers to disagree with me. At one such evening a fellow got up and gave me a dressing-down: 'You underrate the enemy. You over-estimate our strength and underestimate that of the Arabs. You do it to fill us with fighting spirit and a sense of confidence. In 1948 the Arabs may have been stupid. In 1956 the British and French fought for us. But the Arabs have made progress. Their Migs are excellent planes. Their pilots do their training in the Soviet Union. Nasser is a great leader, who is restoring their fighting spirit. We have to see the facts as they are and not cultivate illusions.'

His words were far from pleasing to the ear. 'Not a harsh word!' I told myself; I had asked for frankness and I got it! Uprooting the fears from men's hearts and replacing them with faith and confidence in their own ability was very hard when those fears were backed by reality: a small people, with a small air force, the eternal numerical inferiority in planes; tens of millions of Arabs supported by a Great Power, the Soviet Union; modern planes and missiles. Those who disagreed with my assumptions could always prove that in our eagerness to establish a victorious air force, we had strayed from reality, had let our minds grow hazy, had lost our ability to see things as they really were. In trying to prove that I was right, I couldn't simply brush off the facts. I always had to start with 'Nevertheless ...' and go on to express my eternal, unchanging faith that Israeli youth possessed spiritual powers with which no Mig 17 or Mig 19, or any other weapon of war, could contend.

But faith was not sufficient for an air force commander. I also had to be sure that I had the best men serving the force in their various fields. One of my first steps upon taking command was unpopular: I replaced the chief air intelligence officer. There was nothing personal in my decision. After analyzing his reports, I came to the conclusion that he did not understand the Egyptians, and he was too prone to relate to quantity rather than quality. I definitely did not want an intelligence officer who provided evaluations and analyses that corroborated my assumptions. There's always the danger that the men around you may try to please you by agreeing with your ways and views. It's easy to get false evaluations, including suitable 'facts', not because the man presenting them believes in them, but because they fit the views he knows you to hold and you're his superior. That's not what I wanted.

However, in the same ways, I could not overlook the perverse viewpoint of my intelligence officer. In our arguments he would say: 'The difference between you and me is that *you* are indulging in wishful thinking, while I am supplying you with facts!' I answered: 'You give me the facts, but you don't analyse them correctly. You tell me that the Egyptian pilot (and there are such-and-such number of Egyptian pilots) flies such-and-such number of hours in his plane (and there are such-and-such number of Egyptian planes), which leads you to the conclusion that this represents such-and-such an amount of strength and such-and-such superiority over our forces. But your equation needs thought and analysis. What does the Egyptian pilot do during those hours of flying? Are they effective hours? Is he really learning and making progress? A correct evaluation of an air force isn't just knowing how many planes it has, and what type, and how many pilots have been trained to fly them. You must add further factors to your equation: the pilot's aptitudes, his morale, his motivation, his character; the abilities of his officers, the tactical and strategic notions of his commanders. That is the sum total of its strength, and not dry figures.'

Naturally, one of the principal concerns of the air-force commander is the acquisition not only of good men, but of new planes. Unlike his fortunate opposite numbers in other air forces, the Israeli commander cannot plan his requirements without considering his country's political circumstances. For ten years we were trapped inside the French market, unable to get into others. We bought French planes not out of choice, but because of the force of circumstances. All the same, our luck held; the French aircraft industry was excellent and provided us with first-class planes. So good were the French planes, and so well did they fit into our air force, that if I had the choice today, with additional markets open to us, I would again prefer to buy French aircraft.

When an air force commander is shown a new plane, whether it is already on the production line or only in the planning stage, he is overcome with doubts and uncertainties. On the one hand, he is tempted to recommend its purchase, for he wants to strengthen his force and improve its aircraft. On the other hand, he hesitates, fully aware of his country's poverty and its meagre resources. He is afraid that deciding to buy the plane could create a *fait accompli*, which will be an obstacle if new markets open up later.

If I were asked to point to one single act that I regard as my crowning achievement in the air force – in addition to teaching our pilots to believe in Zionism, our strength and our unassailable rights – I'd say the integration of the Mirage into the Israeli air force. The Mirage was an ultra-modern plane, and not only us, but even its French designers, had no previous experience in its use. The truth is that in approaching the plane, we had to overcome a barrier of fear – fear of the unknown. It was a delta-shaped plane, without flaps or tail. Its speed was Mach-2, and it featured various innovations. From this point of view, our air force's transition from Mystères and Votoures to the trail-blazing Mirage had a greater significance than the later entry of the Phantom.

I was shown the first prototype Mirage as far back as 1957. Dan Tolkovski knew that it would fall to me to buy the plane and bring it into service. Aside from political alliance, the French were also guided by simple commercial considerations. Israel was a good market for French planes. Before the Sinai Campaign the French planes were unknown, and world markets were closed to them. The campaign made them famous. The French naturally regarded our air force as a kind of recommendation for their planes, and they assumed that if we bought Mirages, it would pave their way to other air forces.

I first saw a completed Mirage at the French air salon in 1959. I travelled to France before the end of my first year as air force commander, accompanied by Motty Hod, who was then a colonel, and by Danny Shapira, who had just completed a test-pilots' course. The new plane's appearance was attractive, and we had a private 'rule': an attractive plane must be a good plane. (The converse of this rule is that an ugly plane must be a poor plane, but that assumption was smashed to smithereens when we encountered the Phantom, which is far from handsome but a wonderful plane.)

We stood transfixed, on the Villa Coablais airfield, while Danny Shapira took the new 'bird' up to 38,000 feet. A radar check showed that Danny was the twelfth pilot in France to exceed Mach-2, which earned him a golden Mirage tie-pin. Aside from a few sample planes, the French air force was not then (1959) equipped with Mirages. With the Mystères, the Super-Mystères and the Mirage, the French and Israeli air forces received delivery of the planes simultaneously.

On the strength of French recommendations and of our own impressions, we decided to purchase the Mirages, which had the traits we required. We were fully aware that our air force would have to be based on a mixture of expensive and cheap planes, because of Israel's limited financial resources. (Nowadays, the mixture consists of the costly Phantoms and the less-costly Skyhawks.) The idea was that the faster, dearer planes were intended for air combat and interception, while the slower and cheaper planes were for attack and bombing.

In addition to endless frustrations in adjusting the Mirage's cannon, the new plane gave us a bellyful of troubles at first. There were engine failures, and several fellows were forced to abandon their planes in mid-air and bail out. The first of these was Reuven Harel, and the circumstances illustrate that, where aircraft are concerned, there is a fine dividing-line between life and death, or, if you will, between laughter and tears, with the line zigzagging like crazy. I was in the air over Haifa in an Alouette helicopter, with Shimon Peres, when I was informed, in a coded radio message, that somebody had jumped from a Mirage. Within a few moments, we landed at Ramat David. It ranspired that Reuven's engine had stopped. He desperately wanted to save the Mirage, and he tried with all his skill to get it onto the Ramat David runway, but he soon discovered that his attempt would fail. At an altitude of 300 feet – which is extremely low – he bailed out, and the plane crashed near the camp's main entrance. Of what was, a few moments earlier, a magnificent weapon of war, there was nothing left except some burnt-out wreckage, scattered in all directions; but Reuven was saved. A few moments after Reuven had unstrapped himself from his parachute, his wife returned from a shopping expedition in a nearby town. Near the gateway, she identified the wreckage of a plane, which she knew to have been a Mirage. Overcoming her terror as best as she could, she asked the sentry on duty: 'Who's the pilot?'

'Somebody by the name of Reuven Harel.'

He obliged her with the details, but she didn't hear the end of the sentence, '. . . he jumped at the last moment, he's alright.'

When she came round, Reuven was standing there, alive and well, stroking her hand.

There was one miracle, an utterly incredible tale; for believers, it must seem like the hand of God. Ran Pakker was flying back from a photographic reconnaissance mission over Port Said, piloting his Mirage masterfully. In the vicinity of Hazor, his engine packed in, due to a fault in one of its pumps. (This was a recurrent fault, which robbed us of three or four costly Mirages before we succeeded in overcoming it.) There was nothing for Ran to do but save himself. To make it easier to jump, Ran straightened out the plane, put it into a gliding position, bade it a sorrowful farewell and bailed out.

The plane glided down until it reached a ploughed field, where it slid along the furrows on its belly, as though it had been there before. To the best of my knowledge, this was the only case, in any air force, of a Mirage landing and coming to a halt without anyone climbing out of the cockpit. True, the creature was not over-careful in landing and didn't even trouble to lower its wheels, so that we had to spend half a million dollars on repairs, but it wasn't long before the 'pilotless plane' took off once more. I sent Ran a poem I had written for him, about how, by virtue of the pilot's strong spirit, the plane comes down in its appointed place, even without him.

At that time, one Mirage cost one and a half million dollars. When I spoke of buying 100 Mirages, that involved an expenditure of 200 million dollars (including spares and other appliances). Even within the air force, some officers whose opinions carried weight felt that I was going too far. There was a school of thought, with many adherents in the General Staff, which held that we should buy a larger number of cheap planes and fewer expensive ones. In any case, they said, the Mirage will fly at low altitudes, where its speed doesn't approach Mach-2. It would be better, therefore, for the air force to spend less money on more planes. They went so far in proving the 'correctness' of this theory, that in 1960 there were some who even suggested returning to the B-26 piston planes, which were slow and possessed high carrying capacity and which could be bought in considerable quantitites at bargain prices. A large number of such fantasticaly cheap planes, with the addition of a small number of Mirage interceptors to protect Israel's skies, was all they felt the air force needed.

This idea was very attractive to the sensitive ears of ground commanders, who are always an absolute majority at General Staff. The arrogance of those over-inflated 'laddies' from the air force irritated many of the ground commanders, who would often say: 'All the money goes on planes, and there's nothing left for other needs. Who do they think they are, those big-heads?' For them the air force was a distasteful necessity. They wished they could do without it, but if that was impossible, it should at least be kept on a tight leash, receiving only essentials, so that some of the cake would be left over for tanks and guns.

There was a kind of alliance between those inside the air force, who simply misunderstood, and those outside the force, who backed up their own arguments by citing divergent air force opinions. Officers from the General Staff and Defence Ministry officials quoted an air force major and a colonel as saying that my demands were exaggerated. These two officers erred and misled others. I was sure of it, but they were cited as proof that not even the whole air force thought like Weizman, indicating that he wasn't necessarily right.

In short, I argued, explained, shouted, begged, submitted proof. No good. I was prepared to come down to ninety planes, but the decision was to buy no more than twenty-four Mirages. It was a blow made all the worse by the irritating comment that accompanied it: 'First of all, let's see how you cope with these'.

We only broke through the 'two-dozen barrier' when Zvi Zur ('Chera') became chief of staff in January 1961. His period as chief of staff was colourless and tranquil. The glamorous chiefs of staff, whose names shine in letters of fire on the pages of our short history, are the ones who led the army to war. That's natural. But Chera's was also an important period, which saw the armed forces considerably strengthened, and not just the air force. This was the period when the first of the British Centurion tanks were delivered. Chera and Shimon Peres established close cooperation, which led to our Mirage force being quadrupled. A force of Nord transport planes was built up, anti-aircraft defences were strengthened, and the construction of a new airfield was finally approved, after long and stormy arguments with previous chiefs of staff. Thus, we gained a strong Mirage force. Even though the French engine was weaker than its American, British or Russian counterparts, we made enormous use of the plane, and its service in the Israeli air force turned the Mirage into a magic word for many other air forces.

At the same time – in effect, up to the Six Day war and again after the 1973 war – there were considerable doubts and uncertainties about our ability to face the Arabs' growing strength and their powerful anti-aircraft systems. There were even parts of the air force that fell prey to these doubts, and they were doubly strong outside the force. There were times when I felt the sceptics were positively hunting for proof that the balance was tilting in the Arabs' favour. One of their arguments was that the Egyptians' war against the monarchists in Yemen would give their pilots experience, which they would use against us. I replied that their experience in Yemen would be an obstacle to the Egyptians if they tried to apply its lessons against us. The conditions in Yemen were quite different from those the Egyptians would have to face in fighting us, and, needless to say, we would conduct the war in a different manner. Besides, even if the quantitative gap widened between the Egyptians and us, the quality of the Israeli air force's pilots and commanders would decide the fate of the war.

Not everyone was convinced. Gnawing doubts sometimes show such persistence that only deeds can overcome them, not words. War, with its great feats, smashes them, but peacetime, with the absence of proof to the contrary, permits them to grow and flourish. There are times when an air force commander who has a profound belief in his force is obliged to produce such proof in order to fortify his arguments.

One day in October 1958, we downed a Mig 17, while a second one fled for his life. Everybody was in a dreadful state of tension. It was the first Mig 17 we had shot down. At six that evening, I was summoned to the office of Chief of Staff Chaim Laskov. Uzi Narkiss, assistant head of military intelligence, was also present. I told them about the Migs penetrating our airspace and our pursuit. I didn't have an easy time with my 'boss', and when he said 'We're going to Ben-Gurion', black clouds appeared on my horizons. On the way I tried to guess Ben-Gurion's reaction, while Chaim only uttered a few short sentences. 'What will the Russians say? What will the Americans say?'

'Alright Weizman,' I told myself, 'it could be that in the short annals of the Israeli armed forces, it will be noted that you were in command of the air force for four or five months, and it was nice knowing you . . .'

At Ben-Gurion's Tel Aviv home, we found him in a good mood. I felt my chances slightly improving. 'Weizman,' he said sharply, 'a battle? What battle, where?' Chaim was silently furious. I unrolled the map on the table and waved my finger: around here. He looked closely and said: '*Nu*, people will be very pleased.' He added a few more words, but no hint of reproof. When we left the 'old man', Chaim had got over his anger and was already planning: Israel radio, army radio, the press. That night, at ten, the pilots were interviewed and the stories flowed.

A small lesson: superiority is superiority. A little clash like that, with that kind of outcome, produces more confidence than thousands of words. We *can* do things, but we have to be very cautious and not overdo matters.

Aside from my larger battles to acquire planes and to inspire everyone with my confidence, there was one internal battle that I had to wage from the day I was appointed to my command: the battle for a certain degree of independence for the air force. I had to fight off repeated attempts to clip its wings and make it a subordinate branch of the General Staff, lacking any hallmarks of independence. I was afraid of this. Not that I despised the other sections of the armed forces, nor was it a matter of prestige, but I was convinced that the air force had its own special spirit, which would be dissipated and diluted in a larger framework, making it lose its *élan*.

For years there was a widespread trend among heads of the armed forces that ran more or less like this: 'All air force men have to do is kill the enemy and shoot down his planes. We'll see to all the rest. We'll get your planes ready, we'll see to it that all their systems are combat-ready, we'll arm them, we'll lead them with everything required for battle and we'll supply your food and all your needs.'

This battle reached one of its peaks when we transferred air-force command from Ramle to the centre of government offices in Tel Aviv, the Kiryah. Those who had been waiting for an opportunity swooped down with cries of 'the time has come to bring those anarchists into the regular army set-up! An end to the autonomy they enjoyed at Ramle! Why should they be any different from the other sections of the armed forces? Don't they belong to the Israel Defence Forces?'

'Of course we do!' I replied. 'But you won't turn the air force into a branch of the General Staff. Air force command is an aerial general staff, precisely as the General Staff is the headquarters of the ground forces. Of course, the air force is subordinate to the General

Staff and to its over-all instructions, but it isn't just one more of its branches.'

What a battle there was over building a fence round air force command, and over a separate air force ensign fluttering above its command, not to speak of a sentry-box and a guard at the gate! These were external trappings, trifling in themselves, but they expressed our distinctiveness and our independence. Moshe Goren, then head of the Quartermaster's Branch of General Staff, was truly shocked: 'Weizman,' he said fervidly, 'Believe me, you've gone out of your mind! Truly! What is this – a fence inside a fence?' There *was* a fence inside a fence, and on the day in April 1959 that air command took up its new quarters, six Mystères in perfect formation flew over the Kiryah, to show that the air force had arrived.

As part of this fight for independence and distinctiveness, I insisted that air force officers were not to be interviewed by the head of the Manpower Branch of the General Staff administration officer. 'My dear friends,' I contended, 'for this purpose – talks with officers and planning their stages of advancement – I am the General Staff of all those serving in the air force.' Arguments, opposition, accusations, but it went over. Of course, every man in the air force retained the right to ask for an interview with the head of the Manpower Branch, or the chief of staff, but very few made use of this right.

What disturbed my rest was not only the logistic argument (will I get fifteen vehicles to carry bombs to the planes, or will they give priority to an infantry brigade or armour unit?), but above all the big problem was one of aerial operations. I always had the feeling that the General Staff did not correctly evaluate the air force's role in future wars and did not understand that a strong air force could decide the battle.

A misunderstanding of the forms of aerial combat aroused one of the most bitter arguments ever between the air force and other sections of the armed forces. While we were trying to prove by all available means that any non-offensive employment of the air force was a grave danger to us, President Kennedy stirred up a tremendous argument in Israel by agreeing to sell us Hawk ground-to-air missiles. This was in the years 1960–1, when Ben-

Gurion was defence minister and Zvi Zur chief of staff. As commander of the air force, I hadn't the faintest intention of underrating the value of the president's decision. The first time that an American president decided to sell arms to Israel was, without doubt, a breakthrough of the first magnitude. Our entry into the sphere of highly sophisticated weaponry was an additional reason for welcoming the decision. Furthermore, at that time the Hawk was an excellent defensive weapon. In short, it was a great day for Israel.

But while I didn't underrate President Kennedy's decision, I did not join in the rejoicing. I was apprehensive, and my apprehensions lay in two mutually complementary areas. The contention that Israel was now protected from air attack would be advanced by critics of our whole concept of an aerial first strike. Even without such a move – which, in their view, was both dangerous and uncertain – enemy planes would be handicapped in their ability to strike at Israeli territory, because of the Hawk batteries. I feared that at the critical moment, when the senior executive echelons had to approve an offensive strike by the air force, Israel's possession of Hawk missiles could impede a swift and positive decision. On another level, I also knew that President Kennedy's generosity would cost Israel a lot of money. Israel's treasury is always hard pressed, her needs are always greater than her resources and there are ten contestants for every dollar, each crying 'Mine! It's mine!' If this threadbare treasury had to pay for the Hawks, I feared that the allocations for the purchase of planes would be cut, and the air force would be the one to suffer. Moreover, those who wished to make cuts would justify them by pointing out that this excellent anti-aircraft defence system reduced the need for large numbers of planes.

It should be pointed out that the anti-aircraft units were only transferred to the air force's responsibility in 1970; previously, they were under the artillery command. Obviously, shooting upwards, whether with anti-aircraft cannon or ground-to-air missiles, was an operation that did not belong to the air force. It required a great deal of trouble and explanation to convince people that anti-aircraft defence is a single, integrated entity, including detection of raiding enemy planes, giving the alert, rapid and correct identification and a firing order, which may take the form of unleashing anti-aircraft guns or pressing the firing button of a ground-to-air missile or giving planes the order to 'scramble' to intercept the enemy. It was only in the hands of the air force that this whole system could ensure effective protection, by controlling all the options available and in each case, using the appropriate type of defence or a simultaneous combination of two or three types.

The battle to unite all the anti-aircraft units under air force command began before the first Hawk missiles arrived. My successor, Motty Hod, kept up the pressure throughout his first six years as air-force commander, and it was only in his seventh year that he succeeded in getting anti-aircraft defences wholly under air force control.

President Kennedy displayed true generosity, declaring, 'We'll sell you as many batteries of Hawks as you need.' He didn't impose any restrictions, leaving it up to Israel to decide how many it would purchase. The temptation was enormous, and there were some who spoke in extremely large figures. The planning branch of the Operations Department conducted a survey and concluded that so many batteries of Hawks would provide optimum defence, while so many fewer were the minimum. I contended that even fewer would be enough. 'In any case, we shall attack first, and the stress should be on numbers of planes for a powerful attack, and not on the number of missiles for defence. There is, of course, no justification for neglecting our defences, but they should be minimal, and under no circumstances at the expense of the offensive option!' Furthermore, I added, 'It isn't a problem just of spending millions of dollars on purchasing missiles. This is more than a one-time outlay. The batteries will demand a large maintenance allocation for construction, manpower, vehicles, training and whatever else such units need. Batteries for Tel Aviv, Haifa and Beersheba will do.' My view was not accepted by Shimon Peres, the deputy defence minister, and Zvi Zur, the chief of staff. We argued and brought detailed proofs and learned opinions and there were fiery speeches and voices were raised, until, as always, there was a compromise. In effect, we entered the Six Day War with a few batteries operational, while one was for training.

In any case, the Six Day War proved that we had no need of a larger number of Hawks, and even the few we had practically didn't come into use. In the Yom Kippur War, the circumstances and the character of the war were different, giving a different, much more active role to the Hawks.

Long drawn-out arguments have accompanied the air force since the first day of its existence – regarding its distinctive character and everything stemming from it, both on logistics and in strategic notions. We were not always successful in these arguments, but we never neglected our obligation, which was to prove the correctness of our view, to contradict the contentions of our opponents and to work for solutions we found suitable. For those who commanded it – indeed, for every officer in air command – the air force's distinctive spirit was the apple of his eye. If the 'plot' to blur its distinctive character had succeeded, this spirit might have been marred.

It is inevitable, in a way, that as commander of the air force I found myself dealing with problems and questions that I had been concerned with throughout my career in the air force – like this ongoing battle to preserve the force's sense of independence and distinction, which had been going on ever since Yadin was chief of staff. The other major concern that accompanied me practically from the time of the War of Independence ended, and I first began to think in terms of building a force, was the training of pilots. In those days I was busy writing training manuals, integrating into the force young Israelis who had to replace the experienced foreign volunteers, mapping out an ideal for the Israeli pilot to aspire to and the means of getting him to reach it. The air force had changed drastically from those early days of piston planes and all but *ad hoc* command, but the subject of pilot training was always a burning issue and, in its way, had to develop along with the changes in the force itself.

I didn't know exactly how long I would serve as commander of the air force. I wanted my successor to continue on the same path where I left off. Not a mimic who would 'chase after Weizman' and would always be thinking: 'What would Ezer do in this case?' On the contrary, someone new, able to contribute his own ideas and initiate in his own right and by virtue of his own authority.

But at the same time a man who, in basic issues and matters of principle – the special spirit of the force, its orientation towards its men, the belief in its power and its operational concept – would believe in the things I believe in; and even if he interpreted matters in his own individual way, a man to whom I could pass on this tremendous asset without reservation. Not everyone saw things as I did. Again and again, I was accused of going out of my way to surround myself with 'yes-men', people without backbone who blindly chanted 'Amen' to my doctrine and who were eager to serve my every whim.

Over and over again, at every opportunity, and in every possible form of expression, I repeated: 'The human factor will decide the fate of the war, of all wars. Not the Mirage, nor any other plane, and not the screwdriver or the wrench or radar or missiles or all the newest technology and electronic innovations. Men – and not just men of action, but men of thought. Men for whom the expression 'By ruses shall ye make war' is a philosophy of life, not just the object of lip-service. Men who are constantly seeking out new stratagems, discovering and innovating. Men to whom the notion of resting on their laurels is inconceivable; who are never satisfied with what has already been achieved but constantly search for improvements, more and more.'

It was to that kind of man that I wanted to 'turn over' the air force. It was important to me that he should grow up close to me, that he should absorb things from me. In Motty Hod I found the model I was looking for. He was a man close to my heart from the first moments of our acquaintance. While serving as commander of the air force, I discovered in him those traits by virtue of which, I believed, the continued development of the force would be assured, if he were appointed to serve after me. How much I believed that my successor would do well to make his own contribution and leave his personal stamp on the life of the air force can be seen in a statement I made upon leaving the force in 1966. At a farewell party, I told a group of senior officers: 'I wish for the air force, its new commander – and myself – that in five years' time, when I come to visit an air force base, I won't recognize the force anymore.' But again, I was off in my estimate of time: only two or three years later, I didn't recognize many things about the air force, and anyone who thought I was only pretending surprise was dead wrong.

Motty was then a lieutenant-colonel and head of a branch in air force command. Three base commanders were stung – and they smarted. They believed that they were more deserving of advancement than Motty was, and the nature of Motty's step up indicated that he would keep on going up. And they were not the only ones who claimed that I had misjudged Motty's capabilities and had credited him with what he just didn't have. I saw Motty as a rough diamond; others claimed that he was just another stone.

When I appointed Motty head of Air Branch in 1961, I promoted him together with the base commanders to the rank of colonel; and I promoted the base commanders two weeks before Motty – though that didn't help much. They came to me to let off steam: 'You're a real snake in the grass, you are. You promoted us first just to soften us up for the blow.' The characterization didn't bother me, but I can't say as much for the tension that permeated the various levels of the force. It was obvious that Motty's appointment was hard for many people to swallow, but I didn't – and don't now – feel an ounce of regret about my decision. Motty was not only the man who brought to realization in the Six Day War all that we had planned and built together – and more – but he prepared the force for the Yom Kippur War, and despite the tremendous difficulties, the air force expressed itself outstandingly in that war, too. If only on the logistic and organizational side – arms and ammunition, pilots and planes – its success was complete. Motty's first days in his new position were accompanied by a crisis, which worried me much more than the accusation that I acted as I did in order to surround myself with people who were loyal to me personally. I was at peace with myself, and the bad feelings dissolved after a while. More important, Motty grew polished, proving the justice of the appointment.

It was therefore settled, as far as I was concerned, that I was going to 'pass on' the air force to Motty Hod, but there were many difficulties along the way. The events of the Yom Kippur War have given new immediacy to the question of the position of the minister of defence vis-à-vis the IDF. Is he a kind of commander in chief à la super-chief of staff, the last word in any military matter? Since the nature of the relationship was not defined in the nation's laws and regulations, the degree of any defence minister's involvement in the daily affairs of the IDF was a matter of personal behaviour and was a reflection of the quality of his relations with the chief of staff and the senior echelons of the military. In fact, the whole question was left to habit and adopted procedure, rather than codified law.

The IDF's relations with Ben-Gurion were, naturally, very close. In all of my meetings with the 'old man', both before and after the Six Day War, I always felt that I was in the presence of greatness. One just naturally felt a need to 'walk softly' with that man. In 1963 I was with Shimon Peres, then deputy defence minister, and Chief of Staff Zvi Zur at the Air Salon in France. We were greeted like royalty and our way was paved with a shower of compliments and pleasantries, so that we felt like representatives not of some tiny country in the Middle East, but of a major air power. We were staying at the Continental Hotel in Paris, and on the 15 June I received a call that Shimon wanted to see me immediately. I went down to his room, took one look at Shimon – who was shaking and as white as a ghost – and was sure that a war had broken out, catching us unprepared, and the situation was critical. When I got him to talk, and he spit out between clenched teeth the two words: 'Ben-Gurion resigned', I shared his sorrow, but I also felt a tremendous sense of relief that my worst fears could still be classified as fantasy alone. To relieve the tension, I announced in a tone of mock gravity: 'Shimon, now you must make a fateful decision: a double whisky or a dry martini?' He managed a weak smile, opted for the martini and decided on the spot to return home immediately. Back in Israel I was attacked for joining him, on the grounds that it was unseeming for the commander of the air force to be involved in political matters. Quite true. But it is equally true that I chose to accompany Peres on the grounds of friendship alone. Once home, however, I joined in the attempts to talk Ben-Gurion out of his resignation, but like others – both better than I and closer to him – I failed.

The parting with Ben-Gurion was difficult for us. Involved as he was with every detail of life in the IDF, right on top of every aspect of security affairs and because of his incredible powers of understanding, we were all thoroughly accustomed to view his word as first and last in every question of security. And the appointment of Levi Eshkol as prime minister and minister of defence did not especially inspire confidence. I should add immediately that in time I found Eshkol to be a marvellous man and an outstanding defence minister who, due to an unfortunate alignment of circumstances, has been deprived of his proper place in our perspective. Peres was torn over whether to follow his mentor and leave with Ben-Gurion or remain deputy defence minister under Eshkol. To me, Shimon was a man who had done truly great things for the army and the air force, and along with many of my colleagues I asked him not to go but to try and find a common language with Eshkol. He granted our request – though even without the pressure he had reasons of his own for continuing to serve – but the Eshkol-Peres partnership didn't last for long.

Eehkol assumed office in June 1963, and the succeeding months found him – perhaps insufficiently prepared – on the threshold of a change of guard in the senior echelons of army command. Zvi Zur was winding up three years of service as chief of staff, and Yitzhak Rabin waited in great expectation to be appointed his successor. Rabin had already thought once that his hour had come, but he was passed over and Zur was brought back from France and appointed chief of staff, while Rabin was made his deputy. But he was sure he wouldn't be passed over again – and this time he was right.

At the end of 1963, therefore, Rabin was ready to take on the chief of staff's position and there was no doubt that the magic wand would be his. But the case was far from clear-cut in regard to his immediate subordinate, the deputy chief of staff and head of the General Staff Division. A number of possibilities were open here. Chaim Bar-Lev was studying at Columbia University, and the longer his 'exile' went on, the shorter his patience grew. And I, too, worked myself into the race. When Eshkol became minister of defence, I was about to conclude my fifth year as commander of the air force. The truth is that when I had mapped out my career at an earlier stage, I thought that I would serve as head of the air force until the age of forty, and then, at the height of my powers, and with years of rich experience behind me, I would leave the military for a civilian career – though I hadn't thought about exactly what it would be. But Shimon Peres, Zvi Zur and, afterwards, Yitzhak Rabin (in the days when the relations between us could even be called warm) thought otherwise, and each of them in his own way, in the manner of speech characteristic to him, began to plant the seeds of a new ambition in my heart: 'Weizman, why don't you become a future candidate for chief of staff? Who decides that the next chief of staff can't come from the ranks of the air force?' And the seeds fell on fertile soil. The stronger the suggestions, and the more diversified their sources, the more they aroused my desire to reach that top post. At first the great challenge still seemed far off, but the more I toyed with the idea, the closer it grew, as these things do, until it was almost within reach.

I had six meetings with Eshkol on the subject of General Staff Division and the air force command. My relationship with him was perhaps the only consolation in those days for the hours of tension, which were plentiful for me. Eshkol was a lovable man – easy-going, open, a grand conversationalist – and it was simply a pleasure to be around him. Some of our meetings were over lunch, spiced by a glass of cognac. He just loved to eat, and because he never made the slightest attempt to hide his pleasure, he usually infected his guests as well. Once, as we were finishing a meal, I said to him: 'You've got a phenomenal appetite, God bless it!'

'You call *that* an appetite? That's nothing, my boy! My grandfather – there was a man with an appetite! When it grew late and came time to go to sleep, my grandmother would press him to go to bed, but he would repeatedly put her off. "Why not?" she would shout. "Who knows," he used to say, "I may yet get hungry."'

Our meetings, either in his office or over a meal, were always held in an atmosphere of warmth and good fun. A little Hebrew, a little English, a Russian accent, a little Arabic for spice and musical strains of Yiddish – an international brew of languages and wit. His stories about my father and Uncle Chaim, which he told like folk-tales, captivated my heart.

Eshkol always acted naturally. That's the way he was, and he never used his magic charm to pull me into line. The appointment of my successor was not, of course, dependent upon his will alone. But it was clear that as long as my colleagues were not in full agreement with me about Motty, I wouldn't leave my post at the air force, and there was obviously no movement afoot to 'fire' me. I explained to Eshkol repeatedly: 'This is not a personal whim of mine. And my desire to have Motty follow me is not because I owe him something. I just feel that I have the right to decide what's good for the air force, and I know that Motty is what's good for the air force. Sure I want to be chief of staff. But what the air force will be after I leave it is more important to me than what I will be'. Eshkol was probably bloated by the brew fed into him by those who wanted to block Motty's advancement. He claimed that Motty had to study to make himself worthy and fit for the honoured task. I told Eshkol that perhaps he was right. 'But no matter what, Motty will never quote Shakespeare and Bialik to you. Arabs, on the other hand, he'll screw, in simple, unsophisticated Hebrew.'

There was a lottery going on in the IDF. The land forces were afraid of that 'winged wild man' who might land behind the desk of the head of General Staff Division. Since most people judge others by their own achievements and behaviour, many started to say: 'Weizman is just flirting around. In the end, he'll give in and become deputy chief of staff.' In the meanwhile, however, Chaim Bar-Lev returned from the United States, heard that there was a good chance I would be appointed deputy chief of staff, and announced his resignation from the army. It was easy to understand how he felt: he had already been commander of the armoured forces and was a general a year longer than I was. He therefore felt he had no choice but to express his bitterness by announcing that he would leave the army. At lunch one day I suggested to Chaim that he shouldn't go speeding out of what only appeared to be an open door, for if my judgement about Motty wasn't accepted, I had no intention whatsoever of leaving the air force. Throughout that whole bloody campaign over Motty, I stood pretty much alone. Even Shimon Peres wondered outloud: 'Why are you putting up such a fight over it?'

Meanwhile, the plot thickened. The time had come for Zur to

go and for Rabin to take over as chief of staff, and there was a desire to announce a new chief of staff, his deputy and the head of General Staff Division in the same breath. But in the middle of it all sat 'Weizman' blocking up all the pipes with 'his Motty'. Eshkol called me in for a session. The good man was on the spot. He was afraid that if Bar-Lev were appointed head of General Staff Division, after I'd been promised the post, I'd leave the IDF, and he put it to me straight: 'I want you both, and I'm not prepared to give up either of you.' So I took a load off his mind by promising him, 'I won't leave. I'll stay in the air force. There are only two possibilities: either Motty will become commander of the air force and I'll be the deputy chief of staff, or Bar-Lev will be deputy chief of staff and I'll stay in the air force. I'll get along with Bar-Lev. Don't worry.'

In the end there was a 'wee compromise'. Bar-Lev was appointed head of General Staff Division, without the title deputy chief of staff. Eshkol – and I say this without bitterness – walked off with the game: the half tea-half coffee solution worked. Not everyone understood me (which was not unusual by this point). Some thought I had passed up a great opportunity. Sheika Gavish, at any rate, came up to me and said: 'Good for you, Weizman! I didn't think you'd take it so well.'

The barrier that I put up against my personal temptation – and which, in the end, served to pave Motty's path to the command of the air force – I feel – subjectively, of course – was one of my most important contributions to the air force. Had I succumbed to the temptation then, I would have been deputy chief of staff during the Six Day War, and, naturally enough, I would also have become chief of staff before Bar-Lev, and all the paths in my life from that point on would have been dotted with different sign-posts. I might have reason to regret that things did not work out that way. My consolation was the work of the air force during the Six Day War – an air force that demolished the power of the Arab states and achieved for the IDF and the state an astounding victory. In the midst of that war, or perhaps just after it, Rabin said to me: 'Weizman, you were right.' I had to pay a price for being right, and it didn't come cheaply – not at all. In the end that phenomenal war found me neither deputy chief of staff nor commander of the air force, with fantastic pride in my heart but a bitter taste in my mouth. Sometimes the pride overcame the bitterness, sometimes it didn't.

Yitzhak Rabin became chief of staff at the beginning of 1964, and during his first year in the post I already had the opportunity to prove to him the power of the air force. In November the Syrians began to shell Dan and Dafna, two kibbutzim on Israel's northernmost frontier. Rabin decided upon massive retaliation and wanted the air force to bomb the Syrians. Never before, during Ben-Gurion's tenure, had the air force received permission to bomb in peace-time. Rabin found Eshkol while he was visiting my Aunt Vera, in her Rehovot house, and had only to present his case to receive permission to bomb. My car radio announced that the chief of staff was looking for me. It was on a Friday afternoon, and I was on my way home. When I got there I called in, and the duty officer passed the call on to the command. Forty-five minutes from the moment the chief of staff decided on the aerial response, our planes took off and fire and smoke rose from the Golan Heights. There was no forwarning, no special preparations. It was an exact expression of the constantly tightened spring of the air force.

The permission of the political echelon was needed not only to bomb the enemy but also to photograph over enemy territory, as no act requiring the crossing of a border – whether on land, sea or in the air – could be carried out without its approval. We needed aerial photographs for a number of reasons: to keep our boys in a state of readiness; to provide them with the element of tension and offer ways for them to prove their skills; and to remain prepared on the basis of fresh data on the enemy's strength, airfields, equipment and planes. It may sound strange, but Ben-Gurion was a 'miser' over this issue. Getting his approval for air reconnaissance was a tough mission, and permission, once given, did not set a precedent for further activity for the same purposes. Every new photograph required new permission. So it's not surprising that I went to Eshkol to ask for his approval to photograph Hilwan, in Egypt, with a heavy heart and little hope for success.

I was truly astonished when he agreed so quickly, but the reasons for requesting the operation were, after all, good ones. We had begun to receive information about the presence of anti-aircraft missile systems of the SA-2 type, and even though at that time we didn't take in the full significance of such systems in a future war, it was clear that we couldn't be satisfied with intelligence reports alone. We had to see those systems for ourselves – in photographs.

The plan was the most daring to date. Since the systems were reported to be in Hilwan, to get there our planes had to cross the Sinai – no mean distance – which was then, of course, entirely in Egyptian hands. There was another problem: night photography had not been sufficiently developed at the time, and we decided to carry out the mission by day. After studying the problem in depth, it was decided that two Votoures would fly south of Eilat, cross the centre of the Sinai at low altitudes, reach the Nile, turn north and photograph Hilwan – still at a low altitude – continue west and, close to the Mediterranean, leave Egypt through the Delta. The mission was set for eight in the morning. Before I even recovered from the shock of the quick approval, Eshkol surprised me again. He wanted to be present at the air force command-post while I directed the operation. Because of its daring, dangers and the equipment involved, a mission of this kind was directed by no less than the commander of the air force himself.

I was delighted to host Eshkol in the command-post. Ben-Gurion never asked to come and never came. Eshkol was obviously totally inexperienced in such operations, but he absorbed a lot by sheer virtue of his intelligence, which was a source of great pleasure to all of us. I involved him in various stages of the operation, pointing out the position of the planes on a map every time we received a report. The great tension and closeness to a suspenseful operation pleased him, and he didn't try to hide that pleasure. Then our planes were spotted by the Egyptians, who sent up their own to intercept. I was very tense, as commanders are when their men are exposed to great danger, but the prime minister and minister of defence remained quiet and closed within himself. The planes did not make contact, and only after the boys had returned safely to base did Eshkol reveal to me how nervous he had been.

As a partner in the operation, Eshkol soon asked me to bring the photos to him. Their clarity and detail were amazing. They had been shot from a low altitude and not only exposed new missile batteries clearly and exactly but showed them in their correct proportions. These were the air force's first low-altitude photographs so deep inside Egypt, and Eshkol feasted his eyes on them over and over.

During the second operation, which took place soon after the first, Eshkol again came to the command-post and followed every stage closely. Two Mirages entered Egypt at Alexandria to look for Egyptian missile installations west of Cairo. They photographed Cairo West with great precision, flew along the Cairo-Suez highway, discovered an SA-2 installation – among the first of those days – and started to make their way home. But from El Arish two Migs began to pursue them and fired – for the first time in the history of air warfare in the Middle East – air-to-air missiles from a distance. We had never used Mirages for a photography mission before, and their experience in dodging the Egyptian missiles was an important lesson.

During my sixth year as commander of the air force, I was growing more and more convinced that five years is the ideal term for a commander to hold the post. Were it not for the difficulties in appointing Motty in my place, I would have left the air force with the beginning of Eshkol's term in 1964 and become head of General Staff Division. In the end, I was the commander of the air force for eight years. It's not to be recommended. The daily grind, even if you fight the good fight, is a strong opponent, and as much as you struggle against its effects, you can never be sure you've blocked them out of your world.

After completing the integration of the Mirages, I had the feeling that I had completed my task. The air force had an excellent complement of planes and sky-high morale (there used to be a saying that it was dangerous to cross an Israeli air base at an altitude of less than 40,000 feet; you might collide with some morale!). Its men shared a pride in belonging to it. It was a force that was keyed up in spring-like readiness; a long sword, ready to be whipped out of its scabbard at tremendous speed – and strike home. I was satisfied and content with what I'd done. I had gained respect, even adoration. This was the time for a further step – on the way to chief of staff. Yitzhak Rabin repeatedly said he wanted me as deputy chief of staff and head of General Staff Division. Relations between

Yitzhak and Chaim Bar-Lev weren't smooth, and those between me and Bar-Lev weren't entirely free of friction. Even though Bar-Lev had been appointed head of General Staff Division, he knew that I would be given that job, at some stage, and then, after a test period, both of us would be placed in the same balance. Whichever one of us tipped the scales would replace Rabin as the chief of staff of the Israel Defence Forces.

The sixth year passed, the seventh was just around the corner and I was still commander of the air force. Motty had been head of Air Branch – in essence, my assistant – for five years, and he was also growing impatient and restless about his fate. I began to put on pressure, send out signals to Eshkol and Rabin and try to set the machinery of change in motion. But nothing moved. My relationship with Bar-Lev had begun to suffer badly, and I regretted it deeply. As long as we weren't thought of as contestants for the position of chief of staff, the relations between us were smooth and open – and I had a sincere respect and feeling of friendship for him. But competition creates enemies, barriers and sometimes sour feelings. Perhaps that was my fault. I made no attempt to hide my desire to become chief of staff from anyone; on the contrary, I openly pushed in that direction. And when all is said and done, I could understand how Bar-Lev felt. He was head of General Staff Division, waiting to jump up a step to the top position; and there on the sidelines, a strange animal, an 'unbridled Weizman' with a big mouth – not from the infantry, armour or artillery, but from some closed fortress that goes against all the rules – was whistling in the air as if waiting for him to jump and miss. Had Eshkol decided definitively, then and there, 'Bar-Lev will become chief of staff after Rabin, and Weizman after him,' or vice versa, one of us could heave a sigh of relief and the other could either accept the decision and wait his turn patiently, or go his own way. It was the prolonged uncertainty that left us both so strained, and instead of our feelings being calmed, they were whipped up further and further, until the battle got out of hand.

In the end, things fell into place and the tension lifted. At the beginning of 1966, it was decided that Bar-Lev would shortly leave to study in France and I would be appointed head of General Staff Division, while Motty would become commander of the air

force. I felt good. I was to be the first commander of the air force
not to go out of uniform but to remain in the framework of the
IDF and be appointed to a post never before held by an air force
man.

'I'm leaving the air force.' It's easy enough to say, but no one
who has not actually gone through it can understand how difficult it
is to do. During the preceding eight years, the force had grown
strong in quantity and quality. I got to know many of its members,
and many more got to know me personally. I went through such a
long round of farewells that I was afraid I would never get to
everyone. I parted from each wing separately, but I didn't stop at
that. For hours and hours I went from mechanic to mechanic,
electrician to electrician, pilot to pilot, here a word, there a word, a
million pats on the back, warm expressions of closeness, regret
over my leaving and sincere wishes for success in my new post. I
felt the deepest sense of pleasure at the sight of this magnificent
family. At each place my visit wound up with a party. Near the
time of the actual change of command, we held a dinner for 150
senior officers, and I don't know what flowed more freely that
night, cold wine or warm words.

A strong wind was blowing on the day that the ceremony of
command was to take place. Such ceremonies are not only festive;
somehow they are coloured by a sense of theatricality, and Motty
and I had to arrive by air (in this case by helicopter). As we landed,
my heart was working overtime, and I wondered how Motty was
feeling. (You can't always trust his outward expression, he's much
'cooler' than I am.) I, at any rate, was overcome by a storm of
emotion. I was closing a twenty-four-year chapter of my life, from
1942 to 1966, on the very same runway from which I took off in an
RAF uniform and later in the air force's first Messerschmidts. And
now I was passing on the command of the Israeli air force to a good
friend.

It was a short ceremony, with the traditional handing over of the
force's flag. At the end of reading the order of the day, I added,
'General Motty Hod will lead you to victory.' To the best of my
ability in forecasting the future, I think my words were very
fitting. I didn't say he would deter the enemy. I didn't say he would
prevent another war. I said he would lead the air force to victory.

And all the time I had a feeling in the pit of my stomach that a future war was not only unavoidable, but would come upon us soon. Had I known then just how soon – thirteen months from the day I turned over command – Motty would have had no choice but to have waited his turn patiently until after the victory of June 1967.

Motty read out his order of the day, we saluted each other and I left the parade on my own. My 'black Spit' was awaiting me at one side, flanked by two mechanics who had been serving since 1948. They knew the Spitfire and me, with all our crazes, pranks and tricks. They strapped the parachute onto me, I got into the Spit, started up and took off. I did one run with a roll over the base and landed at Ramat David.

At one o'clock I was at home, having lunch with Re'uma and the children; at two o'clock I was behind the desk of my new office: head of General Staff Division. 'Ezer,' I said to myself, 'to work – on the double!'

11

TWO AND A HALF HOURS IN JUNE

THE DISENGAGEMENT OF FORCES is a relatively new concept in our military lexicon. But from the moment I took on my new post, I knew that Motty would not be able to carry out his command and I would not be able to fill the shoes of the head of Operations Branch if I didn't disengage from personal involvement in the air force. And although it hurt like hell, I decided to cut myself off from anything related to the air force – except, of course, those matters that came across my desk as head of operations – for the first year of my post. It was a terrible struggle for me, and more than once I was on the point of losing it. The boys didn't understand it. They would call, they would come over to lay out a matter before me or ask advice. It broke my heart to have to turn them away and tell them, delicately, that there is a commander of the air force, and it's not me anymore. It was clear to me that had I not acted this way, my ties with the air force and its men would have been an obstacle for Motty. So drastic was my dissociation from the air force that the boys began to grow anxious about it and asked me, 'Ezer, are you angry? Are you bitter?' And again and again I would have to explain why this break was absolutely necessary.

In order to find my place in the new order, it was imperative that I first 'liberate' myself from my old and so familiar framework. It was difficult to bridge the gap. Now that I no longer belonged to the air force, I could clearly see the full meaning of the expression 'the Israel Defence Forces – and the air force', as if one were talking about two completely separate frameworks. The commanders of the air force never wanted to turn it into an army of grenadiers. But through education and discipline, we cultivated a smart and healthy appearance in our men. In the final analysis, this fashioned not only a military atmosphere, but also a feeling of order and cleanliness. This is also true of air-bases, with their gardens, flower beds and trees lining the sign-posted paths.

I had grown accustomed to all of these things, and over the years they had become a permanent part of my way of life. The life-style of the ground forces is different, even when the officers take special care about matters of order and cleanliness (and they don't always). The ground forces don't have this sense of polish. Their special stamp is tied to a coarser, dustier way of life, having to put up with mud and sand, the merciless sun and the unavoidable conditions of the field. Everything was so different: the way of talking and the rhythm of work, the terminology and even the quality of relationships. I almost began to believe those who claimed that it wouldn't work – to take this bird, clip its wings and turn it into a field animal.

In order to nip this feeling in the bud, before it took hold of me completely and made it impossible for me to succeed in my post, I returned to the path I have believed in throughout my life: I started to get to know people, to grow closer to them, to learn about their way of life. That was also difficult. Every acquaintance, every effort to get close inevitably led me to make comparisons with the acquaintances and the deep social involvements I had with men in the air force. This was different. It had to be different. In the air force the people and the affairs of the force were flowers that I had planted, watered and cultivated, until they passed the most vulnerable stages of youth, and then I followed them throughout their careers. Here I came to a veteran forest, which others had planted and cultivated; I was an 'alien' invading this territory and feeling, quite naturally, distant and uncomfortable in it.

There was no escaping the feeling. I was from a different outfit. Even my appearance was different: everyone else was wearing green khaki, and I was the only one in light-coloured air force uniform, which I persisted in wearing, together with my air force cap. Occasionally, when visiting units in the field, I would exchange my air force uniform for green-khaki clothes, but even then I remained loyal to my blue air force cap. (That was when they were still being worn. We hadn't yet reached the times when hats were out, skirts short and hair long.) Chaim Nadel Haka (Yitzhak Hofi, commander of the northern front in the Yom Kippur War) and Ghandi (Rehavam Ze'evi) were to fill a certain vacuum in my heart and fill the place of close friends in the air force. I doubt that the 'earth-bound' knew or even suspected how I felt, what was eating me and how difficult it was for me to adapt.

There was another big adjustment for me when I moved to the General Staff. I ceased to be a commander. When no officer fills the post of deputy chief of staff, the head of General Staff Division is the number-two man in the army. By this standard, he's more important in the hierarchy than the commander of the air force. Even though he's the staff officer of the highest commander in the Israel Defence Forces, he's deprived of many of the components of independent decision-making; and I had grown accustomed to these components during the previous eight years and saw them as natural to, and derived from, my very position as head of the air force.

In the air force I had known every subject – combat, technical, logistic – thoroughly, inside-out. To avoid setting myself a pretentious objective I knew I could not reach, I got myself used to the notion that I would never gain a similar level of know-how and mastery over the ground forces, with the complexity of their combat doctrine and everything connected with it. The command of large units always has a number of common features, but there was no overlooking the differences that characterize every type of warfare, according to its means, its weapons, its men and its own distinctive forms of combat. These are basic professional matters, which demand study, repetition, renovation and updating, so that we remain well practised in the art of war and maintain the qualitative gap, as in the air force.

So I went back to the classroom, in all seriousness and without any compromises. It was a great challenge to learn about the traits of the tank – its range of operation and of fire, the calibre of its shells and its modes of deployment and operation in armoured battles; mortars and their range; artillery and its traits; the structure of a company, a battalion, a brigade; organizational forms of the ground forces; problems of terrain and their effect on forms of combat. I drummed up every drop of modesty I possessed (and I don't have an abundance!) and told myself, over and over, no pretensions, no make-believe, no bashfulness. Listen and learn. Let the experts talk to you, hour after hour, in the office, in the field and in the units, and don't hesitate to ask questions, lots of questions, on every subject, in every sphere. Be careful not to impose your decisions on matters where you are not yet certain in your professional knowledge. Don't be hasty. Use a lot of common sense. Here, like the air force, like anywhere else, matters have their own logic. Learn it, master it. The more and the faster you learn, the quicker you'll dispel the sense of being an outsider. Even if you continue to wear an air force uniform, beware of spreading your wings without need. Don't arouse opposition. Seek understanding and agreement, try to see eye to eye with the men around you.

I had lots of arguments – first and foremost with myself. When I visited an infantry brigade or an armoured battalion and encountered things I regarded as undesirable, or noticed the differences between this unit and the air force – in spirit, in morale, in identification and participation – I would tell myself: 'That's it! Get used to it! You can't do the same things here that you could – and did – in an air force squadron!' But this conviction did not survive long. It was rapidly contradicted and displaced by a series of questions: 'Why do you think so? Why can't you make the same changes here? Why accept less than the very best? These are the same excellent Israeli youngsters. You can get anything out of them! Talk to them!'

My first year in my new post – May 1966 to May 1967 – was fascinating for me. Essentially, it helped to prove the justice of the assumption that rotation in command is a blessing. Everything was a challenge, new and interesting. In the final analysis, I think that I was right in feeling that many people in the ground forces who had their hesitations about me in the beginning came round to seeing that it was possible to live with this winged creature, and that despite his 'genetic differences' he was capable of understanding the problems of bipeds and of those cramped into a tank.

Notwithstanding later disagreements – which I won't conceal, at the proper point – it was a very fruitful year for me in my relationship with the chief of staff, Yitzhak Rabin. After five years as deputy chief of staff, Yitzhak was an unchallenged authority as a ground commander. His organizational work gained him much praise, and he had brilliant analytical ability, helped by his superb articulation. It was a delight to hear him analyze a situation, even when I didn't agree with him. Much of what I lacked in my post, I learned from Yitzhak, and it was a pleasure to learn from him.

The Israeli armed forces may be an excellent school, but they never cease grappling with current problems and realities. In the operational sphere, my first year in the General Staff, the year preceding the Six Day War, was overshadowed by the struggle for the sources of the Jordan. I spent one of my last days in the air force flat on my belly on a little hillock, with Rabin and Bar-Lev lying at my side. We were near one of our positions close to the old Syrian border. Three generals were hugging the ground very, very closely, because not far away the Syrians were shelling the '120-acre field'. This field was inside the demilitarized zone and became the issue of a long dispute with the Syrians over Israel's right to cultivate it. To tell the truth, a dispute over 120 acres is beyond the comprehension of an airman, who thinks in terms of thousands of square miles. It was the first time I had ever been so close to a bombardment, and I admired the driver of the armoured tractor, who continued working while shells exploded all round, as though the Syrians were aiming at someone else.

The Syrians had begun work on diverting the tributaries of the Hazbani and Jordan rivers on the Golan Heights to deprive us of vital natural-water sources. The 'war of the metres' in the north was, without doubt, of the greatest importance. A whole host of names was created to designate various points on the border; for example, 'De Gaulle's nose', 'The 120', 'The beet', 'The 360' and so on. The water problem was so acute that it gave rise to the joke that if Israel didn't succeed in protecting her water sources, every citizen would have to be issued with a daily ration of so many water-bottles.

Matters heated up, and within forty-eight hours of my appointment as head of General Staff Division, Israeli forces carried out a reprisal raid on quite a considerable scale in the Jordan Valley. It was my first experience with a ground raid. I went to the scene together with Rabin and the head of the Northern Command, General David ('Dado') Elazar. I was present at the briefing session before the operation and at the debriefing that followed it, where I heard details of the attack and listened to the soldiers' accounts. Unintentionally, I was comparing their experiences with the stories of our pilots on their return from combat. It was only forty-eight hours since I had left the air force, and my previous experiences were still fresh in my mind. The new ones were so different that over and over again doubts arose in my mind: perhaps I'm in the wrong place.

'Weizman, what are you doing here?' echoed with renewed force a short time later. A vessel that was patrolling the Sea of Galilee with a ten-man crew ran aground on the eastern side. According to the Syrian-Israel Armistice Agreement, 10 yards of the sea's north-eastern shore belonged to Israel, but it was feared that the Syrians would nevertheless attack the boat and its crew. Efforts to get the vessel afloat again failed. Yitzhak, Dado and I boarded her in civilian clothes, to make a close inspection and see whether she could be towed off. The chief of staff, the head of General Staff Division and the head of Northern Command – just three men in a boat, with armed Syrians 50 yards away. Taking such a risk may not have been very sensible, but at that time it was the general view that the most senior officers should be personally and closely involved in every incident. But I felt strange, and, as usual, I said to myself: 'Pardon me, Mr Weizman, but what are you doing here, within pistol range of the Syrians, instead of being overhead in a Mirage?' It was only after the Six Day War that we found a most interesting object in the Kuneitra office of Syrian intelligence: a photograph of Messrs Rabin, Elazar and Weizman in bathing costumes on the boat's deck. I presume the Syrians were satisfied with the picture and didn't try to discover the identities of the three 'experts'.

I was entering even deeper into the subject of the ground forces, and my intensive studies were bearing fruit. I had good teachers: I got to know Arik Sharon, the head of the training department; Ghandi and Dado; Sheika Gavish, then head of Southern

Command; Uzi Narkiss in Central Command; Haka, head of Operations Department; Aharon Yariv, head of military intelligence; Matti Peled, head of Supply Command; Shmuel Ayal, head of Manpower Branch; and Yisrael ('Tallik') Tal, commander of the armoured forces – all experts in their fields. One superb teacher I had was Tallik. He called me 'Bluebird', and I responded by addressing him as 'Black Panther'. Whenever I wanted to know anything about the tank and its munitions, I'd say: 'Tallik, a lesson?' and we would immediately closet ourselves in a room. Tallik would scrawl on a blackboard, and I'd acquire a welcome addition to my knowledge and comprehension.

The *fedayeen* sabotage forays were being stepped up again, and when one of our vehicles hit a mine and three men were killed, a reprisal raid was clearly called for. I had a certain amount of influence on its character. 'In 1966, we can't carry out a 1955-style reprisal raid,' I contended, 'going in at night, laying a few pounds of explosives, blowing up a house or a police station, and then clearing off. When a sovereign state decides to strike at its foes, it ought to act differently. We have armour, and we have an air force. Let's go in by day, operating openly and in force.'

This approach largely influenced the 'Samoa Operation', where armour and air units went in, openly and in force, and struck a heavy blow at the Jordanians. We also paid the price: the commander of a parachute battalion, Yoav Shaham, was killed, and a pilot who was taking part in the operation lost an eye from a bullet wound (nevertheless, he brought his Ouragon down safely, earning a citation).

Then, at the end of 1966 and the beginning of 1967, when it became clear that the Syrians were very serious about diverting the sources of the Jordan, Prime Minister Levi Eshkol gave permission for the air force to enter this decisive struggle. Votoures and Mystères went into action, inflicting heavy blows on Syrian excavation equipment. Armour and artillery also took vigorous action to disrupt the Syrian diversion scheme. As the conflict heated up, in March and April 1967, there were several aerial clashes, the best-remembered of which resulted in six Syrian Migs being downed, with our planes chasing the survivors as far as Damascus. There was great suspense, as everyone awaited a Syrian reply; but no one predicted a full-scale war before 1969. Moshe Dayan was then a Knesset member. One day I happened to run into him, and he was quick to respond to our move: 'Are you people out of your minds? You're leading the country to war!'

At the regular weekly 'forum', presided over by the defence minister, discussions were not conducted with any sense of urgency, and there was no feeling of war around the corner. The meetings usually took place on Friday. The participants, aside from the defence minister, were the chief of staff, the head of General Staff Division, the deputy defence minister and the director general of the defence ministry. The chief of staff would bring along a senior staff officer, according to the subjects on the agenda – intelligence, air force, armour or any other sphere. As second in command of the armed forces, I felt very much at home, and my opinions were listened to. Eshkol, who served as minister of defence as well as prime minister, delighted us repeatedly with his alertness, his sensitivity and his wide interest in logistic problems. He visited the units, inspecting them and studying their problems, and his conclusions, reservations, questions and suggestions were brought to the forum to be discussed. When he heard of the air force's supply situation, he was thoroughly shocked and gave immediate instructions for more spare parts and ammunition to be purchased or manufactured. Even though the June 1967 war was short and did not require the air force to flex all its muscles or use up all its stocks, I have no doubt that Eshkol's intervention was very useful. (On the eve of the Six Day War, intelligence evaluations were incorrect about forecasting the imminence of war, as they were before the Yom Kippur War; but before the Six Day War, the Israeli forces were in a better state of preparedness, and, to some extent, this made up for the mistaken intelligence.)

Eshkol's interest in the military household was not always pleasing to army chiefs. His genuine concern for the needs of the armed forces had another side – his vigorous demands for economy and avoiding waste. Once he came to the forum and dropped a bombshell: 'Can anyone explain why every colonel has a regular army man for a driver?' There was silence. And Eshkol added: 'If it's essential for every colonel to have a driver, he ought to be a conscript!' The reckoning was simple and familiar: a regular army man cost the army £10,000 a year, a conscript cost £1,000. Ben–Gurion never took an interest in such trifling items. If, for some reason, a matter of this kind had come to his attention, he would have given a general order to 'make cuts' and leave its practical implementation to his deputy, Shimon Peres. Not Eshkol. He ordered the chief of staff to act. 'I'll show you how to economize!' He followed through on the order by demanding reports on its implementation and asking whether 100 colonels had had their drivers replaced by conscripts. The colonels griped, and Eshkol smiled. The order was carried out.

By Independence Day 1967 – which is celebrated on the anniversary of Israel's first day of independence according to the Hebrew calender, and once every nineteen years (as happened in 1967) it falls on 15 May, which is its date by the Gregorian calendar – a great sense of confidence, satisfaction and contentment enveloped the parade in Jerusalem. High-flown speeches (on second thought, they may have been too high-flown) were the order of the day. That evening, at the air force's traditional Independence Day gala, war seemed remote and unreal. It was the first such gala I attended as a visitor, rather than commander of the air force. Eshkol sat in the front row, together with Rabin, Aharon Yariv, Motty and myself, as well as other generals. Festivities were at their height – noisy, turbulent, enthusiastic – so that no one took any notice when Yariv was called to the phone. When he came back and called Rabin, everyone was still rejoicing. Rabin called me to join the consultation. Egyptian forces were pouring into Sinai. We waited for the interval to inform Eshkol. Nothing serious. It doesn't look like a prelude to war. Back to the festivities. But the wheels of the Six Day War had begun to spin.

The steps leading up to the Six Day War followed all the rules of escalation. Step by step, day by day, strand by strand, the war was woven, steadily and systematically. The provocative acts of the Egyptians set the wheels turning – removing the UNEF troops from Gaza, sending large forces into Sinai, closing the Straits of Tiran and spitting out arrogant challenges. After it had exhausted all the political alternatives, Israel was forced into a war it did not want.

The prelude to the Six Day War was like a thermometer warming up, with preparations ascending from cool to hot. At that gala on 15 May 1967, it never occurred to anyone that the Egyptian army's flagrant move into Sinai, in broad daylight, was the opening chord of the great symphony of war. We didn't even consider calling up a significant number of reservists. Rabin called me aside and said: 'Move such-and-such forces, just in case there's any trouble.' A typical routine move, dictated by basic prudence, but resting on the assumption that there wouldn't be any trouble.

Everyone thought we were witnessing a repetition of 'Operation Rotem'. Some six years before, the Egyptians began to move their forces into Sinai, on a scale similar to their movements on the eve of the Six Day War. The air force was instructed to send two Votoures for a daylight photography mission over the Suez Canal. Rabin, then head of General Staff Division, told me: 'Pending further notification, the ground forces have been caught with their pants down. Everything depends on the air force.' But the matter ended without anything happening. The Egyptians withdrew their forces, while we were trying to pull our pants up.

There are two popular folk-sayings that are as fatal to military concepts as they are to political ones: 'There is no wisdom like experience', and 'History repeats itself'. In war, history plays its tricks and doesn't repeat itself, so that for the man of experience who relies on the stability of history, wisdom becomes a broken reed. Although the events of the twenty-four hours that followed 15 May pointed to the trend, no one took the prospects of war very seriously. We were sure that there was very little likelihood of hostilities. I didn't think that this was the war I had predicted only two years earlier. I didn't sense anything of the sort.

As war was assumed to be unlikely, we inclined to overlook various preliminary signs that preceded 15 May 1967. We received various indications that the Egyptians were planning high-altitude reconnaissance flights (the Mig flies at 50,000 feet and is hard to intercept). Together we reviewed the Egyptian steps that would be regarded by Israel as a *casus belli*: a blockade of the Straits or forces about a certain size entering Sinai. We were convinced that the Egyptians would not take any one of these steps alone, but both simultaneously, or one after the other.

The entry of Egyptian forces into Sinai, which preceded the blockade of the Straits on 23 May, was accompanied by reports of an offensive, war-like mood in the Egyptian army, suggested by the remarks of certain officers. As the atmosphere began to warm up, events were nibbling away at our initial conviction that war was not in the cards. I never believed the Egyptians would get the chance to invade, if the political echelon only understood that we had to pre-empt such an attack. But on 17 and 18 May, when our entire standing forces consisted of scarcely more than two armoured brigades, there were some unpleasant doubts and a general feeling that the reserves would have to be called up, even if the final outcome justified the assumption that there would be no war.

During the four or five days that followed 17 May, we started mobilizing reserves on a considerable scale. In stages we called up tens of thousands of men, a large-scale mobilization by Middle Eastern standards at that time. Our small standing army could not withstand the Arab forces, and we had to consider the likelihood that in the case of war, the Egyptian front would not be the only battlefield. A few months before the war, in February and March, I had completed the armed forces' work schedule for 1967–8. Such a schedule depends on whether or not war is to be expected in the course of the year, which naturally affects the size of forces planned. Our schedule assumed there would be no war. To understand what that means, it's enough to remember that the whole Jerusalem defence line was manned by seventy-one men, a ridiculous number to defend Jerusalem from a Jordanian attack! The escalation in Sinai was not only worrying in its own right, but it also aroused concern about the Jerusalem front and the border with the West Bank parallel to the coast between Tel Aviv and Haifa. And of course we could not expect the Syrians to watch such a war from the sidelines.

If I had to describe the eight days from 15 May to the day the Egyptians blocked the Straits of Tiran on 23 May, I would simply have to use an understatement: there was a great deal of confusion. It stemmed largely from uncertainties about forthcoming steps. No one was certain as to what would lead to Israel instigating an attack. Any attempt to attach the blame for the confusion to the top political echelon, the government alone, and to absolve the top military echelon, the General Staff, would be misleading. If there is such an impression, it may not have been created deliberately. Perhaps it was nourished by the fundamental difference between the image projected by the government and that of the General Staff. On the one hand, the government, dithering and undecided, headed by a 'stuttering' premier and defence minister, Levi Eshkol, appeared to be a fear-stricken, timorous lot. On the other hand, a young, confident, intrepid General Staff appeared to be prodding the government to draw sword from scabbard and lunge at the enemy, and it was only the government, with its fears and doubts, that was delaying our redemption. That's not the way things were at all. There were, indeed, doubts among the political echelon, but it was the top military echelon that nourished them. If the government was groping in the dark, it was the General Staff that strengthened and reinforced its doubts, because it, too, was perplexed and confused and didn't put things before the government clearly. In the long run, the prolonged period of stand-by may have been useful, as it gave the army the maximum opportunity to complete its preparations. But the doubts were not solely on the side of the political echelons, just as decisiveness and intrepidity were not the sole preserve of the General Staff.

As the suspense built up, and especially as mobilization went ahead and intelligence reports poured in telling of Egyptian forces entering Sinai, I sensed that the chief of staff, Yitzhak Rabin, was progressively losing his balance. He displayed this by changing previous decisions, in his expressions of concern over what was in store for us and in an inability to make up his mind. Rabin created insecurity all around him – in his talks with the prime minister and at General Staff meetings.

What happened on the evening of 23 May and on the following day reflected the peak of Rabin's personal crisis, which also affected his later ability to conduct the campaign. On 23 May, at about eight in the evening, Rabin phoned me at home. Speaking in a faint voice, he asked me to come to his home immediately. Within moments I was in Zahala, where I found him sitting alone in the larger room of his apartment. Everything was silent and still. He looked broken and depressed. He sat on the edge of the couch, and I sat down beside him. We remained alone.

Yitzhak spoke in a weak voice. 'Due to a series of mistakes, I've led Israel into an entanglement, on the eve of the greatest and hardest war the state has ever experienced. In this war, everything depends on the air force. The air force will decide the war. I believe that if a man has erred, he should go. I've erred. Will you take on the post of chief of staff?'

I was very upset. It was so unexpected, and I paused for a moment or two to compose myself. Then I said: 'Yitzhak, you know I want to be chief of staff. But under these circumstances, I won't accept the post. If you resign, it's worth a few divisions to Nasser. In the present difficult circumstances, it will be a heavy blow to the army's morale. The government is hesitant about going to war, and this will make it hesitate even more. As for you, Yitzhak, if you resign now, you'll be finished for the rest of your life. Summon up all your strength. I promise to do the best I can to help you get through. You'll be the victorious chief of staff. You'll reach the Suez Canal and the Jordan.'

I asked Rabin to rest and promised to return in the morning. I instructed the telephone exchanges at General Staff and military intelligence not to contact the chief of staff and to transfer all calls to me for the time being. Then I returned home. All that night, I couldn't shut my eyes. I didn't say a word to anyone, and the next day, at seven in the morning, I returned to Rabin. When I got there, I found his aide-de-camp, Colonel Raphael Efrat, and Dr Gilon.

Again Rabin asked me, 'Are you prepared to take the job?'

I replied, 'The answer is negative, like last night.'

Dr Gilon, Efrat and I agreed that we had to report to Eshkol. We decided to spread the story that the chief of staff had been taken ill with nicotine poisoning.

I drove to General Staff, where I called the heads of Operations Department, military intelligence, Southern Command and the commander of the armoured units and ordered them to complete the over-all plan for the campaign in Sinai. That morning we finalized the plan. I instructed Southern Command to move various brigades and divisions and gave orders for a general stand-by to go into effect the next day. I told the commander of the air force to convene his officers and brief them on the details of the air force operation to destroy the Egyptian and Syrian air forces.

At 5.30 that afternoon Eshkol came to the war room. Except for generals Yoffe and Sharon, who remained with their divisions in the south, all the armed forces' generals were present, including Chaim Bar-Lev, who had returned from abroad the previous night. Eshkol was accompanied by the deputy defence minister, Zvi Dinstein; the director general of the ministry of defence, Moshe Kashti; Colonel Li'or and Addy Yaffe.

I opened with a few words about the purpose of the meeting. The head of military intelligence described the situation on every front. The commander of the air force presented the plan to destroy the enemy air forces and expressed his full confidence in its success. The head of Southern Command presented the plan for the ground action. The heads of the Northern and Central commands and of the navy filled in details about the situation on their fronts. Eshkol asked everyone for his opinion about the prospects for the southern-front plan. No one opposed it. At eight I concluded the meeting by saying that from the following day, 25 May 1967, the Israel Defence Forces would be ready and prepared for war.

That evening I went to the chief of staff's home and reported on everything I had done. He smiled and gave his approval. The next day, when he came to the General Staff, a few colleagues and I persuaded him to go down and visit the forces in Southern Command.

It's hard to pinpoint the precise day, but around 26 May there were no further doubts left in the General Staff about the necessity of Israel breaking out of the noose Nasser had placed around its neck. At that point, two things were clear: first, diplomatic activity had no hope whatsoever of resolving the crisis; second, from our viewpoint, the blockade of the Straits was not, in itself, the principal problem. The large concentration of Egyptian forces in Sinai, even if there were no immediate attack, would require Israel to keep enormous numbers of reservists under arms, undermining the economy. This situation was a dangerous one and of far-reaching consequences to the credibility of Israel's deterrent capacity. I repeatedly told the prime minister, Levi Eshkol, that every additional day gave the Egyptians a better chance of organizing their forces in Sinai, and that meant increased difficulty in breaking through their defences, with additional Israeli casualties. This view was not accepted by all the senior officers. Motty Hod, for example, thought otherwise. When I told him, at one stage, that one Egyptian squadron had moved into Sinai and another into the Suez Canal zone, he could not conceal his satisfaction: 'Excellent, they'll be additional prey for our planes!' Motty, like the others, assumed that the more forces the Egyptians moved into Sinai, the faster the air force would shoot up their defence lines and smash them – and all the more so if they moved their planes within the range of our aircraft.

There were disagreements in the General Staff about how long to 'give' the government to try out all the possibilities of a political settlement for the crisis. Not that anyone thought of acting in defiance of the government should it remain hesitant and continue to pin its hopes on a political solution, but there would be a recommendation, something like: 'Keep trying for a political solution for such-and-such a time longer. At the end of this period the armed forces will be ready to act. Beyond that, time will be against us, for the element of surprise, which is the basis of our plan, may disappear, or at least dwindle, and Egyptian military deployment will make things hard for us.' Opinion in the General Staff was not unanimous on this subject, and Moshe Dayan's appointment as defence minister also affected the argument.

At one point I went down to the forces in the south, to encourage them and be encouraged in return. In the rear, in the government and the General Staff, there may have been doubts and uncertainties, but here, among the officers in their units, I found veritable war-horses champing at the bit. Men like Arik Sharon, Tallik and Avraham Yoffe were afire: 'Now! Let's do it now!'

Uzi Narkiss at Central Command wandered around in a constant state of excitement, as though knowing that his great moment was drawing near, and put everyone into a good mood. He and Amos Horev, who had no clearly defined post, 'worked' on me: 'This is the great opportunity to do something terrific to the Jordanians! We mustn't miss it!' I asked Amos, 'What do you think is the best break-through route into Sinai? Where should we attack?' He replied, 'The solution to re-opening the Straits is . . . to liberate Jerusalem and the West Bank.'

The harbingers were growing more numerous: it was assumed that the Egyptian air force was deployed in readiness for an attack on ours and that its plans were complete. The whole world was sitting back, preparing its heartfelt eulogies for the State of Israel. Intellectuals and good friends were wiping away a tear and saying: 'What a pity. It was a fine state. Nineteen years. What a pity it was only a fleeting episode. The Jewish people deserved a better end.'

The world beheld a state that had lost its impetus, whose enemies had to do very little for it to drop into their laps like a ripe plum. All this whipped up Egyptian fervour to white heat. Together with the general feeling in the world that Israel's day of reckoning was drawing nigh and with the inactivity of our friends, I don't hesitate to number our government's hesitancy and apprehensions as direct causes of Egyptian escalation. In Egyptian eyes and, to some extent, to their Soviet friends as well, this was an Israel that lacked the power of resistance. Its enemies could tighten the noose and sap its strength; whatever happened, it probably wouldn't fight.

On 24 May, when Eshkol visited the war room, I presented him with the final plan we had prepared. It rested on two principal assumptions: (1) the main objective was re-opening the Straits of Tiran; (2) the time available before the United Nations and the Great Powers intervened to impose a cease-fire was very limited. Military intelligence was convinced that we had no more than forty-eight hours at our disposal.

Concerning the question of the Straits and the limited time we had, there were different ideas: a break-through to Sharm el-Sheikh, or a parachute drop there. I supported a different plan: the air force would annihilate the Egyptian air force in its bases, putting it out of action; by midday, it would be free to join in the ground war. The ground forces would break through to the Canal, the main effort being to reach it. Even if it had a slogging contest with the Egyptian army at various strategic points on the way, the army would push on, helped by powerful air strikes on enemy forces. Within the forty-eight hours available, it should be able to reach the Canal. If the Egyptians were still holding on to Sharm el-Sheikh when the cease-fire was imposed, there was a chance of a deal: Israel would withdraw from the Canal and allow it to be re-opened to navigation if the Egyptians withdrew from the Straits of Tiran and permitted free passage to Eilat.

The plan was finally completed only when Moshe Dayan took up his post as defence minister on 31 May. By then it comprised all the previous elements: annihilation of the Egyptian air force, a thrust into Sinai, destruction of the Egyptian ground forces and re-opening the Straits. Dayan had only one worry: he feared international complications if we held on to the Canal and wished to avoid them in the event that war resulted in the Canal falling into Israeli hands.

Rabin returned to work on 25 May. Two days earlier Chaim Bar-Lev returned from France. He had no clearly defined post and no one knew what he was to do. Up to 26 May it was always the same team that went to Cabinet meetings for reports and discussion: Rabin, Yariv and I. On 26 May I heard Yariv say to Bar-Lev: 'Come along with us.' Whether he invited his friend on his own initiative, or whether he was acting for someone else, I felt the ground beginning to crumble under my feet. I never underrated Bar-Lev's political connections, perhaps because I didn't have such contacts.

Around 30 May, amidst the discussions and disagreements inside the Mapai Party and the pressures to replace Eshkol as defence minister with either Yigal Allon or Moshe Dayan, Rabin took the initiative to settle the Bar-Lev question as well. He summoned me and suggested that I be appointed deputy chief of staff to co-ordinate the land, sea and air arms, while Bar-Lev, who was an authoriy on ground warfare, would replace me as head of General Staff Division. 'I'll buy it!' I told him. He went to Jerusalem, but came back with his tail between his legs: he hadn't succeeded on selling the notion to the government. If Rabin had presented it a little more vigorously, I presume that no one would have stood in his way. But he didn't, and that angered me. Twenty-four hours before Dayan's appointment as defence minister, Bar-Lev was appointed deputy chief of staff, I was left head of General Staff Division, my status undermined.

As long as I am not convinced that some objective test found Bar-Lev more suitable to be chief of staff (and his appointment as deputy chief of staff was the ultimate indication that he, not I, would be Rabin's successor), I may be permitted to assume that my political opinions and the tendency to regard me as belonging to a rival party did not help. As for my views, no one needed spies or hidden microphones. I did not hatch secret plots, and I didn't conceal my views from anyone. Everyone knew that I wasn't a member of Mapai, the dominant political party, and that my roots weren't in the dominant Labour movement. The loyal party stalwarts understood that it was an unusual animal they had in this Weizman. To them I was a wild man, with horrifying opinions: a senior commander who claimed that we have the right to Hebron and Nablus and all of Jerusalem, and that we must endeavour to implement that right by force of arms, if there is no other alternative; a character who could influence young people with his claims that Zionist rights cannot be divided between Beersheba and Hebron, but between hypocrisy and honesty and who said that anyone who claimed we had the right to Beersheba but not to Hebron was sinning against Zionism, against the state and against his own conscience. They viewed me as a 'national desperado' who preached that the best pilot in the world isn't just a man who knows how to squeeze the right button and send off his missile at the right moment, but must believe in the justice of his deeds in defence of the rights of the Jewish people to the land of Israel.

At the beginning of June 1967, I walked around feeling like a whipped dog. Things were caving in on me, one after the other. I felt so lousy that a sinful thought crossed my mind: should I leave the army in protest? Every man has his weaknesses, and I had a deep need to say: 'If that's the way you treat me, you can go and run your own war!'

But nothing came of these thoughts, and I don't regret it for a moment. Although a protest was called for, I managed to regain my balance and overcome my anger. In doing so, I was helped by the advice of three men for whose qualities I had a high regard. I poured my heart out to the National Religious Party leader and interior minister, the late Moshe Haim Shapira. He listened and thought the matter over. Then he begged me not to resign on the eve of such a fateful war. Menachem Begin added a note of drama to his request: 'Swear to me that whatever you do, you won't leave the army now. The time isn't right for personal protests, however justified they may be.'

But it was a Haifa man who had the greatest influence on me: the late Abba Hushi. I had always been on excellent terms with him, like my late father before me. Abba was Haifa's father (*abba* is Hebrew for father), and its citizens were his sons. That was the way he treated me. Whenever I came to Haifa, he always gave me a joyful welcome. Hushi was one of the people who wanted to see me appointed chief of staff. I know that he spoke to Eshkol in my favour, even though he was aware of my political 'deviation'. I don't know exactly how he found out that I was toying with the idea of resignation. In any case, he phoned me and rebuked me in his usual frank manner: 'If you resign from the army, this will be the last time I talk to you, and I'll never see you again!'

The die was cast. Whether I liked it or not, I was going to swallow my anger and stay on in the army, at least until the war was won. There was something else I did – a small act, but of value nevertheless. The fact that I'd been screwed was of course no secret to other senior officers. I convened those of General Staff Division and told them: 'This is the way things are! Chaim is deputy chief of staff and I'm head of General Staff Division. Together with the chief of staff and the heads of army commands, we shall lead the armed forces to a great victory. God help anyone who tries to stir up any trouble between Chaim and me!' There was some astonishment, but my words were well understood, and if anyone was plotting something, he was given notice that he wouldn't get away with it.

Even before Dayan was appointed defence minister, I had one or two opportunities to urge Eshkol to shake off his doubts and hesitations and go to war, which was inevitable in any case. Whether it was to 'build up' my reputation, or to make the matter more dramatic, a story made the rounds about my ripping off my rank-insignia and throwing them in Eshkol's face. Verity requires the embellishments to be stripped off the events of those days, which were painful and turbulent enough. The fact is that one day at the end of May, when it was totally clear that there was nothing to hope for from further political efforts and that no one would solve any problems for the beleagured State of Israel, I went, on my own initiative, to Eshkol's Tel Aviv office. The justice minister, Yaakov Shimshon Shapira was with him, I said to Eshkol, 'The armed forces are ready and prepared for war. If you give the order, Jewish history will remember you as a great leader. If you don't, it will never forgive you!' It was no mutiny, nor any form of *putsch*, as various adroit commentators tried to describe it; it was a clear and, in my opinion, legitimate attempt to encourage the prime minister to take action. My words produced total consternation. Eshkol bowed his head. Shapira covered his face with both hands. As I left the room, I thought I heard him sob – or perhaps I only imagined it.

I never threw my rank-insignia at Eshkol, or anyone else for that matter. A few days before my talk with Eshkol, I walked out of a long, tiresome and frustrating meeting of the Cabinet and entered a side room, where only the late Moshe Kashti was sitting. I was boiling with rage. With my right hand, I pulled the insignia off my left shoulder and flung them on the vacant table. At that precise moment, Finance Minister Pinchas Sapir walked into the room and saw my gesture. Needless to say, it wasn't I who reported the incident to the press.

When Moshe Dayan was appointed defence minister, he brought with him a sense of the urgency about going to war. He gave us the feeling that it would not be long before the Israeli forces struck. He came at the right time; he gave people heart and dispelled their doubts.

After the victorious conclusion of the war, when political accounts were being settled, those angered by Dayan's success used to say: 'Can you imagine that Dayan altered things completely in the few days between his appointment and the outbreak of war? Did he make new plans? Did he supply the armed forces with equipment they lacked?' Of course, the answer is no; he didn't change things around completely, and that wasn't his great contribution. But he gave a tremendous push to the will to fight. He gave tremendous impetus to the demand not to restrict ourselves to some limited, incomplete operation instead of the total annihilation of the Egyptian army.

But Dayan had two serious worries. His first fear related to the southern front: the occupation of the Gaza Strip and the banks of the Suez Canal. He was very knowledgeable about Sinai, from back in 1956. Whatever he lacked, he made up diligently. About a fortnight before he was appointed defence minister, Moshe went down to the southern front and got to know it inside out – in some spheres, better than anyone else. He 'angered' Sheika Gavish, head of Southern Command, by openly expressing a wish to replace him. (At one point I received a request from Dayan asking to be mobilized as a reservist and to have his uniform and insignia sent to him. Both requests were fulfilled.) Dayan's second worry concerned the northern front. The head of Northern Command, Dado, made repeated appeals not to forget him and the Syrians. Nevertheless, it was considered doubtful whether we would go up the heights and occupy the Golan. (The decision to do so, at a later stage, was taken under somewhat strange circumstances.)

Later, when political conditions permitted Dayan's appointment as defence minister, he brought with him to General Headquarters a distinct flavour of leadership. There was something about his appearance, his speech and his confidence that dispelled gloom and replaced it with smiles, that drove away uncertainty and, in its place, created a sharp awareness that our path had been shortened. When he first entered the undergound command-room, a few days before the war, his entry was typically Dayanesque: 'Do you have a plan?' he asked, as though it were conceivable that, with war so near, the General Staff of the Israel Defence Forces didn't have a clear plan of what to do and how to do it. However, even on the morning of 5 June, when war broke out, not everything was clear. We knew that we were about to annihilate the Egyptian air force and hammer the Egyptian army until it was utterly destroyed. But it wasn't clear how near we would get to the Canal and whether the army would take up positions on its banks. On the other hand, it was certain that we wouldn't fight Hussein or occupy the West Bank, unless the Jordanians launched military operations.

The task of the air force was clear: the faster it finished off the

Egyptian air force, the sooner it could divert its attention to the Syrian air force and to aid the advancing ground forces by clearing their routes, preventing the Egyptians from bringing up reinforcements and scoring vigorous attacks on their armour. I was fully confident of the air force's ability to do the job. But the air force commanders, men who had risen under me, already showed more faith than their 'pope'. A few days before the war, I visited Benny Peled, then commanding an air base. I asked him, '*Nu*, Benny, how will it work out?' and he answered bubbling with confidence, with details of what the Egyptian and Syrian air forces would look like after we finished with them. When I took off in my little helicopter, I thought to myself, and later said to Re'uma, 'It could be I've trained a group of men so cock-sure of themselves, they even outdo me!'

Above all, 'everything depends on the air force', as several senior officers so justly put it. That was what I felt on the morning of 5 June, in the air force command-post. That was the feeling of everyone who was there that fateful morning. At 7.30 on the morning of 5 June the suspense was incredible. The planes were on their way. At 7.40 they were to deliver the first blow at nine Egyptian airfields. For five years I had been talking of this operation, explaining it, hatching it, dreaming of it, manufacturing it link by link, training men to carry it out. Now, in another quarter of an hour, we would know if it was only a dream, or whether it would come true.

For the strength and striking force of our air force to come to full expression at 7.45 am of 5 June 1967, we did a thorough job of studying the Syrian and Egyptian air forces and their way of life. We assumed that their commanders' notions would be influenced by Soviet advice and supervision. The more we learnt and analyzed, the more the picture grew fuller and more complete. The Egyptians were not prepared for such a crushing blow. They sat at the feet of their Soviet teachers, instead of learning the lessons of the Sinai Campaign. We would catch them on the ground and destroy them before they could take off, before they even understood what was going on.

Nevertheless, we did not rely on this analysis alone, however correct it appeared. When Dan Tolkovski was still commander of the air force, we feared an attack on our planes while they were still parked on the airfields. Ben-Gurion was no combat pilot, of course, and he acquired his military education while contending with Israel's problems and troubles. In 1954, when I was in command of Ramat David, he came on a visit. At the time we had three squadrons: Meteors, Mustangs and Spitfires. The whole lot were parked in straight lines, wing to wing, like soldiers on parade. The 'old man' glanced at them for a moment, and then he said: 'God protects fools'. We explained that it was a matter of economy, and, indeed, this was the reason for lining them up like that. When they are all bunched up, you need fewer tractors, less compressed air and less electricity to do maintenance work on them. Ben-Gurion listened carefully and remained unconvinced. We were confident that no Egyptian or Syrian plane could reach the field and attack the planes on the runways, but we knew that confidence was not enough.

We had extensive knowledge about enemy capabilities, but we had to know about our own ability to carry out the task successfully. An operation like attacking Egyptian airfields, within a brief time span and with all our forces attacking in a series of waves, demanded a high degree of precision in timing take-off and arrival at targets. Because of various restrictions, we rarely sent up such large numbers of planes for practice. This is the time to mention an air force staff major during the sixties (now a lieutenant-colonel), who is 'to blame' for thinking up the idea of attacking in waves and of doing the precise and complex job of co-ordination involved. He also produced the operational orders for the job and proved that it was possible to achieve a high degree of co-ordination between planes possessing dissimilar traits.

At one stage of our preparations for such a situation, information began to pour in about Egyptian preparation of an anti-aircraft defence system. Once again, we had a taste of the sceptism that is a regular feature of our lives: could the air force do its job, despite this new and powerful factor? We were confident that the way we were planning the operation would not permit the Egyptian defence systems to foil the plan.

The whole plan rested on total surprise: sending up a large number of planes from a number of bases and dispatching them, at low altitudes, stealthily. All those planes, taking off from different airfields, flying at different speeds, would get into formation as planned and, at precisely the identical moment, they'd arrive at nine Egyptian airfields (the tenth, Beni Suaff, near Fayum, was a little further away, and the attack there was deferred slightly). If the scales should tip against us, and we failed to destroy the Egyptian air force, only four planes were held in reserve for the defence of Israel's skies. Never has there been such an audacious attack, where everything was thrown into the balance.

On the morning of 5 June, all we had were 196 operational combat planes, from Ouragans to Mirages. Dozens of planes were in the air in foursomes. Each foursome was headed for its own field, followed, at precisely co-ordinated intervals, by additional foursomes. These were my boys, the ones I had brought up, trained and taught, who downed hundreds of litres of whisky and cognac with me, whose hearts were linked to mine in a deep sense of partnership. I loved them at that moment more than I had ever loved them before, and I knew that even if the operation were a complete success, an astounding victory, even then some of them would never again have a drink with me, never shake my hand and say: 'It was worth it, all of it.'

Radio silence was imposed. I wanted at least to know where they were, how they felt, to hear their voices and let them hear mine. But I couldn't. Everything depended on the degree of surprise.

Whether or not you are a believer, you pray – for the boys. For the State of Israel, whose fate lay in the balance.

The man who drove me out of my mind during those moments was the commander of the air force, Motty Hod. I've never seen anything like it! My part in preparing the air force and its men for this war is a matter for the history books. Here, at the command-post, all the responsibility rested on Motty. And that man – what a man! – was calm and quiet to an amazing degree. His expression was impassive; no one in the world would ever know what was going on inside him. But what strange habits he had! He wasn't addicted to cigarettes, he was hooked on water! He was a kind of gigantic radiator. There was an enormous water-jug beside him, and he picked it up with both hands, put it to his lips and bottoms up! You heard a kind of prolonged gurgling, and then ... it was empty. The radiator had been filled up. The jug was replenished for him and, without blinking an eyelid, without even going away for a drain, he gulped it down once more. He must have been burning it up! I relieved my tension with a momentary thought: 'What will happen first – will a couple of hundred Egyptian planes go up in flames, or will the radiator burst?'

At 7.45 it was hard to live with the suspense any longer. The defence minister was there, as was the chief of staff and his deputy and senior air-force officers. Breathing was uneven, faces pale. And then the first reports came in. A foursome had eliminated five planes. Another destroyed four. Another two and three and four. Radio silence was over, and our hearts contracted. The first of our planes were downed, and pilots were missing. But the news was basically a stream of great successes.

The plan was that each field would be attacked by the first foursome, followed seven or ten minutes later, by a second foursome. The nine Egyptian airfields – four in Sinai, three near the Canal and two close to Cairo – were taken completely by surprise. We purposely did not decide to strike at dawn or dusk, which are the conventional times for attacks of this kind because of the refraction of the sun's rays. We assumed that the Egyptians would be prepared for an attack at the conventional hours: 7.45–8.45 was chosen to deceive the Egyptians and gain complete surprise. If they were ready for an attack at sunrise, that had passed and nothing had happened, giving them the feeling that it would be another routine day. To complete the deceptive impression of routine, we sent up innocuous Fugas that morning for regular practice. We hoped the Egyptians would continue to labour under the delusion that it was just another day of training. Nothing was going to happen.

While they were enjoying their delusions, the Egyptian air force was turned into a flaming torch. Without total surprise, it would have been impossible to achieve such success in such a short time. Most of the stories published shortly after the war in the world's press about the new types of weapons our air force used in its attacks were a lot of nonsense. Our victory was so impressive that people had an urge to find some kind of special explanation or revelation that would remove the curtain of mystery from this fantastic triumph. The papers cooked up canards, and the public, both in Israel and abroad, swallowed them greedily: special bombs, amazing gadgets and all kinds of brilliant Israeli inventions – all titbits for the palate and the imagination.

The truth was simple and colourless. Perhaps in that lay its strength. Eight years earlier, the French had declared the simple aerial cannon to be completely superfluous, a waste of time, money, ammunition and training, and suggested replacing it with air-to-surface and air-to-air missiles. Used for strafing from a low altitude, employing standard ammunition in the skilled hands of the Israeli pilots, these cannon were our principal weapon in the Six Day War. More than anything else, it was these simple weapons that destroyed the air forces of Egypt, Syria and Iraq.

It was all so simple that it's almost a pity to puncture the glamorous tales of brilliant inventions. To maintain complete surprise by keeping out of sight of Egyptian radar, the planes had to fly at extremely low altitudes. But the lower one flies, the more fuel the plane uses up; because of the distances, the planes were unable to carry large loads of bombs. In any case, bombs are not an effective weapon for destroying planes on the ground. Strafing with cannon and machine-guns is far better for this purpose. That was the importance of total surprise, which would find the Egyptian planes parked on their runways, exposed to the accurate fire of our cannon. Our planes carried few bombs, and there was no point in wasting them on enemy aircraft. They were kept for ravaging the runways, if only briefly to prevent the Egyptian airplanes from taking off between one attack and the next, whether to engage our planes in aerial combat or to flee the fate that awaited them from the cannon of our planes.

The truth is that simplicity triumphed in this war: navigation by clock and by the good old compass, unusual discipline, precision flying in take-off, forming into foursomes and flying the low-altitude routes, and the cannon, simple and superb. We knew all about this simplicity during those hours down in the air force underground command-post. Reports came in and were quietly computed. Four, another four, another five, another five, another two – the numbers swelled. The count of the first hour showed that 100 Egyptian planes had been destroyed. No one said it, but there was a terrible fear in our hearts: 'Have the fellows picked up the

Arab habit of exaggeration?' Even those who believed in this operation, recommended it and fought for it to be put into action suddenly found it too big and inconceivable.

But it was a fact. At about ten o'clock in the morning, I phoned Re'uma: 'We've won the war!' She was considerate enough not to say what she thought of her husband going mad under the tension. She only said: 'Ezer, are you crazy? At ten o'clock in the morning? You've gone and finished the war?' The war wasn't finished. There were still a number of unsolved problems. But at ten o'clock, two and a half hours after it had begun, the war was a complete and stupendous victory. Down in the command, you could read it on men's faces. The tension was relieved. The frowns of fear and doubt disappeared. How shall I express the way I felt then? It was like facing a grey sky, laden with clouds, and then the sun begins to rise, slowly, hesitantly, one ray, another and another, and the sky begins to clear up; finally, there is the sun, big and bright, master of all the heavens.

The Egyptian air force was finished, even if it still had a few Migs, which later attempted to influence the battle. In destroying it, we lost nineteen planes, 10 per cent of all our air force, a higher percentage than we lost in the costly Yom Kippur War, relative to the number of planes we possessed at the beginning of the war and the number of combat sorties. With the approval of the high command, Motty correctly decided to divert the air onslaught to Syria: it was her turn to see murderous blows descend on her planes and their airfields.

As soon as I was sure that the Arab air forces had ceased to be a factor in the war, my attention as head of Operations Branch was directed to what was happening in the ground battles. In setting zero hour for the ground attack, we had to prefer one of two considerations: if we pinned our hopes on air force participation in the land battles, it would be better to set the zero hour for our ground forces later than for the air force. Only when the planes completed their task, or when their success was no longer in doubt, would the ground forces go into action, secure from air attack and aided by our planes. The other consideration: a few hours after the attack on their airfields, the Egyptian command would be ready for a ground attack. If zero hour for both air and land attacks were the same, the ground forces would also benefit from the element of surprise. After thinking it over, we preferred the second option, both because we were confident that the air strike would succeed and because we thought that surprise would be of great help to our ground forces. Accordingly, both 'Red Sheet' (zero hour for the ground forces) and 'Focus' (zero hour for the air force) were set for the same time, 7.45.

Tallik was to be the first to make a breakthrough, without awaiting the outcome of the air attack. He was still slogging it out with the Egyptians in the northern sector of Sinai when Arik Sharon began to advance in the central sector. With Sharon went David. Thus, in the midst of the great war, with its ringing triumphs and its promise of new opportunities, I was involved in a 'private war', in which my personal interest went well beyond my official duties. David is the son of my sister, Yael. I had brought him to Israel and to the Israeli army, and I regard him as my own son, flesh of flesh. And I knew that in this 'easy' war, Sharon's battle for a break-through in his sector would be very hard.

12

YAEL

YOCHAI-YAEL WEIZMAN. That was what I called my sister, Yael, with the affection of a younger brother for a sister three years his senior. Yael excelled at school, she was often brandished before me by my father, held up as an example I would do well to follow. I loved her and was closely attached to her. She was a great beauty, and I was much concerned with the 'great question' of who she was going out with. She was irritable, often moody and depressed, undergoing successive emotional crises. Her relationship with our parents was not always as good as mine. Perhaps that's the way it is with girls. Or perhaps my lousy nature at least did me the favour of permitting me to enjoy life.

It was through Yael that I got to know Chaim Laskov, who was chief of staff of the Israel Defence Forces when I returned from command college at Andover and who was still chief of staff when I was first promoted to commander of the air force. Chaim won my heart, and not just because he was Yael's steady boy-friend. He was strong, healthy, sturdy, the very epitome of Palestine's sporting Jewish youth. Thus I had good reason to regret it when Yael and Chaim broke off their relationship. In 1939 Yael went to Jerusalem to study at the university, while Chaim remained in Haifa.

Throughout World War Two there were always Englishmen in and out of our home. Despite the disagreements between them and us, my parents believed that our joint effort to destroy the Nazi monster required the Jews of Palestine to suspend their campaign against the British government. I presume that the use of the English language in our home, the common cause and the frequent visits by Englishmen all contributed to what our family regarded as a terrible tragedy: Yael fell in love with a British officer, a non-Jew. There were attempts to break the tie, to ward off the danger, but they all foundered on their rock-like love. I can't claim to be guiltless. If I were to pretend that my view was different, and that, unlike other members of the family, I treated the relationship with tolerance and understanding, it would be untrue.

While Yael Weizman and Captain Connell William Allingham were involved in their great love affair, I was a cadet-pilot in Rhodesia, enmeshed in my own dreams, in my pursuit of the war. I discovered something of what was going on from more-or-less overt hints in my parents' letters. It was only later that I discovered the rest, when the pieces fitted together to produce a complete picture.

Yael – slim, blonde and beautiful – was sunning herself at the beach when she met the tall, handsome Englishman. He was serving in the 7th Armoured Division and had been badly wounded in the battles in the Western Desert and sent to Haifa for treatment and recuperation. One glance from each side, and it was love at first sight.

Father's world caved in on him. He was the first to grasp that this was no fleeting love affair but a serious relationship. As a first step, he cautioned Yael. Speaking bluntly, he warned her of the results of her recklessness – to no avail. Then he presented himself before the commander of the British forces in Palestine. Walking in with his head held high, he addressed the general bluntly, without any preface: 'I am Yehiel, the son of Ozer Weizman. I have a daughter named Yael. There's an armour captain of yours, by the name of Connell William Allingham, who's dancing attendance on her. If you don't get him out of the country, there's going to be trouble.' Short and to the point.

The English general understood. He sent the captain off to the Western Desert. In retrospect, I wonder if this act of father's didn't help bring about Yael's marriage to Connell. There can be no certain answer. If Father had pretended indifference and let her handle her own affairs, Yael might have changed her mind. But when he tried, with his habitual forcefulness, to impose his view on her, it was like challenging her to a duel. She was obstinate to an extreme and quick to flare up. She rebelled against his attempt to fetter her and force her life into precast moulds. In many ways, her character resembled Father's – if it was going to be war, then war it would be.

Father was working in the south at the time and lived in Uncle Chaim's house in Rehovot, where he made the acquaintance of the commander of the Tel Nof (Akir) airfield, a pleasant middle-aged Englishman named Harry Owen. Yael, sharp-witted and crafty, foxily pretended that the captain had taken control of her heart. There was no way Father could have suspected that her friendship with Harry Owen was closely bound up with Allingham, then exiled to the Western Desert. Behind Father's back, Yael hatched a plot with Owen: Harry helped the captain to hitch-hike flights to Palestine, Connell came on leave regularly, and their love overcame all obstacles.

Total pandemonium broke loose. Aunts and uncles were tearing their hair. My sister – gifted, with an excellent academic record, an honours graduate of the Hebrew University Organic Chemistry Department, the family's pride and joy – went to Father and announced: 'I'm marrying Connell'. What could he do? He shouted. He begged. He threatened. If I'd been at home and not in Rhodesia, I would probably have had a fit of rage, and we would have quarrelled. Father tried the ultimate weapon: 'If you marry him,' he told Yael, 'your fate will be bitter. You'll be cast out of this house and out of our people, as befits a renegade.' It was no good. There was no way back. Yael and Connell were married by the Jerusalem district commissioner.

Accompanied by Connell, Yael walked into 4 Melchett Street to proclaim: 'I am now married to Connell William Allingham.' Silence. Tension by the ton. Father, his face tormented, paced heavily towards Yael and ordered her to leave the house, never to return. Yael took Connell's hand. There was no point in saying good-bye. They departed.

Father wasn't orthodox; he did not observe religious law. He did not sit *shiva* (the seven-day mourning for the dead), as a religious Jew would when a child 'married out'. But although he was not observant, it was as though darkness had descended upon him, as though Yael had departed this world and he would never see her again.

It was October 1944. The war was still spreading destruction. Connell was posted to England, and Yael, as a 'war bride', accompanied her husband by train from Haifa to Alexandria, where they were to take a troopship to England. There was a sorrowful leave-taking at the Haifa railway station. Yael was seen off by her cousin, Uncle Moshe's daughter Mika, and by Mother, sufficiently emboldened by love for her daughter to defy Father – probably the only time she did so in all their time together. They were the only ones there. Mother often described those sad moments, the painful farewell leaving her with an aching heart and a bruised soul. I don't know exactly what went on between her and Father at that time, but, during those emotion-laden moments at the station, Mother probably also sensed a doubt: was only Yael to blame? Yael and Connell Allingham? Or was it Yehiel Weizman too? And perhaps herself, as well? For years after, she drenched her pillow with tears, weeping through clenched teeth.

I heard of all this in Rhodesia. In my heart, I found no justification for Yael's behaviour. I felt as if she had betrayed everything: the Jewish people, Zionism, our parents, our family, our country and me. I was convinced that from her own point of view, she had also acted foolishly: this marriage would not hold together. Whenever I thought of my future relationship with my sister, I felt sorrowful. I was sure that her reckless step had destroyed our friendship. My indignation flared at the thought that she had broken this unique bond, which always served me as a source of warmth and gratification. There was no longer anything in common between us, so I thought then.

Paradoxically, it was Uncle Chaim, the president of the World Zionist Organization, who treated Yael and her husband generously. When they reached England, he took them under his wing, to a certain extent. I presume that he did so under the influence of his wife, Aunt Vera. She was a clever woman: assimilated, a snob and an introvert. She didn't know Hebrew and spoke English with a heavy Russian accent. I wouldn't say that her traits exactly befitted the wife of a president of the State of Israel.

She kept a sharp eye on Uncle Chaim, watching his every move with the devotion of a faithful bodyguard and keeping him from too-close contact with people. She made great efforts to shut him up within her own enclosed world. She may have thought his high position made it unfitting for him to be too gregarious; or perhaps she was too well acquainted with his 'flesh-and-blood' nature.

When Yael slammed the door on Judaism, rejecting the solid Weizman values and rebelling against the conservative conventions of Yehiel and his family, it was a welcome breath of fresh air for Aunt Vera. Vera was alien to our family, and our customs were strange to her. She shrank from us and our clamour. She would withdraw into a corner and cast a disdainful glance at our noisy clan. She despised our habits, our shouting and our heated arguments. What a tribe they were, those Weizmans! Each would grab his *pulke* (chicken leg) and bury his teeth in it, with the fat oozing down his chin and unmusical sounds filling the air. She maintained a firm hold on Uncle Chaim to keep him from plunging into the Weizman revelries. He was somewhat afraid of her and her endless grumbling, but more than that, he was attracted to his natural family, whose customs he loved like any of the other brothers. At first he would try to do her bidding, but gradually he melted and gave way, until he broke away from her and became a true Weizman – lively and effervescent and full of *joie de vivre* – to join in the eating and drinking, the laughter and shouts. Yet Uncle Chaim did not turn his back on Yael. He helped her to get a job as a chemist at a Manchester refinery, and he was her sole support in her new life in England.

In 1946 England was still licking her war wounds. My brother-in-law had no trade or profession. For twelve years he had served king and country, but this entitled him to no more than a relatively insignificant post. All in all, Yael and Connell had a pretty difficult time of it. They struggled to scrape together a living. I'm not saying that a frugal life must necessarily cause a couple to break-up. On the contrary, I know it's not unusual for family ties to be strengthened by such exigencies. But in my disapproval of their relationship, it crossed my mind once or twice that if they suffered economic difficulties, their ties would weaken. But they withstood their tribulations, and their love endured.

I was furiously angry with Yael, but it never entered my mind to break off contact with her. After my release from the RAF, I went to London to study. When I got there in June 1946, Yael was already nursing her firstborn, David, then seven or eight months old. We hadn't met since 1943; in effect, our links began to weaken in 1939, when she left home to study in Jerusalem. I phoned her. For some reason she sounded cold. Troubles, I thought, and perhaps a touch of embarrassment.

I got on the train at Waterloo and set off for Pinner, a dreary suburb. As the train wheels rumbled along, thoughts and emotions raced through my mind. I was on my way to my sister. We had spent all our lives together, in her pink room and my blue room, side by side. We were always hand in hand, our hearts closely linked; we were always frank and open with each other. And here I was, jammed like a sardine into an English railway carriage, dirty and dingy and dilapidated, as was most of England during those arduous years. A voice in my head whispered: 'You're going to see Yael!' But it was soon replaced by: 'Who? The one that married that Englishman and presented your father with a half-Jew, half-gentile grandson?'

I rang the bell. The door opened to reveal a tired face, drawn and drained of its former freshness. I flung a glance inside. A grey house, misty, with the smell of coal and English cooking. A grey house in a grey environment. A depressing sight. I almost let out a shout of bewilderment, of anger, of surprise: 'Yael, why? This in place of our wonderful home on Melchett Street in Haifa?' In her arms she held her blond baby. To tell the truth, little babies, with their peculiar smells, have never inspired me with any feeling of intimacy. But I suddenly realized that this baby was my nephew, the first to make me an uncle. Perhaps I stroked his head. I don't remember. On Yael's cheek I planted a little kiss, more a token of estrangement than of cordiality. There was a barrier between us, a kind of wall.

We sat down. My brother-in-law was away, delayed on his way back from work. We didn't speak. She was rocking little David. My glance darted around from place to place. Finally, I couldn't stand it any longer. I told her what had been on my mind for years.

'What have you done? What do you need all this for?' I felt a little better. But not a word from Yael. She was silent, withdrawn, remote, as though she wasn't sitting in that house, but hovering in a world of her own. Then my brother-in-law came home. A tall man, cool and detached. We exchanged a flabby, rather reserved handshake.

That first meeting left me frustrated. I managed to tell Yael that if she wanted to get out of her predicament, 'just say the word, just give a sign. I'll help you.' And again, I saw those dulled, expressionless eyes, and once more, her silence cut into my heart.

At the end of 1946, or perhaps early in 1947, my father came to England. He professed to be there on business, but I suspected that, secretly, his purpose was different: his son was in England and so was his daughter, as well as his first grandson. But he had his self-respect, and when we met at his hotel, he promptly informed me: 'I'm not going to her. I'm not going to see her. For me, she doesn't exist.' I didn't display much filial respect. 'It's your grandson,' I told him. 'Your first grandson. His father may not be Jewish, but his mother, you may remember, is your dearly beloved daughter. So kindly get ready. We're going to Yael.' His resistance was feeble. We went to Yael.

In my lifetime I haven't had many opportunities to cry. It's not exactly the sort of thing I like to do. But at that meeting between my father and Yael, I shed tears. Just like that. With no premeditation. All of a sudden, my cheeks were wet. My throat burned with a lump I couldn't swallow. Once again the door opened; once again she stood in the doorway, in the same pose, with her baby clutched in her arms. My old man had a terribly fierce and passionate nature, but he also had a tremendous heart, and he melted on the spot. He was simultaneously tender and angry, a mixture of clashing, contradictory feelings and desires. They clasped each other in a long, ardent embrace. It was a highly charged kiss, full of love and a lot of tension. After that the old man picked up his first grandson and fastened his wise eyes on him. He looked and looked and looked, as though he were trying to see what lay behind that innocent little face; as though he wanted to foresee what the future held for this half-breed child and where his destiny would take him.

On the train, on the way back to the hotel, Father said to me in a peremptory voice: 'If it's the last thing you do in your lifetime, you are to bring Yael back home, either with all of her family or part of it.'

Events raced by. The War of Independence began at the end of 1947, and there was no time to think of Yael, Connell and little David. But every now and then I would remember her in surprise and indignation: the Jewish people was shedding its blood, fighting for its state, and she was far away, as though the struggle didn't concern her. She had a small child, I knew. Then, later, their daughter Diana was born. But how could she disregard it all?

In 1949 Yael came on her first visit to the independent State of Israel, with her son and daughter. It was only a few years later that I heard the full story from her: Father invited her and the children to come on a visit. She never imagined that he was laying a trap for her. He bought the tickets and met her in Paris. Suddenly, it occurred to her to ask: 'What about the return tickets?'

He was embarrassed. 'There's only a one-way ticket to Israel.'

She was firm and forceful: 'Either you buy me a return ticket, here and now, or I'm not going on.'

Father's attempt to impose his will on her failed, as it had on previous occasions.

Yael came and spent a short time at our parents' home. She looked around, she listened, but she wasn't swept off her feet. This gave me further cause for indignation, and I didn't let the opportunity slip by. How indifferent she was, this 'English-woman'! We had a state! A sovereign state! We were building up the country. Her uncle was its first president. Her younger brother was a squadron commander in the air force. But she didn't display any enthusiasm, she wasn't carried away; she treated the whole matter as though it had nothing to do with her. Then she returned home to England. That sounded strange: 'Home to England'.

We corresponded. We met again. In 1950 I was the first Israeli officer to go to England on an official visit after the War of Independence. As on all my other visits, I went to see Yael. I observed her dreary, humdrum, existence, and it jerked at my heart-strings. By this time I had my Re'uma, and our lives centred around Shaul. It may have been thanks to Re'uma that my ties with

Yael grew stronger. In our sporadic talks with her, Re'uma and I took care to avoid offending her. I told her that even if it didn't happen immediately, ultimately she would find her home again in Israel with us. I didn't press her to make immediate, unequivocal decisions. Without entering into any obligations, we tried to inquire what work Connell could do in Israel and how he'd fit in.

David, Yael's son, came again in 1955, about the time our daughter Michal was born. I was the commander of Ramat David, and I took David there. Every nine-year-old is enthusiastic about planes. I cannot claim with any certainty that David found any significance in the fact that the planes were Israeli, but something may have remained with him from that visit. It may have had some influence on his future development.

Yael was in England, and I was in Israel, eagerly building up an air force. It was only at infrequent intervals that I had time to think about her. Every now and then, I would see her face and fret over our separation.

Father died in 1957. I hurriedly phoned Yael, but she did not arrive in time for the funeral. She came a day or two later, unaccompanied. The sorrow we shared over Father's death helped to topple the barriers between us. We talked a great deal. Things I had only grasped hazily now became clear to me: the deep conflict between Yael and Father; the mighty clash between two strong personalities, each with those cloudy eyes, which flared up strangely, like a pair of flaming torches, whenever they grew angry. Later, I happened to overhear a conversation between Yael and a cousin of ours who also married a gentile and lives with him in South Africa to this day. After the two hadn't met for fifteen years, I heard my sister ask her: 'What right did we have to do what we did?'

My father's death reminded me of his behest. 'Weizman, my lad,' I said to myself. 'This is it. You have to get to work to bring Yael and her family back to Israel.' In 1960 I invited David, then fifteen, to come and stay with us for a time. We made no mention of Zionism. I was at great pains to remove any suspicion that I might be plotting anything. I satisfied his curiosity on various points. He enjoyed himself. I wanted nothing more.

In 1963, when David was about seventeen, I discovered that he was thinking of joining the British air force. If this notion stemmed from my efforts to familiarize him with airplanes, I thought it would be profitable to take a further step and familiarize him with the Israel Defence Forces. I wrote to him: 'David, you've grown up. You must decide what you're going to do in life. Before you make a final decision, come and visit us. If you want to, you can learn Hebrew. You don't have to if you don't want to. If you want to return home to England, you can do so without any difficulty.'

In February 1965, he arrived in Israel. Re'uma, Shaul (then fourteen) and I – very excited – met him at the airport, a young man in flannel trousers, sports jacket and tie: a typical Englishman. We brought him home. A probe here, a feeler there, a short talk, a word from him, another from us. One thing became clear. David was discontent in England. His life there was far from easy. He was undecided, troubled. He knew that his grandfather had been a fervent Zionist, that his own uncle was the commander of the Israeli air force and that his mother's uncle was the first president of Israel. He had read the book *One Hundred Hours to Suez*, which I gave my sister after the Sinai Campaign (with the inscription, 'Next time, fifty hours – and forever!').

I have no doubt that he felt at home with us. Re'uma and I were very warm towards him. He had a room of his own, his financial needs were all covered and not a word was said about Zionism, Judaism or Israel. Planes, flying and the fact that his uncle was commander of the air force, enjoying a degree of popularity and glory, all probably attracted him. I sensed that there was a breakthrough, and, applying the basic principle of war, I decided to exploit this initial success. 'Listen, David, I'm not your father, I'm only your uncle. I can only offer you my advice and promise you my help. I propose you try life in Israel. Just as a trial. If you agree, there are two elementary things you have to know and do: to learn Hebrew and get to know people.'

He agreed to try. We made enquiries and concluded that it would be best for him to learn Hebrew at a special course in a kibbutz. And if he were going to a kibbutz, then it ought to be Mishmar Ha'emek, where Re'uma grew up and went to school, and where I have many good friends – ideological differences notwithstanding. My sister was pleased at the arrangement.

Without saying so expressly, she may also have thought, in her heart of hearts, that if David struck roots in this country, it would be a first step, opening the way for her and Connell and their little daughter to return home to Israel.

David was thrilled with his life in the kibbutz, where he shared a little shack with a Norwegian boy. Hanna Wolf, who went to school with me in Haifa and was now a member of Mishmar Ha'emek, also bent to the great task of bringing Yael Weizman back home. Other Haifa people who cared about Yael did likewise. For them, what had happened to her was a misfortune, and they proclaimed their readiness to help.

David learnt Hebrew and helped tend the sheep. I couldn't help the association of David the shepherd. He grew so attached to the kibbutz that he was to claim he had three mothers: Yael, Re'uma and Hanna from Mishmar Ha'emek. He was about nineteen when he came to me and said, 'Listen, Uncle Ezer, I've decided I like the life here.' My heart palpitated with agitation and excitement. Uneasy at revealing my weakness, I tried to conceal it. He continued, 'If I'm going to live here, then I have to be like everyone else and join the army.' Have you ever seen a man truly overjoyed? I looked at David, and in my mind's eye, I saw Yael and Diana, and Connell, too, leaving England and coming to Israel.

Like his father, David joined an armoured unit. In November 1965, this English-looking boy with his faulty Hebrew reported for basic training. I suppose he had more difficulties than we ever knew about. But he has two good qualities: he is an introvert, who wrestles silently with his problems, without complaints or grouches; and he's likeable, and he soon became popular. And David was a loyal soldier. He would bring home piles of dirty clothes, and Re'uma saw to everything. Was it I who brought Yael home? No, Re'uma did it. She looked after David like a mother. She tended him when he was ill, played hostess to his friends – boys and girls. She looked after his clothes, ironing and darning and patching. David went on to a tank commanders' course and then a tank officers' course. The lad was doing well.

I had a delightful experience at that time. In the winter of 1966, when I was head of General Staff Division, I visited the training camp, accompanying Chief of Staff Yitzhak Rabin. We walked into the officer-cadets' room. David was there. He didn't bat an eyelid, as though he'd never seen me before. At the time, there was much argument over the methods in force in the armoured units with regard to discipline and spit and polish. The chief of staff asked some questions, and a few of the cadets replied. All of a sudden, my boy got up, red as a beetroot – he may be quiet, withdrawn and self-controlled, but when he warms up, he reminds me of his mother – and said there was a lot of nonsense being spoken, and that the way things were, with polished boots and immaculate uniforms, was the right way – and a very good one it was. Then he sat down. Yitzhak didn't say a word, and it was only when we went out that he asked, 'Ezer, isn't that your nephew?' Naturally, he knew the whole story.

When David completed the course, I felt like a father whose son has made officers rank. I was also overjoyed to see that my bait was well anchored. The time would soon be ripe to throw the hook into the water and angle for Yael.

On 15 May 1967, at the beginning of the stand-by period that was to lead to the war, David, already wearing officer's insignia, was in the last stages of the course. I signed the order for the course to be dispersed, with the cadets being posted to Arik Sharon's division. He was in a fine Centurion unit, facing some formidable tasks. At that stage I was convinced that war was on its way. Even if it were deferred, it was inevitable. And I was equally certain that David, the son of my outcast, 'renegade' sister, this young man for whose presence in Israel and in the army I was responsible, he, and not my son, nor any other Weizman, would be the only member of our illustrious family to fight in this way, on the most dangerous front, in its most dangerous sector. What a crazy world, I thought. How the wheel of fate turns! Where is it hidden, the computer that calculates these strange whimsies, forging the links and joining the ends together?

I was convinced that we'd win. I said we'd win. But let no one think I wasn't worried. I knew the war would take its toll. It was a heavy burden. On 2 or 3 June, when the General Staff already knew the exact hour and day of the attack – and I knew very well that David's battalion would have the task of making the first breakthrough in the central sector of Sinai, and precisely where David would be in all this – I took a plane and flew down to visit the units in the field. I questioned the commanders, listened to their answers, proffered advice. I didn't refrain from inquiring about such-and-such brigade, such-and-such battalion, such-and-such company – and tank number such-and-such. I found him. He was walking underneath the camouflage netting, with my father's Parabellum pistol dangling from his belt. A boy going to war with his grandfather's Parabellum.

The pistol was bequeathed to me by my father, who left instructions what was to be done with it: 'It shall be given to the first of my grandsons who graduates from an officers' course'. Before David came to Israel, I intended to give it to my son Shaul, but he was too young to take part in this war. I got Shaul's permission, and then, not knowing whether I'd reach the area where David was stationed, I sought out Shmuelik Gorodish (commander of the southern front in the Yom Kippur War), a man with a truly Jewish soul. I told him the whole story and gave him the pistol to deliver to David.

'A thousand and one nights,' my lips whispered unthinkingly, as David climbed out of his tank, wearing Grandfather Yehiel's pistol. He had a favour to ask: 'Ezer, it's my turn to go on leave on Tuesday. Ask Re'uma to prepare a lot of hot water to get this dirt off me.' I tried to smile, but all hell was breaking loose in my heart. I said: 'Okay, chum, that'll be alright.' And inside I was thinking: 'God knows where you'll be on Tuesday! Or how warm you'll feel – and not from warm water either!' I was dying to tell him. To give him a hint. But my lips were sealed. I mustn't. I gripped his hand, firmly and warmly.

When the war came, David mounted his Centurion and charged. He shot up three Egyptian T-34's and stormed ahead, as far as the banks of the Canal. In all the pandemonium, amidst the great victories, each day I'd glance at the casualty lists for David's battalion. His name did not appear.

Shortly after the war, Yael came on a visit. David was the draw. After that, matters didn't take long to unfold. In 1968 Diana followed in her brother's footsteps and enrolled as a first-year student at the Hebrew University. She now works at the Weizman

Institute in Rehovot. Both she and David are married, and each of them has a son. In 1969 Yael and Connell came. Yael is employed at the Organic Chemistry Department of the Weizman Institute. Connell works in the engineering department of the Israeli Aviation Industries. The whole family is here. I went to Father's grave and told him: the task is completed.

13

GREATER ISRAEL

WHILE WE WERE COUNTING UP the number of Egyptian planes destroyed and Motty was ordering the attack on the Syrian airfields, while Tallik was thrusting into Rafiah and Arik Sharon was preparing to lunge forward, a new sound reached our ears. The 'little king', the darling of Israeli politics, Hussein of Jordan, was making vulture-like sounds. Nasser at least had guts: he put a noose around Israel's sensitive neck, threw down the gauntlet – and got his due deserts. Hussein waited. Israel sent him reassuring messages. 'Sit still and don't worry. We're not going for you.' But Nasser filled Hussein's head full of fanciful tales, telling him Tel Aviv was in flames and Israel was on the verge of collapse, and it would soon be time to divide up the spoils. As soon as he heard 'loot', Hussein lost his head and bounded to the carcass for his hunk of meat. Thus Hussein altered the course of the contest, giving it an additional national and historical dimension: as a result of the war, we returned to our ancestral home, to Jerusalem and the Land of the Bible.

At the first reports that the Jordanians had opened fire, there was an inclination in the General Staff to make light of it: 'Hussein's just pretending, to keep in with Nasser; but he doesn't mean it in earnest.' I must admit that I very much hoped he was in earnest. As long as we had been forced to go to war, I wanted it to give me the chance to write a wish on a slip of paper to be stuffed into one of the cracks in the Western Wall. It soon became clear that Hussein was in earnest – and we were in even greater earnest. The conflagration spread, and the Israeli forces set about restoring Jerusalem, Judaea and Samaria to the Jewish people. Now we were at war on two fronts, with Dado in the north sending heart-rending pleas throughout the week of war, until he was allowed to launch his blow at the Syrians on the Golan Heights.

During the fifth or sixth hour of war, the Jordanian air force met its fate. The Egyptian air force was already finished; the Syrians had undergone thorough treatment, and its backbone was about to break. Motty poured another jug of water into his 'radiator', gave a slight twitch of the little stick he was holding, resting it on two points on the map, Amman and Mafrak (two airfields, with thirty or forty planes each), and drawled casually: 'Do the Jordanians.' 'Do,' he said, and they were done. One of the components of the air force's power is its ability to switch units from one sector to another, and here was a classic example: one of our pilots was leading a foursome of Mirages for a strike in the Gulf of Suez area. When he was near Eilat, he was called up and asked: 'How's your fuel?' He had a look and reported back. There was enough. '180 degrees,' he was told. 'Go north, to Amman, and shoot up the planes there.' Additional air units, some on their way to objectives in Egypt or Syria, also joined the attack. Around one o'clock, halfway through the first day of the fighting, they finished off the Jordanian air force – their third that day!

The ground campaign was also going well: Tallik was battling his way towards El Arish on the northern coast of Sinai. There was a plan for the 55th Brigade, paratroopers under the command of Motta Gur (now chief of staff), to be dropped behind the Egyptian lines at El Arish, while water-proofed tanks were put ashore from landing craft and ships. After a time the plan was shelved. It was assumed that Tallik would manage to reach El Arish unaided. The 55th Brigade was deeply disappointed when the drop was called off and it was sent to Jerusalem instead. But there was some 'small' consolation for the cancelled drop: in the annals of the Jewish people, the brigade will be remembered as the liberators of Jerusalem.

The absence of any plan to occupy the West Bank left us with no choice other than to scrape together forces, some of which had been assigned to other fronts as reserves, and to send them into action. There was no talk yet of conquest and occupation, only of a limited operation. The order was to grab a few morsels, in various areas, to prevent Jordanian artillery from shelling Israeli centres. In the small hours of the morning between 5 and 6 June, Dayan, Rabin, Bar-Lev, Haka and I were sitting at headquarters when one of the commanders radioed in to inform us that his forces had surrounded Jenin, one of the major towns on the West Bank. Moshe looked at us with his single eye, a foxy kind of glance, and said, 'I know exactly what you want ...'

'What?' we let him guess.

'To take Jenin.'

'Correct!' we nodded.

'So, take it!'

That was the turning point. The plan for snatching morsels died at birth, and it became clear that we were to capture and liberate the West Bank.

The fact that our occupation of the West Bank was not premeditated, but the result of Hussein's desire to flex his muscles, justifies the titles I bestowed on Jordan's king after the war. One was 'the modern Balaam': Hussein wished to share in the spoils of war, but instead he blessed Israel, for through him we returned to the land of our ancestors. The other was 'The Hyena': Nasser convinced him that the carcass would soon be ready for stripping, and he shouldn't forgo his share of the flesh. Hussein hates us no less than other Arab rulers, although he covers it up with crafty phrasing, to please the Americans. After the Yom Kippur War, I concluded that Hussein had made two mistakes: the first was that he believed Nasser in 1967 – and barely saved his hide. The second, was that he *didn't* believe Sadat in October 1973, for amidst the events of the first days of that war, he may have missed an opportunity to improve his military position. It seems that he's prone to error. Let's hope he continues to err.

On the second day of the war, 6 June, Moshe Dayan tired of his role of rear-echelon defence minister. 'I'm going to Jerusalem,' he informed me. I jumped at the idea. 'Jerusalem? Then I'm going too.' I piloted the Alouette helicopter; with us were Ghandi and Shaya Reviv. Normally we would have landed at the Givat Shaul airstrip at the west of the city, but the field was within range of

Jordanian artillery, so we came down at the car-park of the Jerusalem convention centre, Binyanei Ha'uma, where General Uzi Narkiss and his staff were stationed. The flight itself was an experience. Below us were convoys of our troops going up to the capital. I flew low. Apparently they recognized Moshe, and we could see their excitement as hundreds of soldiers waved their hands in greeting.

At Uzi's command-post the atmosphere was tense. They began to spread out beflagged maps before Moshe, but he was impatient. He didn't want maps or briefings. There was only one thing on his mind: 'I want to go on a tour!'

'Where to?' asked Uzi.

And Moshe, as is his caprice at such moments, said, 'Guess!'

Uzi guessed: 'Mount Scopus.'

'You've got it!' said Moshe.

I heard him say Mount Scopus, and my ears pricked up. For twenty years I'd been dreaming of that hill, yet had never set foot there, although officially the area was Israeli territory. Mount Scopus, which dominates the Old City of Jerusalem and the eastern quarters of the Arab city, was the original site of the Hebrew University and Hadassah Hospital. We didn't lose it in the 1948 war, but we were cut off from it, and it had remained an enclave in the middle of Jordanian territory ever since. We were allowed to maintain a military guard there, which was relieved about once a month, but the tragedy was that this once vibrant centre of learning and healing was just sitting and rotting away for twenty years.

Uzi made all the preparations, and then he said to Moshe, 'Everything's ready, you can get into the half-track.' Moshe was in an impish mood: 'Get into a half-track yourself! I want a jeep.' It was 9.30 in the morning, and the war was still raging. Clouds of smoke were swirling up, snipers' shots were reverberating, casualties were being evacuated and a sharp smell was tickling our nostrils – cordite, smoke and burning.

A jeep carrying a recoilless cannon drove in front, and a half-track covered our rear,' while we, 'four in a jeep', were in the middle. We drove slowly down the road through one of the quarters of the Arab section of the city, and our little convoy

caught the Arabs' attention. Windows were opened. Sitting with
our helmets on, exposed, we drove on calmly, expecting a
fusillade of shots at any moment. The commander of the small
force on Mount Scopus didn't know exactly who was coming to
join up with his unit. Soldiers and officers emerged excitedly from
their positions, and everyone fell into each other's arms, hugging
and kissing. Almost unthinkingly, my legs carried me to the
laboratory of my uncle, Moshe Weizman, who was a professor of
chemistry at the Hebrew University. It was as though time had
stopped still. The clock, weary of ticking, had halted. On the table
I found a bundle of Uncle Moshe's papers. Chalked up on the
blackboard, in his handwriting, was the name of the lecture and its
date: 1948. The room was still permeated by the sharp smell of
chemicals. My sister Yael had studied here. It was from here she
graduated and later earned her masters degree. Elsewhere, friends
found some of her notebooks, dating back to 1948. For a moment
my thoughts turned to her son David, now taking part in the
onslaught on Sinai.

In the course of the years that we hadn't seen the university, it
had swelled in our imaginations, growing large and splendid.
Now, as we toured its departments and the National Library, it
returned to its true proportions, small and cramped. We went up
to the roof of the National Library. The road to Jericho was still
open to the Jordanian army. Jerusalem's encirclement had not yet
been completed. Dayan and Narkiss held a short consultation.
Then Dayan gave the orders for the encirclement of East
Jerusalem. We had our lunch with the Mount Scopus garrison and
then went back the way we came, in our jeep. I flew the helicopter
back to Tel Aviv. Down in the underground headquarters, I saw
Motty locked in battle with the entire Arab world and consuming
Tel Aviv's water by the jugful. In front of him I put down an
envelope I had taken from the Ambassador Hotel on the way up to
Scopus inscribed with the words: 'To my friend Motty, whose
victory laid the foundations for the Third Temple'. He read the
inscription, gulped down another jug and went back to conducting the war.

The Israeli forces struck on three fronts in the Six Day War:
Sinai, Jordan and the Golan Heights. On all three fronts our

victory was dazzling. But the Jordanian front was unlike the others. In Sinai and on the Golan, we fought for military reasons. There was no other choice: we had to eliminate the Egyptian army, and we had to call the Syrians to a bloody account and save our settlements from their menace. All this was true of the Jordanian army, too, but the liberation of Jerusalem, Judaea and Samaria (the West Bank) was more than that – far more. For me it meant returning home, to my own country, to places whose very names filled me with excitement and made my heart tremble.

These were places I had known as a child; in my early teens I used to accompany my father from Haifa to Jerusalem by way of Tel Hanan, Jenin and Nablus. At Han Luban, between Nablus and Jerusalem, we would halt to buy dried figs and then enter Jerusalem from the north. In Sinai and on the Golan Heights, we were guided by military and political considerations, here, in Judea and Samaria, our very souls rejoiced and palpitated. The prospect of returning to Kfar Etzion, where I had dropped supplies for the first time in January 1948; to set foot once more in Bet Ha'arava, which the air force had evacuated in 1948; to see Atarot again all held additional significance for me. Whenever I lectured at staff college, I would stress that, without all of Jerusalem, without the Western Wall, without Shilo and Anatot, Israel was a crippled, truncated state that could scarcely survive. In reply, I was told that was all nonsense, and the whole thing was 'historical hysteria', without any rational foundation. I was frequently hauled out on the carpet for 'misleading' our youth.

It was one of the whimsical fancies of history that my military vagaries took me to the back of beyond at the precise moment when the first Jews were returning to the Western Wall. It was eight on the evening of 6 June 1967. The war was already thirty-six hours old and almost completed. The Egyptian air force had given up the ghost. Tallik, Arik, Yoffe and Sheika Gavish had passed the half-way point in Sinai. Jerusalem would soon be in our hands. Jenin had been taken, the West Bank was collapsing. From his headquarters at Northern Command, Dado was clamouring: 'What about the Syrians?'

In underground General Staff headquarters, Defence Minister

Moshe Dayan asked: 'My friends, where is the force now
nearest to Sharm el-Sheikh?' We gave him the unit's name and
number. We looked at the maps: clearly it would take many hours
to reach Sharm. The defence minister was concerned. 'Friends, we
started this war principally over free navigation in the Straits of
Tiran. We've gained great victories. The West Bank is falling. In
my opinion, we shall soon be under pressure for a cease-fire – no
later than 8 June. (His prediction was accurate, as it transpired.)
We're going to destroy the Egyptian army in Sinai, and we shall
reach the Suez Canal and the Jordan – and I still don't know what
political results these tremendous victories will bring. But how
will it look if we don't reach Sharm el-Sheikh, after making that
our *casus belli*?'

He was right. It was then we thought up the idea – I think it was
hatched in the cool and brilliant mind of General Haka Hoffi, the
head of Operations Department, a man who got less than he
deserved of the glory and praise for the Six Day War victory – of
throwing together a force of paratroopers and flying them to
Sharm by helicopter, to take the area on the following day, 7 June.

Our intelligence reported an Egyptian battalion, possibly two,
in Sharm. It was quite a problem to get our paratroop force
together. Two of our paratroop brigades were engaged in fighting
in Sinai and shedding much blood, while Motta's brigade was
engaged in the battle for Jerusalem. At the same time, some of the
best officers in the army found themselves, for various reasons,
without any units to command. Likewise, Aharon Davidi, Chief
Paratroop Officer, was a staff officer without an active command.
The first step, therefore, was to gather these officers. Then, from
odds and ends of various other units, we got together 150
paratroopers. This force was to be sent down in sixteen helicopters.
Should it need reinforcements, some 350–400 additional paratroopers were assembled from various brigades, to be flown down
by ten Nords. In addition, a transport unit of Stratocruisers was
prepared to drop jeeps, command-cars, water, fuel and food as
soon as the area was captured. The plan called for four Mirages to
deliver a softening-up raid before the attack, and the navy was
instructed to move its torpedo boats from their anchorage at Eilat.

Then I dropped my private little bombshell: I was joining the force going to Sharm! The chief of staff and the minister of defence were surprised: the head of General Staff Division, the General Staff's senior general, joining an operation like this? 'Why you?' they asked. How could I explain? How could I tell them that ever since the war started I'd had the strangest feeling? All these years I'd been planning how to flatten the Egyptian air force, and when the time came, I was at headquarters, receiving reports of the victories. When I was appointed commander of the air force, I used to think: I flew in the Second World War, I fought in the War of Independence and in the Sinai Campaign. In the next war, when I look up, it won't be blue skies I'll see, like the view from a pilot's cockpit, but the fluorescent lights of some headquarters command. And here I was, following Israel's war from a command-post while the actual battle was waged by pilots younger and better than myself.

As head of General Staff Division, I was also interested in seeing a real land battle. In addition, I thought I could help in taking any decisions needed on the spot. I could see that Dayan was very worried about the situation, and, although relying fully on Davidi, the commander of the force, I wanted to be present. I joined the operation as a 'supernumerary' general. I took my helmet and my American carbine, and I muttered to myself: 'Weizman, this may be your first land battle!'

The force set off, but I was delayed at General Staff. That night I took my right-hand man, Efraim ('Froike') Poran, and we hurried to Eilat in a light air force plane. When we arrived, the whole force was there, and sixteen helicopters were refuelling. If the Jordanians in Aqaba had been better prepared and not carried away by the streams of lies emanating from Cairo, they could have eliminated the whole force with a couple of mortar shells. Davidi was to fly in the first helicopter, and I was to follow in the second. We'd hug the Saudi coast, on the assumption that there were Egyptian forces on the other coast. At eleven in the morning we took off. We were in contact with the Mirages that were to soften up the target. When we were near Ras Nasrani, north of Sharm on the coast, their commander reported sighting boats at Sharm. We instructed him: 'Attack your targets, as you were instructed!' He strafed the upper camp in Sharm while we flew to Ras Nasrani to see what was happening. From the air we could see the place was deserted, but I wasn't sure that the Egyptians had pulled out. Perhaps they were concentrating at Sharm itself.

We landed at the Sharm airfield, north-east of the outpost itself, on the top of the hill, as planned. The Mirages went in and did a few turns. Then we leapt from the helicopters, ready for combat. I found myself among the paratroopers, sprinting with my carbine and wondering where the first shots were going to come from. Shots, did I say? Not a shot to be heard. Not a single one! All was peace and tranquillity; there was a celestial silence. No Egyptians and no war. It was as though we had come to this charmed spot for a holiday. The paratroopers scattered at a run, taking up positions. But there was no shooting.

So there we were, with ten Nords airborne with reinforcements and the Stratocruisers carrying vehicles, ammunition and food. The first thing was to decide what to do with the reinforcements. Davidi and I decided to fly down to Sharm itself, to see what was happening there. We leapfrogged down with the helicopters, with Davidi, fearful of booby-traps, constantly concerned about me: 'Don't run ahead, don't run into buildings, don't open doors before you know what's inside. For God's sake, sir!' The notion that Sharm was deserted, that there was no one to fight, wouldn't sink in. But the place was empty. There was one camp, which formerly served the Yugoslav troops of the United Nations, and an Egyptian camp. During the stand-by period that preceded the war, the Egyptians evicted the Yugoslavs and occupied both camps. But now there were no Egyptians either – only the Israel Defence Forces' head of General Staff Division, whom war had, once again, impishly eluded.

In Sharm, we had one hell of a surprise. We encountered our navy! As it transpired, they had reached the Sharm anchorage forty-five minutes before us, and, like us, found neither Egyptians nor war. We kissed and hugged them, overjoyed, not only at meeting them, but because they were alive: by some miracle, the Mirages, who did not know of their presence, hadn't shot and bombed them to smithereens. Mercifully, the planes bombed the upper camp, not the anchorage where the navy men were. One of war's miracles.

We were still not convinced that there were no Egyptians about. Perhaps they had taken cover in the hills? Perhaps they were preparing to attack? There were only 150 of us, with sixteen helicopters on the ground, three torpedo boats and only light arms. With a 12–14 knot wind blowing, there was no point in having the paratroopers jump from the Nords, both because of the danger and because it didn't look as though there'd be much fighting here. Later, they almost killed us for not having let them jump.

Davidi and I had a look at the airfield's runway. We ordered one of the Nords to land, and when that went over successfully, we brought the other down. The paratroopers clambered out of the planes (as a matter of fact, there wasn't a single paratroop drop in the war). Then we received supplies, jeeps and command-cars, which were dropped from the Stratocruisers. At one o'clock I radioed Motty Hod, the air force commander, and he said: 'Weizman, disperse as much as you can. Egyptian Migs are on their way to Sharm to shoot you up.' This was the day when a few Migs began to attack. It could be very unpleasant if Migs catch helicopters on the ground. I sprinted from helicopter to helicopter, urging the pilots: 'Get up, get out. Get out, to the hills!' The paratroopers who hadn't managed to jump into the helicopters spread out among the rocks, preparing to open up on the Migs with their rifles. I grabbed a helicopter and ordered the pilot to fly into the canyons. Within a few moments we had scattered into the pink hills to the north of Sharm. The helicopters dispersed some 140–50 men, and the rest remained in the fissures in the vicinity.

We awaited the Egyptians and the terrors of a bombing attack, Ten minutes, fifteen minutes, twenty minutes. No Egyptians and no Migs. I got fed up. I took the helicopter and returned to the largest group of soldiers, where I was informed of a report from Motty that, *en route* to us, the four Migs had been intercepted by two Mirages – two were shot down, and the others fled for their lives. We began to get organized, and I sent out a message: 'Tell Motty to inform Dayan that everything's alright, the Straits are in our hands and open to Israeli shipping.' 'Dayan can't be notified,' came the reply, 'he's at the Western Wall.' I slumped to the ground, literally falling over. 'My lousy luck!' I said to the man beside me. 'For years I've been going on about the Wall; for years,

I've been dreaming about it. And now, at this historic moment, when everyone's at the Wall, where am I? Stuck here, far from everywhere! The company's excellent, the soldiers are excellent, the place is very important for our war aims. But up there, in the north, at this very moment, national history is being made! And that's much more important than military history. I've missed one of the historic moments in the chronicles of Israel, a moment I've dreamt about more than all those now posing for their pictures beside the Wall.'

And how did we get to the Wall? Well, from thousands of feet up, it was my air force that got us there. Without detracting from the heroism of the ground forces, who did excellent work, it was clearly the air force that brought about the Jordanian collapse. Hussein admitted as much. As soon as the Jordanian army was totally exposed to our force, its fate was swiftly sealed. On every route, in every nook and cranny, our planes swooped down on the Jordanian forces and devastated them. Jordanian tanks – 100 Pattons and twenty Centurions – were abandoned on the battlefield; our tank crews got in, started up the engines and drove them off. That was the air force's share in the liberation of the Land of Israel.

After I had shed a couple of tears, and we all celebrated our capture of the Wall – of course, I immediately informed everyone at Sharm – prisoners began coming in. We collected some twenty or twenty-five Egyptians who had been abandoned by their officers. I looked at them kneeling on the ground, with their arms tied behind their backs. Enemy soldiers – defeated, humiliated, alone. It was a dismal sight. I ordered our soldiers to give them food and water. One of the prisoners caught my eye: he was Sudanese, tall, sturdy, strong and dark, with interesting features. He sat there, gazing at me, and in my heart I thought: what does the war have to do with him? Why is he here? I exchanged a few words with him, and he grew agitated. He was married and had a daughter. He took their pictures out of his pocket and, hesitantly, as though unsure of how I'd react, he held them out for me to see. I looked. There was a kind of tranquillity transcending the whole war. In far-away Sharm, a general of the victorious army stood feasting his eyes on the pictures of the wife and daughter of a vanquished Sudanese prisoner.

Three months later I happened upon the Sudanese again while on a tour of the PoW camps with Rabin. We walked along with fenced-in prisoner cages on either side. I was lagging behind a little, exchanging a few words with our guards, taking an interest in what was happening. And then, on my left, his nose stuck to the fence, his gaze confused and perplexed, was 'my' prisoner from Sharm. I stopped and looked again. Yes, it's him – tall, handsome, dark. 'Bring him here,' I ordered the MP sergeant.

'Bring him out of the cage, sir?' he raised an eyebrow at me.

'Bring him out!' And there he was standing before me. Senussi was his name. There was a moment's embarrassment. We had a kind of link between us transcending the fog of war, beyond all wars, above and beyond all the hatreds and animosities in the world. We almost embraced – almost, but not quite, for thousands of eyes were fixed on us from every side. I was glad to see him, glad the Israeli army had brought him all the way from Sharm to this camp south of Haifa without harming a hair on his head. I asked him how things were. What could he tell me? That it's a lousy feeling, being a prisoner of war? That he was homesick for his wife and daughter and his home? 'Alright,' he said. He had one request. He wanted to work in the kitchen, and I saw to it. He looked at me again. Perhaps he wanted to say something else. I don't know what. He only looked. I saw something sparkle in his eyes. He said, 'Thanks.' One word from a defeated corporal.

At any rate, by half-past two or three in the afternoon, I flew from Sharm back to General Staff. Headquarters was a scene of great jubilation. Jerusalem was ours, the West Bank was ours, the war was ours, and there was a flood of joy and happiness and gratification swirling together into one great whirlpool. Thus it was that history mocked me yet again, playfully decreeing that I should neither storm Sharm el-Sheikh, nor be present when the Wall was captured. But the success of the air force was a partial consolation for me. The other part came when Dayan asked Motty and me to accompany Ben-Gurion to the Wall on 9 June. For me, it was a special pleasure, for two reasons: first of all, accompanying Ben-Gurion to the Wall was a delight in itself; and secondly, I kept in mind all the arguments I'd had with him about the Land of Israel

in its full boundaries and the pain he caused me when he used the
expression: 'rocky hills'.

We picked up Ben-Gurion from his home at Keren Kayemet
Boulevard in Tel Aviv. Motty sat in front, beside the driver. As
usual, the 'old man' sprang lightly into the car. I was in the back,
with Ben-Gurion on my right and his wife, Paula, on my left. His
eyes took in the view through the window. Every now and then he
flung out some 'affectionate' comment about Eshkol. In his usual
acerbity, he also had a few 'kind' words for Abba Eban. And Paula
sat at his side, muttering her furious agreement.

In Jerusalem, we were greeted by paratroopers – grimy,
exhausted, tormented, but full of a pride that swept them to
heights of exhilaration. We entered the Temple Mount from the
north-eastern side, opposite Mount Scopus. The city was already
in our hands, but the air was still heavy with the stench of war. It's a
unique smell, which the nostrils detect hours after battle subsides.
Without words, it proclaims the story of the battle and heroism
and devotion, and your breath grows heavy, even at moments of
euphoria. It was the first time my feet ever stepped freely on the
Temple Mount. When I was seventeen, and entry into the area was
strictly forbidden, I had put on the uniform of a British officer and
entered the Mosque of Omar, scared stiff that the disguise would
be uncovered. Now I was there in triumph, a Jew in the uniform of
an Israeli general. Bullets still whistled in the vicinity. We saw
some of the paratroopers who had met us only forty-eight hours
earlier when we were accompanying Dayan to Mount Scopus.
Once again, there were excited embraces and passionate kisses.
From the Temple Mount, we went down to the Wall. We were
getting closer, and I felt my heart and blood and breath revving up
– faster and faster. I couldn't control it; I was breathing in
thousands of years of my people's history.

Ben-Gurion hurried to the Western Wall courtyard, with his
bodyguards sprinting after him. At the Wall the emotional scenes
reached their peak. Everybody hugging everybody, Jew embrac-
ing Jew. Wriggling bunches of hands and legs and heads and
bodies. It was one of the most exciting experiences of a nation's
emotional fraternity. Some men were standing there, binding on
their phylacteries. Others were praying with extraordinary con-

centration. And fellows who didn't know what to do with themselves were just standing there, probably not even sensing how the tears were streaming down their cheeks and their unshaven faces. I wanted to celebrate with everyone, just to celebrate. But, together with the eruption of joy that was overwhelming me, there was a thought troubling my mind: 'Where were you these past nineteen years? Where were you when it was taboo to mention our people's emotional ties to this mound of stones?'

Nearby was a street-sign in English and Arabic: 'Al Burk' – the name of Mohammed's horse (Moslem legend has it that, riding this horse, Mohammed leapt from the Temple Mount to Mecca). It was one of the characteristic Old City signs, in blue-green ceramic tiles, Oriental looking. Suddenly, Ben-Gurion said in that peremptory voice of his, 'Take that down!' As though it were a magic incantation, a soldier instantly sprang onto the shoulders of his fellow. He tried to remove the sign, failed and then smashed it with a little hammer. (It was only some time later that I discovered his identity: it was David Kolitz. Our paths met again later, and he is now one of the closest among my young friends.) Ben-Gurion didn't say so, and I never had the opportunity of asking him about it, but I sensed that his command expressed a need to erase nineteen years of 'Al Burk', nineteen years of uneasy inactivity. The symbolic nature of the deed gripped me. At that moment I felt that we were at the gateway of a new period, that it was a time of spiritual stock-taking for our nation.

The Israeli forces needed no more than three days to trounce the Egyptian army, reach the Suez Canal and totally demolish the Jordanian army. The Jerusalem Brigade and the 10th Brigade were already on the Dammiah Bridge, on their way to the eastern bank of the Jordan. They could easily have ranged as far as Amman, but they were halted by an express order to return to the West Bank. Moshe Dayan also gave orders to blow up the bridges crossing the Jordan, though I never comprehended the purpose of these orders, nor the apprehension that gave rise to them. There was only one neighbour left who had not had a taste of Israeli power – other than in the destruction of their planes – the Syrians, who probably instigated the war in the first place. Never, neither before nor after, was Dado so tiresome. He continually bombarded General Staff with phone calls.

But on 8 June there were two obstacles to an order to scale the Heights. First was the fear that, following Egypt's crushing defeat, the Syrians had taken on such importance in Soviet eyes that rather than see the Syrians beaten, the Russians would overcome their apprehensions and send combat forces into the Middle East. Dayan and others were much preoccupied with this fear. The other obstacle was a general feeling of 'Enough!' After the depressing stand-by period that had preceded the war, with Israel progressively forfeiting all her positions; after the grim predictions of the thousands of casualties that the war would take; after the stupendous victories in the south, the liberation of Jerusalem, Judaea and Samaria and the tremendous upsurge of gratification and pride – enough! Let's celebrate! Leave us alone! Let us rest!

This feeling did more than just reinforce our fears about Syria. It was the reason we stopped where we did, on the banks of the Suez Canal, instead of thrusting deep into Egypt (a move that could have been of crucial importance in gaining peace and preventing the next war, and at least creating a buffer zone that would have hindered the Egyptians in the War of Attrition, as well as the Yom Kippur War). The Six Day War, with its great victories, is, in my opinion, a classic example of a war whose political aims were never clarified or defined. The moral should be clear and explicit: a state should never undertake the supreme effort of going to war until it has defined its political objective, which should dictate all its moves in the war. If a state does not define its political aims before the war, even if its military objectives are achieved in their entirety, and it is flooded with tidal waves of euphoria and showered with the compliments and admiration of the whole world, it has still done only half the job. The unfinished half will continue to hinder it, to deflect it from its national aims and impede its national construction and development; ultimately, it will force the state to fight for its existence under circumstances that may be very critical, as happened on 6 October 1973.

For nineteen years we had spoken of our 'generation-long grief' over our failure to liberate Jerusalem and Hebron during the War of Independence. This grief was replaced, in the Six Day War, by a wide grin of happiness. Six and a half years later, a new grief replaced the old one. I wish I could say that this new grief is at an end; I fear it isn't.

I cannot claim to be guiltless, and I cannot shift the blame onto others. I too refrained from mentioning the political objectives of the war. All I can say in my defence is that if I had contended that we ought to push on to Cairo and there dictate peace, or any settlement we found convenient, I would have been told I was talking nonsense – exactly as my life was made a misery whenever I mentioned the Western Wall before the Six Day War. But that's no justification. Regarding myself and my obligations, I don't accept the notion that one should say only popular things and avoid troublesome conflicts over matters that have no prospect of being accepted. The need to subordinate my opinions to those of others has always been distasteful to me, and even though my frankness has caused me all kinds of troubles and has kept me from achieving various objectives, if I had to face similar tests again, I would not act otherwise.

Dado was keeping up his pressure. Everyone knew he was right and agreed with his contentions. Nevertheless, the prospects were bleak. Moshe was violently opposed to an attack on Syria. On the night between Thursday, 8 June, and Friday, 9 June, after Jordan and Egypt had already agreed to a cease-fire, and despite all the great triumphs, there was an angry mood in the General Staff headquarters. With almost our whole air force available, and the Egyptians, Jordanian and Syrian air forces practically eliminated, our strength was enormous. The Egyptian and Jordanian fronts were absolutely quiet; neither of those armies was capable of breaking the cease-fire. For years we had awaited such an opportunity for settling accounts with our most bitter foes. But the chief of staff left that night in the certainty that the Heights would remain Syrian and the settlements below would continue to suffer from Syrian viciousness.

There is no explanation for what happened to Moshe Dayan that night, nor why an absolute and total ban was replaced the next morning, Friday, 9 June, around ten o'clock, by a laconic order to Dado: 'Forward!' Without consulting the chief of staff, without sending the order to the head of Northern Command through the

usual channels – some even claim, without prior Cabinet agreement – Dyan did a complete turn-about and added Dado to the list
of victorious generals and Syria to the list of routed states.

And then, when the fighting got going in the north, Northern
Command was flooded with all the VIPs who had been freed from
their other preoccupations: the premier, the defence minister, the
chief of staff, his deputy and I. Motta Gur even turned up with a
few paratroopers and asked if he could help in the Golan.

Twenty-four hours earlier the air force had received permission
to strike at the Golan. It was a good preparation for the ground
forces. The Golan, a tiny area compared with the Sinai Desert,
permitted the planes to concentrate their fire and bombs
effectively. However, in such hilly country, with its fissures and
places of concealment, the effect of air strikes is naturally far
smaller than in the open desert. The moment the ground attack
began, the whole air force, with all its planes – anything that could
take off, including Fugas – rushed to the assistance of the ground
forces.

At Northern Command headquarters, I received bad news. One
of my favourite pilots, Aryeh Orbach, had crashed and been
killed. This man had been one of the greatest opponents of my
views. He had skillfully exploited every opportunity to challenge my conviction that the superiority of our men would
enable us to overcome all the enemy air forces. What a pity he
wasn't lucky enough to join the rest of us in celebrating the great
victory. Another friend and neighbour, Colonel Shlomo Biton,
was killed in this last battle, while piloting a Super-Mystère. They
were the air force's last sacrifices.

In the meanwhile the ground forces were storming ahead,
opening up the Syrian 'sardine-tin'. I looked at Eshkol and Dayan,
at Rabin and Bar-Lev, and I knew that each of them felt as I did: a
new era, new prospects, new horizons. No one knew where all this
would lead. There wasn't time to clarify our thoughts and make
precise assessments. But everyone was gripped by the spirit of that
great hour.

We returned to headquarters and Moshe Dayan instructed
Ghandi and me to 'draw up the line where we should halt in the
Golan.' Here, too, after the breakthrough, we could have gone on

without stopping, as far as Damascus. But clearly the Russians were on the horizon, their threats growing louder. Ghandi and I bent over the maps and drew a line much further to the east than we were in fact to hold. Dayan needed no more than one hurried glance to honour us with: 'Stop fooling about!' Ghandi and I began to draw back to the west. Dayan stood over us, peeling off one strip of territory after another, until we got to the 'Purple Line', where the Israeli forces remained up to 6 October 1973. The main consideration in settling for this line was the need to keep a lateral road behind the Israeli line.

On Saturday afternoon we agreed to a cease-fire in Syria. It was the end of one of the greatest weeks in Israeli history. If I went about with a fantastic sensation in my heart, but a bitter taste in my mouth, that was my private affair, and no less reason for the people of Israel to rejoice in its stupendous victory. During the ten years that had preceded the war, this was more or less how I had foreseen it. But when it came about, I found myself not in a cockpit but in the control tower, not in a tank but at Northern Command headquarters. My bitterness was dispelled by a tremendous feeling of gratification over the air force's great share in the victory.

Motty Hod was justifiably content. Under his command the air force had gained stupendous prestige in Israel and throughout the world. At an evaluation session after the war, he did not forget to mention my share in building up the air force and preparing it for war. He may have wanted to repay me for my prolonged battle to get him appointed commander of the air force, when he added graciously: 'I'm sure that a man doesn't envy his son or his pupil'. It was one of those moments when one's throat goes dry and it takes all the strength one has to stop a tear from trickling down, to keep it hidden inside.

14

THE WAR OF ATTRITION

THE END OF THE WAR revived the question of my personal future. It was clear that Chaim Bar-Lev blocked my path to the post of chief of staff. First of all, he was deputy chief of staff. But beyond that, he displayed fantastic powers of leadership in the Six Day War, precisely as the weaknesses of certain generals required him to do in the Yom Kippur War. Bar-Lev, of course, is far from perfect (and I'm as far from it as he is), and evil tongues allege that his expertise in matters of commerce and industry is far from awe inspiring. But above and beyond disagreements about military concepts, or differing views on various battles, he is a man who understands warfare. He doesn't get panicky and he doesn't lose his senses; he is a sound soldier and he inspires confidence. If I had to go into battle with 600 tanks, and I had to decide who should command the force, I wouldn't hesitate for a moment: Chaim Bar-Lev.

After the war, however, he didn't show me much partiality. On the contrary, his attitude towards me was harsh, and I had reason to doubt whether he would want me as head of General Staff Division when he became chief of staff. And if I couldn't be sure of that, I'd better get used to the idea of leaving the armed forces and finding another sphere of activity. I was definitely prepared for it.

The Knesset Defence and Foreign Affairs Committee gave a 'victory banquet' after the war. I was sitting at Eshkol's right, with Rabin on his left, and members of the committee were showering us with compliments. Suddenly Eshkol turned to me, and, in his

melodic Yiddish, asked, '*Nu*, young man, do you want El Al?'
Without a moment's thought, I replied: '*Gemacht!*' ('It's a deal.')
In July 1967 I was prepared to wish Bar-Lev all the best in his future
post as chief of staff and to find consolation for myself in a sphere
that interested me. I did not then consider politics, although I have
always been a 'political animal' (if concern for the people of Israel is
politics, I am such to this day). But then it transpired that Eshkol
had made a commitment he couldn't meet. The transport minister
and chairman of El Al's board of directors, Moshe Carmel,
blocked the way, and nothing came of the whole matter.

While I was given over to doubts and uncertainties, a large cloud
overshadowed all my personal preoccupations, thrusting them
aside. While the Soviet Union was rapidly rebuilding the defeated
Arab armies, sending the Egyptians and Syrians masses of new
weapons, the Americans had decreed a 'suspension of all American
arms shipments to the Middle East, without any exceptions'.
'Suspension' is a fine word, but its true meaning was 'total
embargo', even on arms they had already agreed to deliver, with
contracts signed and sealed. There was no comfort in the fact that
the embargo covered the whole Middle East, as Egypt, Syria and
other Arab countries had all their needs supplied from Soviet
arsenals and didn't buy any American arms. The Skyhawks they
had agreed to sell us were also included in the suspension. We had
lost planes in the war. Migs were pouring into Syria and Egypt;
their shattered armies were being rebuilt at an unforeseen pace.
And here we were, saddled with this 'suspension'! We needed
those Skyhawks. Delivery had been promised for November and
December 1967, but the Americans now turned a deaf ear. At the
same time, the French embargo, which had been imposed on the
eve of the war, had eliminated France as a source of warplanes.
Needless to say, we were extremely worried.

Eshkol and Dayan decided to send me to Washington to try and
overcome the suspension and to convince the Americans that we
could not, under any circumstances, forego or postpone delivery
of the forty-eight Skyhawks. It's clear why I was sent: it was I who
had 'cooked up' the whole deal, in November 1965, some three
months before I handed over command of the air force to Motty
Hod; it was 'my baby', and I had to see the planes were delivered.

Back in March 1965, the American diplomat Averell Harriman came to Israel, at the head of a team of experts, for talks with Levi Eshkol, then prime minister and defence minister. Until then the Americans had only supplied us with purely defensive weapons. They stuck to the view that a combination of their dollars, French arms and Israeli *esprit* was the formula for safeguarding Israel's security. Eshkol was very eager to break the ice with the Americans, so as to eliminate our dependence on France and to open up new avenues for arms purchases. He demanded that America make her arsenals available to Israel. It was agreed with Harriman that late in 1965 an Israeli delegation would visit the Pentagon and try to convince it of the Israeli view. I was instructed to prepare a résumé of our case and present it to the Americans.

With no prospect of the Americans supplying us with Phantoms (these were only mentioned at a later stage), we decided to relinquish our notions of a multi-purpose plane and try to get Skyhawks. These planes have a good range and carrying capacity; they are capable of deep penetration; they're sturdy and cheap (less than a million dollars each, while the Mirage already cost one and a half million dollars). Our purpose was to get a plane whose range permitted it to penetrate deep into enemy territory, and the Skyhawk fitted the bill.

There was a further contention I put forward in my preparatory report. I told the Americans clearly and explicitly that the weaker we were, meaning the more arms we lacked, the greater would be our inclination to launch a pre-emptive strike against our enemies. The stronger we were, the less inclined we would be to do so. (Later, the Six Day War and the Yom Kippur War were to prove both points beyond any doubt: in 1967 we launched the first attack because we felt too weak to withstand an Egyptian first strike; in 1973 we didn't land the first blow, because we felt strong.) We decided to request a good number of Skyhawks, as well as forty-five A-6 Intruders (the latter resembled the Skyhawk in its traits).

When I presented the plan to Eshkol, I was sure he'd fall out of his chair in astonishment and say something like: 'Young man, *di bist meshigge*!' ('you're crazy'). But he just listened and then said in simple Hebrew, 'All right, that's no problem.' – When I saw that he was not perturbed by the figures, I said, 'Sir, there's a small problem I have, and I wonder if you could help? On the one hand, I have to exhibit a certain degree of weakness, to convince the Americans to sell us planes. On the other hand, I have tremendous confidence in our ability, and I don't want them to get any idea that they're dealing with a feeble little air force.' Eshkol didn't hesitate for a moment before proffering me his famous advice: 'Present yourself as *Shimshon der nebichdicker!*' (a pale translation is 'a pitiful Samson', which does not convey the wit of the original).

Armed with our most convincing arguments and Eshkol's novel advice, Benny Peled and I arrived in the United States. Our ambassador, Abe Harman, told us that our foreign minister, Golda Meir, was in New York and that, before setting out to win the Pentagon over to our cause, we ought to go and tell her about our mission and get her backing. I had not previously made the acquaintance of Golda Meir. She was staying in a small suite at the Essex House, and when we went up to see her, I was afraid that the number of planes we were requesting might shock her into placing obstacles in our path. Golda, warm and affable, served us excellent coffee and cake. I screwed up my courage to tell her the hair-raising number of planes: 210. She was not perturbed. She gave us one or two bits of advice, and we set off to meet the Americans.

There were several meetings, both with State Department officials and with senior US air force officers. As a guest of the air force, I paid courtesy visits to the commander and his deputy. A special plane was put at my disposal, and there was no lack of pomp and ceremony. But all this did not solve our problem. I described our predicament and presented our requests. Perhaps I didn't quite adhere to the concept of *Shimshon der nebichdicker*, but I exhibited confidence in our strength, together with concern over the growing power of the Arabs if it were not counter-balanced by our friends.

The Americans were inquisitive about every detail. The French never interrogated us in this manner, with them, we had the feeling that, had we wanted to buy 300 Mirages, instead of a mere seventy-two, they would have agreed, the only question being terms of payment. But with the Americans, we encountered cross-examinations and an exhaustive scrutiny. 'Listen, gentlemen,' I told them, 'I'll undress as far as my belly-button, but I won't take my pants off! That's all!' The atmosphere was good, open and uninhibited, but some of the arguments were quite sharp. They kept trying to convince us that the French could satisfy all our requirements. But in the end they agreed to supply us with a few planes and promised that negotiations would be swiftly concluded and the deal signed. We tried to bring up the Phantom, but the Americans dismissed the subject with a polite smile and a definite 'no'.

Final American notification that they were prepared to sign a contract for the sale of the Skyhawks came later, in January or February 1966. As Motty Hod was to take over the command on 27 April, I instructed him to conclude the negotiations and sign the contract. The Americans undertook to deliver the planes within eighteen months, in other words, towards the end of 1967. The Skyhawks were on the production line at the Douglas plant in California when news of the suspension descended upon us. No personal preoccupation mattered at a time when the State of Israel and its air force desperately needed to persuade the Americans not to hold up our Skyhawks.

I was the first Israeli officer to go there after the Six Day War, and I was given a royal welcome – which added a couple of feet to my normal 74 inches. The Americans were up to their necks in Vietnam, and then, out of the blue, comes Israel, a real featherweight, and delivers a crushing blow to the same awesome Soviet weapons with which the Americans were contending in Southeast Asia. Moshe Dayan's name was on everyone's lips, a modern Ghengis Khan enjoying absolute veneration, equalled in admiration, among all classes of the American people, only by the courage of plucky little Israel. In presenting our case, I went to see the commander of the navy's air force, Admiral Connely, whom I hadn't met previously. I went to his office in the Pentagon. As it happened, he had an eye ailment, and he received me with a patch over one eye. As I walked in, before we exchanged salutes and greetings, the Admiral jumped up and said, 'I didn't put this on in your honour. I really *do* have something in my eye!' We laughed, and the ice was swiftly broken.

There were some critical moments in my meetings with the Americans. I told them about the war – its causes, its successes and its cost. To illustrate my talk, I brought some slides, which Uri Yarom, our air attaché in Washington (previously, commander of our helicopter squadron) offered to show in the course of the lecture. The slide projector was ready, with Uri standing by. I looked over the solemn faces of the fifty or so admirals and generals present and decided that I must break the ice and make the Americans smile. So I told them a little story about Uri. When he was commander of the helicopter unit, he got an SOS from one of our merchant ships at sea: a sailor had been injured, and he had to be evacuated quickly. Uri took off in a helicopter, searching for the ship. But then he found that he was low on fuel and unable to get back to base. To his joy, he found an American aircraft carrier belonging to the Sixth Fleet. Without hesitation he came down on her deck, naturally causing some consternation: Uri clambered out, smiling cheerfully. Then he glanced around and pretended to be surprised and embarrassed, saying: 'Sorry, I thought this carrier was one of ours.' The Americans lost their frozen expressions. Now I could start showing slides and talking to them about our battle for survival in a hostile world.

Addressing another, smaller American forum, I said, 'In this last war, we weren't only fighting the Egyptians and Syrians, we were fighting the Russians too. If there is another war, Russian involvement will be immeasurably greater. True, the war is over, but our borders are ablaze. The Syrians and Egyptians can afford to lose a war; their countries and peoples will continue to exist. We must never lose a war, because we will have no further chance to repair the damage and rectify our errors. We won this war with French arms. We want to *prevent* the next war with American arms.'

As far as I could see, my words did not fail to make an impression. The prevention of war is a concept popular with the Americans; with their deep and troubled enmeshment in the Vietnam war, it gripped their imagination. Somewhat influenced by me, and largely due to various political pressures, the Americans reconsidered. The suspension was lifted, and the Skyhawks reached Israel in 1968. They were the backbone of our air force at the beginning of the War of Attrition on the Suez Canal.

The people of Israel were still intoxicated with their victory.

The leaders adopted Dayan's theories; smug and self-satisfied, they sat back to await a phone call from the Arab leaders. The telephone was silent, and there was no call from the Arab leaders, who were, instead, busy rebuilding their armies and preparing them for the next war. When the first Egyptian shells landed in the Suez Canal area and fourteen of our men were killed, the journalist Shalom Rosenfeld observed: 'The long-awaited phone call has come through – in Russian'.

When Chaim Bar-Lev took up the chief of staff's baton in January 1968, I wouldn't have been surprised if he had wanted to see me far away from him and from the army. But our relationship had been normalized, and it was agreed that I continue as head of General Staff Division, without the title of deputy chief of staff, and that he would appoint no other deputy. In this manner, I would retain my status as his Number Two.

We wanted to learn the lessons of the 1967 war, to rebuild the army and prepare it for the next war, which seemed inevitable. The state had grown, and our problems increased. The Israeli army was unaccustomed to the distances of our new borders. There were more and more questions that called for prompt answers: the size and deployment of our forces; the need for a large number of radar stations throughout Sinai; the diminution of the Israeli air force by comparison with the Arab air forces, which were growing and acquiring advanced planes; preparations for the general use of missiles and sophisticated electronic weapons.

However, as always, ever since the foundation of the state, we were unable to devote ourselves fully to these matters, without paying attention to an urgent and painful problem: the *fedayeen*. Their names have changed, their tactics have grown more ramified, there have been ups and downs, but throughout the years, Israel has had to contend with the terrors of the guerilla warfare that has flared up between the big wars. This kind of warfare has three characteristics that distinguish it from the big wars. First, the Israeli army cannot wage it with the full complement of the components that comprise its strength. Second, it cannot be won by a single, massive and murderous blow, with the army and nation flexing their muscles for one short effort; it is drawn out and troublesome, demanding endurance and fortitude.

Third, it is not the army alone that wages it, and not only soldiers pay the price, it is directed against civilian areas, with the aim of undermining personal security and making civilian life a misery, and also rendering it difficult, almost intolerable, to create understanding with the Arab population.

Yasser Arafat, George Habash and all the rest who vie with each other in their fanaticism and extremism were quick to remind us that our Six Day War victory over the Arab armies was no guarantee of peaceful times. Hussein, the 'righteous' little king, with his Western schooling, granted Al Fatah a haven in the Jordan Valley. Hussein matured and grew wiser, comprehending that the guerillas endangered his rule far more than they menaced us, and in September 1970, he went to war against them. But till then we had to pay the price. At first it was a bit difficult to get used to the new dimensions: there were 3–4,000 armed guerillas in the Jordan Valley. Every night, thirty to fifty of them infiltrated in groups of six, ten or twelve. If the army had not employed its best men in blocking the raids, we might soon have had thousands of guerillas within our territory, inflicting heavy damage on us.

The campaign was waged along a 100-mile-long border, from the Sea of Galilee to the Dead Sea, with the guerilla squads penetrating as far as Arab population centres, where they had a reasonable chance of finding concealment and assistance. The army fought them by ambushes and difficult, perilous pursuits; by fencing off the Jordan Valley and setting up settlements; by advanced electronic devices along the border. This arduous campaign lasted for about a year. About 1,000 guerillas met their death, while government prisons offered hospitality to many others. But that was small consolation. The flower of Israel's youth added fresh graves to the cemeteries.

In this prolonged and difficult campaign, the senior commanders went at the head of their men, as they did whenever our army went into action. Those – unfortunately, there were many – who thought that colonels and generals should sit in their headquarters while soldiers and officers were shedding blood and sweat in ambushes and pursuits through the Jordan Valley, only proved how greatly they misunderstood the make-up of the Israeli army. If I did my modest share in ensuring that senior officers participated in this campaign, I'm proud of it.

Personally, as head of General Staff Division, my share was not as great as that of others. Ghandi (head of Central Command), for example, performed great deeds and set an excellent example. But there were quite a few times when I also participated in these pursuits. Whenever a report came in of a guerilla penetration, a helicopter was on stand by, the Kalashnikov rifles were ready, and we would fly off to help seek them out. Once we netted a guerilla on the way. He was walking along all by himself. I was asked to bring the helicopter down, and we caught him. It turned out that he was on his way to fetch water for the thirteen members of his squad, who were hiding in a fissure. We brought him back to our Bedouin trackers, and he spilled the beans. Then he led us to his comrades, who were waiting for water. We set off – a very formidable group of officers, a sufficient number to conduct a full-scale battle – got down on our bellies and went into action. We were near Jericho and the temperature was 110 degrees. Sweat poured off me by the gallon (where's that 'radiator', Motty Hod?) as I took cover and fired. We killed the thirteen men of the band and returned to base. I was sure that I had been totally dehydrated. After I left the army, a picture was published showing me lying on the ground while a jerrycan of water was poured over my head.

It's a total distortion of the facts to claim that it was Hussein who broke the guerillas' back. Nonsense! The Israeli army did it, with its finest combat units. Hussein completed the job in September 1970, out of selfish considerations and in fear for his throne.

One of the largest operations in this war was the Karameh raid in March 1968. This was the turning point, for after that the Jordan Valley was almost totally abandoned, both by its population and by the Fatah. For the Israeli army, the raid was the first body-blow we had to take after the Six Day War – thirty dead. It was hard.

On the eve of the raid, the whole country was in uproar over a completely different matter. Moshe Dayan had been engaged in an archaeological dig when the sides of the trench caved in and he was buried. I was one of the first to rush to his bedside at the hospital. When I saw him and witnessed the expressions on the doctors' faces, I was convinced that I'd have to fetch my sister-in-law, Ruth, to the bedside of her dying husband, and I feared he wouldn't hold out till she got there. I hurried to the Maskit handicrafts shop, which she managed. When Ruth saw me, she asked: 'Has he been assassinated?' 'No,' I said, 'the trench caved in on him.' That day, when I was asked how Moshe looked, I said: 'Like a plane being overhauled: one wing hanging down, two tubes going in and another three siphoning the fuel out.'

The next day, in the midst of the Karameh raid – the earth shuddered from exploding shells and the noise was overwhelming – Chaim Bar-Lev was in the forward command-post, and I was in the General Staff headquarters when the phone rang. 'Ezer, it's for you. The defence minister wants you.' I was sure there was some mistake. I picked up the receiver and listened. My ears detected a kind of grunting wheeze. I couldn't understand a thing. But, more dead than alive, with his body attached to all those tubes, that man would not give up. He tried again. Now, from snatches of words and grunts and gurgles, I thought I could make out the words: 'Ezer, what's the news from Karameh?' I brushed him off with a meaningless reply. 'It'll be alright. Look after yourself, Moshe!' It was impossible not to admire his strong will and his tremendous determination to live. After a time, he returned to his desk at the Defence Ministry. He was strapped into girdles and attached to all kinds of devices, padded round with pillows and suffering terrible torments. He had lost his voice, and the only way we could hear him was when he whispered into a microphone. Since that time, much has happened. That gigantic figure has been whittled away. But anyone who says that he isn't a brave man, doesn't know Moshe Dayan.

In August and September 1968, while we were battling with the guerillas and building up our army, the new Skyhawks arrived, and our hearts felt a little lighter. We re-organized the armoured units and the paratroopers. Although there was no telephone call from down there, the Egyptian border was quiet. And then, in October, the blow landed. Fourteen soldiers were killed in an Egyptian bombardment at Kantara on the Suez Canal. We sensed that a new era had begun. It didn't have a name yet; later it was called War of Attrition. Fortunately, we did not fall into the snare of thinking that the Egyptians had struck once and would not do so again. After the bombardment in October, there was an interval of a few months before the static battle was renewed, but, all the same, we took matters in hand. The first thing was to erect fortifications. A number of officers, headed by Elhanan Klein, the chief engineering officer, brought up an idea: 'It's a long affair to pour concrete into fortifications so that they can stand up to bombardments. Let's strip down the Egyptian railway line in Sinai and use its rails as steel shields.'

Chaim Bar-Lev hesitated. We didn't know if it would stand up to bombardment. We built a wall like the one they proposed and conducted experiments on it. We fired 120-mm and 160-mm mortar shells straight at it, as well as 105-mm, 130-mm and 155-mm cannon shells, and the Russian 122-mm, and the wall didn't collapse. The detonating layer held out. We stripped down the railway line, ordered used rails from abroad and built the first fortresses. Between March 1969 and 1 August 1970, we lost 250 dead and about 1,000 wounded on the Canal. Only a few were killed inside the fortresses, all the rest were hit when they were outside them or on their way to or from the line.

March 1969 is usually regarded as the beginning of the War of Attrition. I was in my second year as head of General Staff Division. There were two things troubling me. First, never having conducted a static war, our ground forces were unaccustomed to it and could not bring their full potential to bear, as they weren't storming forward to put a stop to Egyptian provocations. Second, our magnificent air force was sitting back; other than photographic missions and intercepting enemy planes, it wasn't doing a thing. It was forfeiting its image as the arm whose absolute superiority could decide every war.

During the months of March–June 1969, 20,000 Soviet advisers poured into Egypt, penetrating into the lowest command echelons of Egyptian armour, artillery and infantry battalions. Soviet planes, with Russian pilots, were stationed in Egypt. Our soldiers were being killed daily. The Egyptians were growing more and more arrogant. We were faced by an army with 1,000 tanks and as many artillery pieces, and, yet, Israeli forces weren't doing what they should and could do. Even when they did act, it was often too little, too late. They made the grievous error of reverting to outdated methods, which may have been good enough for attacks on Jordan or Gaza during the *fedayeen* raids preceding the Sinai Campaign but were hardly suitable now. 'Deep penetration' was the slogan. The army carried out demolition attacks: destroying a transformer station deep inside Egypt; blowing up a bridge; a deep penetration raid with armour. These showed a great deal of courage, daring and resourcefulness, but all this was no more than tickling the Egyptian army. Such actions earned the Israeli army world-wide renown and threw tasty morsels to Israeli public opinion, but they didn't decide the war; they didn't bring it to an end, nor even dampen it.

Whether I was listened to or not, I repeated, over and over again, 'A war like this can't be won by commando raids! It won't work! The Israeli army has to be employed in full and overwhelming force, not only to put an end to the War of Attrition – important enough unto itself – but also to check the Egyptian army before it launches more dangerous offensives!' But mine was a lonely voice. A state with a strong standing army that has just defeated its enemies in a brilliant lightning campaign and yet chooses to conduct commando raids instead of making full use of its strength does so either because it doesn't believe in its ability to employ that strength to the utmost or because of the illusion that some commando raid can solve the problem. The facts proved that the problem wasn't solved until the air force went into action on a large scale.

My efforts to convince my General Staff colleagues to give up these commando pricks and prods and to deploy the army in earnest, so as to put an end to the War of Attrition, were not successful. Another prod and another prick, and the next day, there'd be 1,000 Egyptian shells, 2,000, 5,000, 10,000. Soldiers were getting killed, and the mood in the streets was swaying between grim and grotesque.

If I didn't succeed in conveying to my colleagues how essential it was to employ the army's full strength and to desist from commando raids – and events proved that I did not – I tried to persuade them at least to use the air force effectively, to strike such painful blows at the Egyptians that they would cease to regard the War of Attrition as profitable. Here, too, I encountered opposition. For the first time in the history of Israel, the air force commanders said that, because of the Egyptian SAM anti-aircraft system, they could not conduct operations unless the United States supplied us with some missile or other. I regarded this view as extremely dangerous. Never before had such a contention been put forward. When there had been nothing better, the Pipers of the War of Independence were good enough for the aerial missions required at the time, and no one ever contended that we could not cope because the Egyptian air force had better planes. The Israeli soldier – with his daring, his skills, his devotion, his patriotism, his inner motivation, his readiness to sacrifice his life – was the guarantee of our ability to survive. To trade this mighty treasure for the contention that we lacked some contraption or missile and that as long as we didn't acquire them from our friends or manufacture them ourselves we were powerless to defend Israel's security was, without any exaggeration, acquiescing to a death sentence on the Jewish state.

It may be that the straw that broke the camel's back – and, as I've already pointed out, it isn't only the strength of the straw that counts, but also the resilience of the back – was the following incident, which I had the 'pleasure' to experience. In the middle of July 1969, I was in the Canal area on a routine tour. After we visited a fortified position, I set out in a jeep with Lt-Colonel Asher Levi, chief of staff of Southern Command and a deputy battalion commander, one of the finest officers in the armoured units. About 300 yards from the strongpoint, we were overwhelmed by the worst bombardment I have ever experienced. Hell-fire, such as I've never seen, neither before nor after. We tried to get away, but the manoeuvres didn't work too well. The Egyptians seemed to know there was some high-level officer in the jeep, and the shells pursued us, exploding all around, bringing down a hail of fire, earth and shrapnel. Our driver, the deputy battalion commander, was a first-rate fellow. He didn't lose his head: he twisted and turned, again and again, almost entered one of our own minefields, got us out at the last moment and then plunged into a ditch, where the engine stalled, leaving us stuck. Asher Levi fell onto the two-way radio and broke a rib. I had time to think that dying like this, in a ditch, from some lousy Egyptian shell, wasn't exactly my ideal.

its prospects of success, but permission was not received. From one of the air force bases, the deputy commander called me up on the telephone: 'Sir, it's just like the Six Day War. They're fleeing their dugouts like mice, we can take the whole line!' Indeed we could have. I was sure of that.

Despite the great success of the air operation, when we discussed it that night there were still officers who opposed continuation of the bombings. I pressed for further attacks, contending that we should exploit our success and continue to strike at the Egyptians. Permission was given for bombing to be resumed the next day. But I didn't get much satisfaction from my success. Systematic recourse to the air force involved great difficulties and the loss of planes and pilots. After the air force succeeded in knocking out the ten missile batteries along the Canal, Russian involvement increased, and so did the number of batteries. Instead of regarding the air force as one of the components of the war against the Egyptians, instead of committing ground forces and armour on a large scale to pulverize the Egyptian line, with its artillery and missiles, the whole task devolved upon the air force, which came to be considered the sole solution, while the ground forces continued digging in. The Egyptians got used to living under bombing and did not give up their campaign of attrition. They were also reassured by the success of their attempts to lay ambushes in between our fortified positions. It was here they learnt the lesson they were to apply so successfully in the Yom Kippur War: leave the fortified positions alone and establish footholds in between.

Throughout the War of Attrition, there were apprehensions about the Russians, which was why the ground forces were not used for any decisive purpose, and also why the air force attacked here and there, causing the Egyptians – and itself – casualties and damage, but without employing its full strength.

As the war dragged on, without our army finding a way to put a stop to it, I, unlike others, became gradually convinced that this was the first time we were not winning. I said so countless times: we failed in this war. We did not comprehend it correctly. When the Egyptians agreed to a cease-fire, in August 1970, we interpreted it as an admission on their part that they couldn't stand our bombing any more. Without detracting from the great suffering inflicted on them by our air force, I don't have the shadow of a doubt that the Egyptians wanted a cease-fire in order to move their missile system forward to the Canal, so that it could neutralize our air force when their units crossed the waterway. All this backs up both of my contentions. First, the War of Attrition, in which our best soldiers shed their blood, resulted in the Egyptians gaining a free hand, over a period of three years, to prepare for the great war of October 1973; if so, it is no more than foolishness to claim that we won the War of Attrition. On the contrary, for all their casualties, it was the Egyptians who got the best of it. Second, by our errors between March 1969 and August 1970, and, subsequently, by our tragic acquiescence when the Egyptians violated the cease-fire and moved their missiles ahead, we, with our own hands, smoothed Egypt's path to the Yom Kippur War. When our blindness caused us to misread Egyptian intentions and prevented us from applying an accurate interpretation – or taking action to forestall the enemy – it was then that the Yom Kippur War began, with all its ensuing results.

Towards the end of 1969, my private preoccupations merged with the larger national issues, combining to make me feel altogether depressed. The time was drawing near for my son, Shaul, to be called to military service, and something shuddered within me. For years, I had been toying with the delusion that, when my children grew up, the sword of war would no longer dangle over their heads. Now, when Shaul was recruited, the war was still in progress; we, the first generation of soldiers, had not succeeded in establishing peace.

I experienced a feeling of dejection on another level as well. At the end of my fourth year as head of General Staff Division (the latter years under Chaim Bar-Lev's command), no one in authority was prepared to tell me if I had a chance of becoming chief of staff after Bar-Lev ended his term of duty. Dayan avoided mentioning the subject, and Bar-Lev withdrew behind a heavy veil of silence. I might have been able to pin my hopes on Eshkol's support, but that pleasant conversationalist had passed away. And with Golda Meir, Eshkol's successor, I did not have the same relationship I had had with him. At General Staff I felt more and more isolated in my views. I repeatedly called for an end to the War of Attrition by sending in ground forces to seize footholds on the western bank of the Canal, including the capture of Port Said, and by intensifying and extending our bombing raids. But my proposals were not accepted.

All this cleared the way for me to agree to the notion of resigning from the army and joining the Government of National Unity that was established after the October 1969 elections. On 16 October, when I was at the wedding reception for Yitzhak Rabin's secretary, Ruhama, I got a phone call from my friend, Knesset member Yosske Kramerman: 'Ya'akov Meridor wants to see you. Please come to my home.' I hadn't the faintest idea what it was all about. I took Re'uma, and we drove to the Kramerman's home. Without any ceremony, with his usual bluntness, he said: 'I don't know what your prospects are of becoming the next chief of staff. But I'm doubtful. We are about to join a widely based National Unity Government. How would you like to join the Cabinet as a Herut representative?' It was something of a surprise, and rather bewildering. But, as I said, the ground had been prepared, and I didn't waste more than forty second before replying: '*Gemacht!*'

Re'uma almost fell off her chair. When we went out, she said: 'Have you gone out of your mind?' That single exclamation of hers expressed all her hopes that I'd be appointed chief of staff one day. 'Re'umaleh,' I replied, 'by the time my brother-in-law Moshe Dayan says a word about me having a chance of becoming chief of staff, I'll have died seven times over. Chaim Bar-Lev talks slowly; on this subject, he won't talk at all. I can't get my ideas adopted at General Staff. I'm very concerned about future defence developments. The set-up at General Staff is such that you have every opportunity to put forward your proposals and try to convince others that you're right, but if you don't succeed, you can't fight for your views outside the army. I haven't managed to convince them. Perhaps I'll have another opportunity to do so in the Cabinet. I've got to try!' I presume she understood.

While I was waiting for details to be worked out – I had asked Kramerman to keep the matter a secret until it could be put into operation. I was invited to address an Israel Bonds meeting in Los Angeles in December 1969. I arranged to be called home in case of need and set off with Re'uma. The day after I made my speech, which was my last public appearance in uniform, Peleg Tamir phoned me and gave the code words we had agreed upon. In total secrecy, without the knowledge of the defence minister or the chief of staff, I hurried home. Re'uma remained in Los Angeles. On Saturday evening, 13 December, I arrived in Lod, where I was met by my son, Shaul (in uniform); my faithful aide-de-camp, Raffy; my driver, Avraham, who had given me seventeen years of uncommon loyalty; and, last but not least, Rachel Kramerman.

The following day, the wheels began to spin swiftly. At seven in the morning, following a pre-arranged scenario, I phoned Menachem Begin, telling him I was prepared to resign from the army, so as to take my oath of allegiance as a minister. 'Yes, yes,' said Begin, 'you must resign.' At ten past seven, I phoned Moshe Dayan. 'Brother-in-law,' I said.

He was startled. 'What are you doing here?'

'I came back,' I told him.

'Why? What for?'

'To resign from the army,' I informed him.

'And what are you going to join?' he wanted to know.

'I'm going to join the Israeli Cabinet.'

There was a second or two of silence. Then he said, 'Good for you! And good for the Israeli Cabinet.'

His reply dispelled the last of my doubts. In my heart I had awaited a different reaction, perhaps I even expected it. If he had said, 'Listen, you. You're not leaving the army! I can't promise you anything, maybe you'll be chief of staff and maybe you won't, I'm not promising, but I need you in the army!' I wouldn't have hesitated for a moment to forgo my ministerial ambitions. But when his response was immediate agreement, without the slightest effort to dissuade me, I said to myself: 'That's it! Get going!'

I made one further phone call, this time to Chaim Bar-Lev. He, too, was confused: 'Eeeeezy! What are you doing in Israel?' I told him the story in a few sentences. His reaction was different. 'But this is out of the question! We have to talk.' We arranged to meet at eight that morning, at the Sdeh Dov airfield, on Chaim's way to a Cabinet meeting. He agreed to arrange for my discharge the same day, so that I could appear before the Herut committee that evening. An hour later I got a phone call from Froike, previously my aide-de-camp and now Bar-Lev's, 'It's alright.' I phoned the various members of the General Staff. 'I'm leaving the army today.' They began to pour into my office. 'Are you mad? What's going on?' I called Sheika Gavish, the head of Southern Command, who hoped to become chief of staff. 'Start moving north!' I told him. And a second call to Northern Command, to Dado, who had similar ambitions: 'Start moving south!'

At ten that morning I reported to the office of a woman officer who discharged me from military service, after I had spent twenty-seven years in uniform. I had lunch with Peleg Tamir and Motty Hod, my last meal in uniform. The next day, 15 December, in civilian clothes, I took my oath of allegiance as Minister of Transport in the Israeli government.

15

A QUESTION OF QUALITY

I WAS IN THE CABINET when the War of Attrition reached its height. In itself, the Transport Ministry is a challenging occupation. The country's bus cooperatives, the taxis, the railway, El Al, road accidents and the country's ports can fill a minister's life, even if he doesn't devote time to other matters. But with all my interest in the ministry – and I made a serious effort to study its intricacies and unravel them – I attached at least an equal degree of importance to my membership in the ministerial defence committee – not the behind-the-scenes 'kitchen', but the official body.

I occupied the position of minister in the Israeli Cabinet for less than eight months, a short but intensive period. I learned to regard matters from a different viewpoint, analyzing them in a manner unlike that I had adopted during my long service in the military. Like other senior army officers, I had had a tendency to underrate the ministers (the usual attitude was: 'What do they know about defence matters, these party hacks? They only get in the way of the armed forces.') This was a good opportunity to learn that they were deserving of a far greater degree of respect. They took matters seriously, considering issues from a wide range of angles whilst displaying understanding for military affairs. Whatever they lacked in military knowledge or experience, they made up in common sense. I won't mention the ministers by name, except the intrepid, courageous prime minister, Golda Meir, and Justice Minister Yaakov Shimshon Shapira, who won my respect with his keen intellect.

Nevertheless, membership in the government did not give me much satisfaction. Unfortunately, the Cabinet was also infected by a spirit of demoralization. Instead of influencing the mood of the street, instead of strengthening the nation's spirit and restoring its confidence, the Cabinet itself was under the influence of the weariness and languor so characteristic of public opinion at that time. This negative mood among the ministers was characterized by a remark made by my friend Yisrael Galili, then – as now – minister without portfolio. After hearing a depressing report on an air force attempt to attack the Egyptian missiles system, which resulted in the loss of a further Phantom and one of our best pilots, Galili got up and paced up and down the Cabinet room, an indication that he was tense. He halted beside me, his expression grim, 'Ezer, where's it all going to end? If we don't get that Shrike missile from the United States, what's going to happen?'

That question, and the doubt underlying it, the fear of what would happen if we didn't get some missile or other, hung over the Cabinet's deliberations like a heavy cloud, overshadowing our military thinking at that time. In the final account, this is the reason why the War of Attrition will be remembered as the first war that Israel did *not* win: a fact that cleared the way for the Egyptians to launch the Yom Kippur War. It was the first time in the annals of Israel and her armed forces that the inability to gain an undisputed victory was excused by technological limitations and the lack of some weapon or other. I don't hesitate to say that, if such had been the consideration guiding the senior political and military echelons in 1948, Israel's fate would have been sealed before the Arab armies fired a single shot and Israel would never have arisen.

In 1948 and 1967, and during all the difficult times up to 1970, we never budged from the concept, without which Israel's existence would have been inconceivable, that our safety would be ensured not by parity of armament, but by the quality of the Israeli soldier; that it wasn't technological superiority which made us stronger than our enemies, but our great spiritual pre-eminence; that it wasn't arsenals crammed with the weapons and missiles which maintained us in the Middle East, but resourcefulness and cunning and brains, following the precept, 'By ruses shall you make war'. All through the War of Attrition, there wasn't a day when we didn't talk of our moral preponderance, but we contented ourselves with talk; without being convinced of these truths, all this was mere lip-service. Of the great conviction that we could overcome the Arabs, even if we didn't have some weapon or missile – ground, air or naval – nothing was left but words whose meaning had vanished. Either we got the Shrike – or what? Indecision. Lack of initiative. Acquiescence. Thus, the War of Attrition was the first one in which we gave in to technological limitations.

To use the terms of ground warfare, our Phantoms hacked through the barbed-wire fences of missiles and broke through the aerial fortifications, despite the losses they suffered; but they weren't backed up by the force that should have swept the objectives, demolishing the Egyptian positions and hurling them back from their footholds on the west bank of the Canal. The Egyptian surface-to-air missile system, which was the cause of our air losses and glumness, could have been eliminated in 1970. It would have required sending in infantry and armour, in addition to the air force. Whoever came to the conclusion that we lacked the strength to do so decreed that for the first time in her history, Israel would back down before the superior weapons possessed by the Arabs, thereby condemning the state to face the Yom Kippur War and concede its political positions, until it stood in real peril. And those who did so committed a further sin: in the course of the years 1970–3, they cultivated the delusion that we had won the War of Attrition, thus lulling our senses. Instead of saying: 'We have failed to destroy the missile system. Let's prepare for the eventuality that this system will fulfil a decisive role in the next war, and let's find ways of eliminating it!' we said: 'Once again, we've won, once again, the Egyptians have had to rely on American favours to get them out of trouble' (and they were, indeed, in trouble). Thus, we created a myth, instead of dealing with the facts. We may have improved public morale, but we did so at a high price.

The results were not long in coming. Two or three weeks after the cease-fire ending the War of Attrition went into effect, in August 1970, the Egyptians took a meaningful and highly important step towards the Yom Kippur War: they moved their missile bases right up to the edge of the Canal, under cover of the agreement and in express defiance of it. The Israeli leadership did not have the courage to order a full-scale attack to annihilate the missile system, because they didn't believe it could be done. Then, by appealing to the Americans, they sowed the seed of total dependence on US wishes. This marked the beginning of the great barter-sale: 'We'll sit by quietly and let the Egyptian missiles huddle safely beneath the umbrella conveniently provided by the cease-fire if you give us so-and-so many planes and free us (for the time being) from the threat of the Rogers Plan.' (The Rogers Plan was then being described as a 'disaster for Israel'.) The US government 'capitulated'. The embryonic Yom Kippur War was beginning to take shape. Only three and a half years later, when people met at gatherings on Friday evenings, you'd hear them say: 'Ah, the Rogers Plan . . . now, if we could only go back to the Rogers Plan . . .'

The Arabs have always dreamed of seeing a hesitant Israel, cringing and fearful, and they probed for gaps in her defences. In May 1967 they thought that the situation inside Israel was to their advantage: economic recession, large-scale emigration, an atmosphere of 'The last one out will switch off the light at Lod airport and a weak and hesitant government. That was why Nasser was carried away by the tempting delusion that such an Israel was easy prey. The Israeli armed forces clipped his wings, proving that he had misread the external signs of weakness.

In 1970 the Egyptians tried again. This time it was our turn to misread the Egyptian picture. In August 1970 the Egyptians said to themselves: 'The time has come for a truce. We'll put it to effective use. The Israelis are making a mistake. For us, it will be a source of strength; for the Israelis, a source of weakness.' For three years we played the Egyptian game, cultivating the notion that the Arabs did not have a military option open to them. We fed ourselves on delusions, and everything that happened in Egypt was interpreted to reinforce our view. The Egyptians smiled as they built up their strength and sent up decoys. They used the three-year truce to prepare for the Yom Kippur War. They built up their strength, and we fooled ourselves.

While I was still in the army, I once played the role of the Israeli chief of staff in a war-game that attempted to foresee the next war. By analysis, I predicted (correctly, as it turned out) the hour of the outbreak of war: 'The Egyptians will attack between two and three in the afternoon'. And I explained the reasons the Egyptians would attack at such an hour: maximal exploitation of daylight while limiting the effective activity of our air force to a few hours only, until sunset. So I estimated the time correctly, but I didn't know the date. I assumed that 1976 would be the fateful year, and I was wrong. But on joining the Cabinet, I clearly sensed that we were paving the way for the next war and actually creating conditions favourable to the Egyptians. So I vigorously contended that we must use our power to the utmost, so as to win the War of Attrition and to remove any doubt as to who was the victor.

In its deliberations the Cabinet was never free of concern about Russian reactions. It was therefore uneasy about the bombing raids deep inside Egypt. There were many arguments in favour of continuing the raids and stepping them up by hitting at 'sensitive targets', like power stations, fuel dumps, bridges, railway stations, etc. (as the air force did in Syria during the Yom Kippur War). Israel's ambassador in the United States, Yitzhak Rabin, surprised me with his calls for further bombing, calling for continuous penetration raids inside Egypt. 'Hit 'em hard!' he wrote from Washington. Quite correctly, he held to the view that not only didn't the Americans oppose the raids, but possibly even approved of them. But the government held back, and Israel ultimately conceded this card, too, limiting herself to attacks on the Canal zone alone.

Over and over again, I told Cabinet ministers and army officers: 'The War of Attrition is the first battle in the campaign to retain the fruits of the Six Day War. If we don't win this battle, it will be hard to win the campaign.' When it was essential for her security, Israel could not refrain from taking military action solely because there were Russians in Egypt's operational echelons. Over and over I argued that if, by refraining from action, we accepted the Russian presence as a buffer against Israeli action, we would lead the Russians to step up their demonstrative involvement, steadily whittling down our own freedom of action.

Less than eight months in the Cabinet may not be an illustrious career, but I must add that my brief stint ended despite my better judgement and efforts to prevent that step. I stopped being minister of transport because my party decided to pull out of the Government of National Unity in protest to the acceptance of a cease-fire with Egypt in 1970. I opposed that decision. The acceptance of the cease fire appeared at the time to be tied up with the implementation of the Rogers Plan, and I was convinced that for Israel to accede to the Rogers Plan would be a disaster. But precisely for that reason, I contended that we must remain and not leave the decision on that plan to a Cabinet without Herut ministers. My view was not accepted. Considering the delicate equilibrium inside Herut, and with the Liberals supporting my position, I had reason to believe that by campaigning for us to remain in the government, I could have gained a majority. However, I knew that such a step would cause a split within the party, and I wasn't about to do that. I preferred to refrain from winning people over to my view.

After the Yom Kippur War, I felt a shadow of regret; had we remained in the Cabinet – whatever its composition – perhaps on the eve of the Yom Kippur War things would have turned out differently. Perhaps we would have maintained the existence of the ministerial defence committee and countered the complacency of the days that preceded the Egyptian–Syrian invasion. Perhaps, if we had done so, we would have tilted the balance. Perhaps, with our sensitivity on security matters, we might have done something during the years 1970–3 to make the armed forces better prepared for war than they were in October 1973.

But all these speculations are of minor importance. Neither man nor state can turn back the clock. The Yom Kippur war caught us with our trousers down, bowing to a misconception, ignoring clear signs of enemy preparations, paying the terrible price of the negligence and errors of the years 1969 and 1970. In the course of the War of Attrition we had established a principle. From that moment on, we ceased to be an independent state, deciding its destiny according to its own considerations. If we had been in the government when the Egyptians defied the cease-fire agreement by moving their missiles forward to the Canal, I cannot be certain the Cabinet would have adopted our view that it was essential to wipe out the missile batteries. The fact is that it occurred a fortnight after our resignation. There was nothing I could do but to write and speak – outside the Cabinet.

My brief ministerial career came to an end at four am, in a final vote, when our resignation was decided upon. Within a day or two, I ventured, for the first time as an adult, into private civilian life. In many ways I regarded my time in the government as a continuation of my military service. After my resignation, I found myself, for the first time since the age of eighteen, master of my own fate, not bound to any public or national service. It was difficult. I sensed a distressing feeling of emptiness. All those years time had been strictly measured and apportioned into fixed units, now it was suddenly flowing freely, with all discipline cast away. My driver, who had served me loyally for seventeen years – telling me his troubles and listening to mine – was suddenly unemployed, and it was my concern. At the filling station, I found myself treated in a strangely 'unfriendly' manner: the coarse man filling up my tank really expected me to pay with my hard-earned cash, and it took a long moment to realize that this is how life is outside the service, and I'd better get used to it.

In the small hours of that fateful morning, after the decision on our resignation, Ya'akov Meridor phoned me: 'Come on!' he urged, 'Come and join my business!' It was very pleasant to discover that I had good friends just when I was feeling as though I'd stepped on a mine. One day after my resignation, I gratefully accepted Meridor's invitation and joined his Mercantile Fruit Carriers and other commercial enterprises.

Aside from my business preoccupations, I devoted much time to party activity in Herut and was a member of the party's executive. But despite one or two attempts to paper over the cracks, the conflicts between me and Menachem Begin, the head of the party, began to emerge. I respect him. I presume that respect is mutual. But we are poles apart in our characters, our viewpoints and our personal traits. There was the friction you get between men who lack a 'chemical affinity'. This friction gradually eroded our relationship, climaxing in December 1972, when, after a Herut conference, I found myself a rank-and-file party member. Within the structure of the party, with its hierarchy and the nature of relationships at the top level, it became quite clear that there was no room for a creature like me.

One thing my new life provided for was the opportunity to spend more time with my son, Shaul. He had been badly wounded in the War of Attrition, and from the moment he was injured, up to the present day, Shaul and his sufferings, and the constant worry about his welfare, have become the dominant factor in my life.

Shaul was called up in November 1969. In March or April 1970, he granted me a special favour: as an exceptional concession, he permitted me to be present when he did his parachute jump. He was a good paratrooper and a good soldier. The War of Attrition was at its height when Shaul was posted to the Canal. I knew which strongpoint he was in, and I foresaw what awaited him there. I wrote him a letter: 'When you were born, I said to your mother that I had just one hope – that you wouldn't have to go to war as we did. Now, as you set off for battle, I ask myself, what was the mistake my generation made? Where did we sin, that you too have to go to war?'

That, I think, was the beginning of the 'war of fathers and sons', which reached its peak in the Yom Kippur War. Herzl Shafir, now head of General Staff Division, was then deputy head. I requested that every time that particular strongpoint was shelled or bombed I receive the report. I had to know. In the Cabinet deliberations I was dogged by the feeling that it all involved Shaul and that every decision would affect his life. After a month at the Canal, he came home on leave. He was full of optimism, infecting everyone with his cheerfulness. He didn't have a watch. 'How come?' I asked. 'There was a bombardment, I jumped into a dugout, the strap tore and I lost my watch.' I gave him my air-crew watch. 'On your next leave, we'll buy you another one.'

His next homecoming was painful. I was having lunch in a Jerusalem restaurant with my friend Yosske Kramerman when I was informed that the chief of staff wanted me on the phone. 'It's Shaul!' I flung at Kramerman, and in the three seconds it took from the table to the phone, I realized that Shaul hadn't been killed. How did I know? If, heaven forbid, he had been killed, Chaim wouldn't have phoned. He would have come looking for me. All those months the nightmare had been haunting me: Motty or Bar-

Lev, or Haka at our gate, standing there, not entering, lacking the courage to inform us. When I had to notify families, I, too, couldn't bring myself to go into the homes. Something would make me freeze up.

Bar-Lev's voice came over the phone, quiet, slow, confident. 'Eeeeezy, it's Shaul. He's been wounded. He's been evacuated and treated. He's on his way to Hadassah Hospital in Jerusalem.'

'Fine!' I said. What nonsense a man can blurt out! Of course, I meant it was fine that he was alive.

'Not so fine, Eeeeezy,' Chaim said.

I gulped down a double cognac at the bar. Then I said to Kramerman: 'Yosske, come to Hadassah!'

The evacuation helicopter arrived, and I went up to the ward. Shaul was fully conscious. My watch was on his wrist. In his pocket, he had a little book of Psalms he had received a few days before, when the indomitable Rabbi Goren visited the strongpoint, and the letter I had sent him a short time previously. In a five-hour-long operation, a 0.3-inch bullet, from an Egyptian sniper's rifle, was extracted from Shaul's head. I've kept it.

That bullet was not the only souvenir of the War of Attrition that I kept from that period. Despite all the calm on the surface, from the summer of 1970 through the autumn of 1973, I could never really get rid of the feeling that had plagued me throughout the War of Attrition: we were headed for another war in the seventies. I have never claimed to be clairvoyant, and I've already admitted that I misjudged the date that next war would break out. But not only did I accurately foresee that war would break out at two o'clock in the afternoon, I also predicted how it would unfold. All along our post-Six Day War frontiers, along the Suez Canal, the Jordan and the Golan Heights, it would be the enemy who would initiate the fighting, without the Israeli forces launching a pre-emptive strike. Accordingly, the army had to prepare to withstand the first blow, on the land and in the air. This was the general view, and on the basis of it the IDF worked out its doctrine. The army would build up a standing force, which, together with the air force, would block the enemy attack, providing cover for the reserves to get organized, at which time the army would launch a counter-offensive in full force.

The Yom Kippur War descended upon us at a time when we lacked the two principal factors that together make up the ability to win a war. We didn't have political objectives, and the army was not prepared for it – not prepared to dictate its pace nor to make maximal gains, within the limitations of time.

Long before October 1973 I had said: 'The next war will decide whether we have secured the fruits of the Six Day War or lost them. Under present international circumstances, we can keep those gains only if we occupy Damascus, Cairo and Amman. The Yom Kippur War came. We lost the fruits of 1967 and were left with the pulp. The commanders of the army are to blame for what happened in the Yom Kippur War, and it is ridiculous to try and cast the guilt onto the political echelons. Since the Six Day War, Egypt and Syria had improved their military ability – in their thinking and their planning, in their readiness to fight and in the quality of their soldiers. But that isn't why we failed to gain our objectives in the Yom Kippur War. We failed because senior Israeli officers of different ranks displayed a marked deterioration in their ability to think, to assess foreseeable situations and to predict developments.

Roles have changed. On the eve of the Six Day War, the 'generals' could complain about the 'politicians'. After the Yom Kippur War, the 'politicians' can revile the 'generals': 'An army like this? We never foresaw it in our darkest dreams! This wasn't the army we were used to, the army we relied upon.' Indeed, it wasn't, not because of the error in mobilizing the reserves. For all its gravity, I do not regard that as the most serious omission. I don't accept the contention that the army slipped into its nonchalance because of the general atmosphere of complacency that reigned in the country. The army should have remained apart, in its own preserve, maintaining its standards and not have been carried away by this fashion of *dolce vita*. Previously, we had encountered similar periods – and worse – yet the army's commanders had always provided leadership and maintained its robustness.

Every army lives under the baneful influence of the previous war, event, or situation. Perhaps this is inescapable. The large-scale mobilization of reserves in May and June of 1973, when there were increasing signs that the Egyptians and Syrians were planning to attack Israel, may have prevented war at that time. But in October 1973, it provided the head of military intelligence with dangerous support for his contention: 'I told you *then* that nothing was going to happen, but you didn't believe me. I tell you again, nothing is going to happen.' In October the head of intelligence was believed. It was a typical case of relying on previous experience, and events were to prove how pernicious that can be. We ignored blatant war signals. Our senses were not attuned to what was happening inside Egypt and Syria, and that was how the Egyptians managed to perpetrate their great deception, one of the greatest in the annals of war, on a par with the Japanese deceiving the Americans at Pearl Harbour and the Germans fooling the Russians with 'Operation Barbarossa'.

The greatest and most unforgivable act of negligence occurred in the south, where the whole alignment, resting on a standing force of hundreds of tanks, with artillery support – the cornerstone of all our plans for blocking the enemy, the force that was supposed to go straight into action, allowing the army the necessary time to mobilize its reserves – was not in position when the Egyptians crossed the Canal, even though orders had been issued. Had it been deployed in position, the war would have taken on a different character from beginning to end. Had that force gone into action from positions near the Canal's edge, as our battle plans clearly foresaw, the blocking operation would have ended within forty-eight hours. The reserves would have reached the front line in an orderly manner, ready for combat. The Canal would have been crossed at the scheduled time, by forces that had not been exhausted in an arduous holding operation, and they would have encountered a weakened enemy.

After the war, there is no point in discussing whether the 'Bar-Lev theory', perceived by laymen as the line bearing his name, stood the test, or whether it was overturned. The theory was not put into practice, neither in the timing nor in the force required for its success. The units were miles back in Sinai when they should have been on the Canal. Dozens of punctilious rehearsals in anticipation of such a situation were rendered utterly worthless the moment the Egyptians began to cross. The Egyptians were convinced that Israel was craftily laying a terrible trap for them.

The bitter truth – that the forces assigned to engage them simply weren't in position – never entered their minds. Dozens of senior officers should have paid the penalty and the least they owe the people of Israel is to hand in their uniforms.

The unshakable faith in Israel's intelligence services was undermined. From the first, it was terribly foolish to treat as a certainty their estimate that war would break out at six in the evening and to deploy units on the strength of that deceptive information. On the morning of Yom Kippur, it should have sufficed that war was expected to erupt some time that day, or even the next, for the blocking forces to be moved into position. But the tactical failures of the intelligence services were less serious than the technological surprise. They knew of the existence of the Egyptian infantry's personal anti-tank missile, but nothing about its distribution, its quantities or its use in combat. Lacking this vital knowledge, Israel's armour and infantry, unprepared for such a fatal eventuality, were taken by surprise and suffered heavily. By the fifth or sixth day of the war, our forces, with their genius for improvization, learned how to cope with the missile. If the armour had been forwarned and prepared to encounter the Sagger anti-tank missile from the first day, its effect would have been much smaller, the armour would have suffered far fewer losses, and there would have been a more rapid transition from the blocking stage to a counter-attack.

This was the first war in which part of the Israeli army's senior command failed miserably, engendering great confusion. One front had a commander with another officer supervising him and making sure that his subordinates obeyed him. It was a war conducted by committee, and on both fronts, but especially in the south, Chaim Bar-Lev was chairman of the board of directors. Chaim did it magnificently. Only time will give us the correct perspective to judge his success. His calm, his optimism, his great authority and his accurate judgement were a mainstay of the army during the difficult days of the war.

It's very difficult for me to write about the air force. When speaking of his son – even if he's deserving of criticism – natural inhibitions make a man tone down his words. The air force was prepared for the battle, but it wasn't prepared for the war. Shortly

Finally, we were rescued from that hell and brought to one of our bases in Sinai. I turned to our superb driver and said, 'My son, when we reach the outskirts of Cairo, look out for me. You will drive me in.' It was a way of thanking him for saving our lives, but inside I was fuming. I was approached by an Israeli military correspondent, who informed me that seven Migs had been downed in an air battle. He had hoped to be the bearer of good tidings; instead, he became the target for the first salvo of my anger. In very unparliamentary terms, I told him to go to hell. I added that I was fed up to the back teeth with all this nonsense and that the Israeli people could no longer be pacified with that kind of remedy.

Returning to General Staff, I summoned my friend Motty Hod. I threw everyone out and locked the door. And then I shouted as I had never shouted before – not when Motty was a young lieutenant and I was a colonel, and assuredly not when I was commander of the air force and he was my deputy. 'Listen, this is the end! Today! It's got to stop! Now! Before I ask the defence minister and the General Staff, you are going to send in the air force and shoot up the Egyptian artillery and their headquarters and their logistics! Give me no excuses and no alibis!' Motty is a true friend, and knows me well. He knows what happens when the blood goes to my head. Quietly, he replied, 'Alright. Now let me think.'

Let there be no mistake. The anxiety about the reaction of both the Big Powers shown by Chaim Bar-Lev and Motty Hod was not only legitimate, but perfectly understandable. But I could see how matters were sliding, and I could imagine what the Egyptian campaign of attrition would look like if we didn't send in the air force. With Egyptian strength facing Israeli weakness, the situation being created was intolerable from our viewpoint.

There was another discussion, and another; another doubt and another argument. Finally, on 20 July, we carried out the operation; we sent the air force in for a powerful surprise strike along the whole Egyptian line. We also had sixteen helicopters on stand-by, with 150 paratroopers awaiting permission to cross over to the other side and demolish a considerable portion of the Egyptian line. The plan was ready, and we were fully convinced of before the war I encountered Benny Peled, commander of the air force. I told him: 'In the next war, you have to be ready to pave the way for the ground forces – to Cairo, to Damascus and perhaps to Amman, too. Have you overcome the problem of the Egyptians' and Syrians' anti-aircraft missiles?' 'That's no problem,' Benny replied, 'it's all been seen to.' The air force gained some stupendous successes in this war's air battles. Our pilots – the best in the world – didn't concede an inch of their proud stature. Not a single enemy plane penetrated our populated areas. But the air force was not quick enough in overcoming the enemy missile systems. It had to devote a relatively long time in dealing with the missiles and could not detach sufficient forces to help block the enemy on both fronts. The main burden was borne by the ground forces, who halted the Arab onslaught with their very bodies.

In the 1973 war, in the encounter between planes and anti-aircraft systems, the missile left some dents in the wing of the airplane. That is a fact that has to be studied carefully, and then the appropriate conclusions can be drawn. I believe the dents are temporary, and that the air force will re-establish the enormous superiority of its offensive power over the enemy's missile defence. I have no doubt of that. But in 1973 the air force was also suffering a crisis, which began in 1970 and continued into the war. It was expressed in remarks like: 'At such-and-such a point I can't attack because of the missiles. That objective is hard to hit because of a dense anti-aircraft artillery system.' That crisis requires that conclusions be drawn, with all possible care and despatch.

Since my retirement from the armed forces, I have not, of course, been involved in the deliberations and decisions. But psychologically, there is no discharge after decades of military service, even when a man has doffed his uniform. There are outward expressions of this, such as talks with officers and tours around the army, but the main thing is one's inward feeling. You continue to belong; these matters are part of your very being, even if you know with complete certainty that it won't be you who'll plan the next war, and it won't be your orders that will be carried out on the battlefield.

Before the 1973 war, I had a number of talks with the chief of staff, David (Dado) Elazar. I told him: 'It will fall to you to

conduct the most decisive war in the history of Israel.' Some three
months before the outbreak of the Yom Kippur War, I told him:
'You have to be ready to cross the Canal with a thousand tanks, at
the first opportunity. You have to work with the air force and plan
precisely how it will strike at the Egyptian ground forces and
demolish the bridge-head they'll try to establish on the eastern
bank of the Canal.' In my talks with Benny Peled and other air
force commanders, I gained the impression that they were
properly prepared for the war.

On Yom Kippur eve I had a strange kind of feeling. That
happens to me at times. My stomach rumbles its agitation, and my
heart revs up. A friend happened to drop in – an intelligence
officer. 'There's an alert,' he said, 'but I don't think it's anything
serious.' I disagreed with him. Early in the morning on Yom
Kippur, I was awakened by a phone call from a friend, an official at
the Defence Ministry. In a tense voice, he announced: 'War.
Today. This evening.' I said to Re'uma: 'The war will break out in
the middle of the day, not in the evening.'

Around two, the air-raid sirens wailed. I must confess my
transgressions: I was convinced that all was ready and prepared,
with the standing forces in the north and south following their
well-rehearsed plans. Perhaps I deluded myself that because of all
my unsolicited advice to the chief of staff and Benny Peled,
everything was exactly in place, as I had told them it must be.
Before my eyes, I envisaged a bright and heartening picture: the
standing forces blocking the attack; the army mobilized and
within forty-eight hours going over to a counter-attack, thrusting
for Cairo and Damascus. 'The Egyptians have made the mistake of
their lives,' I told myself.

For twenty-four hours, I stayed at home. But then I listened to
the voices, and, by their tone, I comprehended what was
happening. I put on my uniform and hurried to air-force
command. On Monday, 8 October, when I was visiting one of the
squadrons, I got the encouraging news that General 'Bren' Adan
had reached the banks of the Canal and was about to cross. 'Bull's-
eye!' I said, glancing at my watch. It was two o'clock in the
afternoon. The forty-eight hours assigned for the blocking
operation had come to an end. The army was attacking. I still had

faith. I still hadn't adjusted to a situation full of negligence and errors. I gave the fellows at the squadron a vivid description of our thrust towards Cairo. Later, they accused me of telling them all kinds of fantasies. I still don't know and can't comprehend what had happened to our army.

Later, I attached myself to the chief of staff and accompanied him on his tours around the fronts. I saw the war. I smelled its stenches. All my senses told me that if we had gone to war properly, as planned, we would have won this one, as we won the previous ones.

At air force command, we had long ago laid down a number of principles and tried to impress their importance on the other sections of the armed forces. One of them was that in war the time factor is decisive, both because of the limited breathing space of a small state when it is fully mobilized and because of the probable intervention of the Great Powers. The Yom Kippur War proved that with regard to time, we were pampered, even misled, by the deceptive model of the Sanai Campaign and, even more, of the Six Day War. When the Yom Kippur War began, people walked about with a stop-watch in their hands, counting the hours. As the days went by, a gap opened up between their expectations and the realities of the battlefronts. And as the gap widened, there was a growing feeling that we had suffered a dreadful reverse. This feeling was not a sober evaluation of the war and its outcome, with regard to the specific circumstances and to the balance of forces on the battlefield, but an extreme expression of disappointment at the frustration of expectations. But in a war where the two sides deploy some 6,000 tanks, 1,500 combat planes and about one million soldiers, how short is short and how long is long? Aside from the necessity of finishing a war as quickly as possible, and the enormous difficulties of withstanding a war, is there anyone who has the right to claim, as an objective opinion, that eighteen days of fighting exceed the definition of a short war? Nonetheless, the very length of the war, together with the tragically high number of casualties, again plunged this country into a grim mood.

Even now, over two years after the fighting ended, once again, public opinion is asking 'Where will it all end?' There is only one answer. Whoever doesn't understand the beginning, won't comprehend the end. The beginning is Zionism. The beginning is faith. The beginning is an unprecedented attempt by a people to return to its homeland, after 2,000 years of exile. And this is only the beginning. After 100 years of settlement and twenty-eight years of political independence, ours is the only state in the world whose enemies, denying its very right to exist, plot to wipe it off the face of the earth.

We're only at the beginning of our arduous war for independence. It's hard to accept. We have an understandable human inclination to delude ourselves that, at long last, peace will 'break out' and reach our tormented region, riding on Uncle Sam's shoulders. I wish it were so. I'd greet it with joyful fanfares. Unfortunately, I don't hear the sounds of peace. Instead, I can clearly detect the sounds of the next war. It even has a smell: the sharp stench of Arab oil.

I don't have any scientific recipes for success in the next war. I presume it won't catch us by surprise like the last one. Our air force is a splendid gem: it will spurt ahead, leaving the Arabs far behind, like their missiles, even if they're the best the Soviets have.

Instead of paying lip-service to quality, we must cultivate it in every sphere of life, filled with a fervent belief in the ability of Israeli quality to contend with Arab quantity.

We must be sensitive to any hint of peace and open our hearts to any Arab attempt to put an end to the wars. But there is no prospect of this happening if we don't build up our military, economic and social might. We must be a Middle East 'mini-power', displaying spiritual, professional, technological and military quality.

We need fortitude, and we musnt't be in too much of a hurry. For an embattled nation, impatience is a source of weakness. We have to grasp that there's a long way to go before we can live here securely, relinquish our arms and stop burying our dead. 'What will the next war be like, and how will we withstand it?' These questions require three million replies. When, day by day, three million affirmative personal answers supplement our national reservoir of quality, we'll have restored quality to its true place. Without it, we have no prospect of existing here.

Among the three million replies, it seems only appropriate that I should voice my own. I won't avoid it, though neither will I go into great depth at this point. Many have asked me: 'And you? Haven't you acquired a taste for political life? Have you decided to put all that behind you?'

I'm on a stop-over now. This plane of mine, from whose cockpit I have seen bright mornings and far horizons – and pea-soup fog and threatening clouds – and in which I have done hard landings and soft landings – this plane hasn't been disarmed. For now, I've put it in the hangar – a repair here, a repair there, a bit of polish needed. I'm refuelling, arming, checking out the systems and the latest intelligence data. And in the meanwhile, I've got enough time to check out the route being taken by the State of Israel and plan the direction of my take-off. It's just a stop-over. It may be a short one.

INDEX